Is My Teenager OK?

A Parent's All-in-One Guide
to the Emotional Problems
of Today's Teens

HENRY A. PAUL, M.D.

CITADEL PRESS
Kensington Publishing Corp.
www.kensingtonbooks.com

CITADEL PRESS BOOKS are published by

Kensington Publishing Corp.
850 Third Avenue
New York, NY 10022

All Kensington titles, ... special quantity discounts for ... ns, fund-raising, educational, o ... ustomized printings can also be ... or phone the office of the Kensi ... ishing Corp., 850 Third Ave ... Department; phone 1- ...

CITADEL PRESS and the Citadel logo are Reg. U.S. Pat. & TM Off.

First printing: August 2004

10   9   8   7   6   5   4   3   2

Printed in the United States of America

Library of Congress Control Number: 2003115560

ISBN 0-8065-2513-4

Dedicated to the enduring and loving memory
of Drs. Herbert Rosenthal
and Isidore Portnoy

Acknowledgment

———◆———

MANY THANKS, once again, to the crisply humorous, creative, spiritual, supportive, encouraging, and always available Guy Kettelhack, who made the writing of this book a consistently enjoyable experience.

Contents

Introduction

RAVES, FREAK DANCING—techno, acid house, trance, and jungle—wizz, Billy, horse, and puka bracelets: just a few current buzzwords that characterize "having a good time" to today's teens and often scare the wits out of their bewildered parents. From the simulated sex of freak dancing to new and highly addictive "cocktails" of recreational drugs (as available to the farm boy in Iowa as they are to club kids in San Francisco or New York), pedophilic chat rooms on the Internet, and teen shoot-outs in suburban malls, the landscape of adolescence today looks and is very different than it was even ten or fifteen years ago.

That the years from twelve to twenty mark a crucial passage in any human being's life is hardly news. On every front and in every realm—physical, intellectual, social, sexual, and emotional—teenagers' experiences of themselves and the world they must navigate is almost always as tumultuous and confusing as we hope it will be enlightening and empowering. But the forced sophistication, stimulus overload, incessant blasts from the media, instant Internet access not only to information about every imaginable kinky lifestyle but to the people who practice them, all have had revolutionary, unnerving effects on the emotional lives of our teenaged sons and daughters—effects that no parent can ignore.

Add to this intimidating menu the typical anxieties most parents of adolescents themselves face—the day-to-day challenges of career, marriage, paying bills, and (increasingly often) dealing with ex-spouses and stepfamilies—and the stress of rearing teens can become monumental. Of course, not all problems teens face are new. Anxiety about physical appearance, dating, algebra, clothes, gym class, and "what other kids think about me" are concerns as potent and universal to today's teens as they ever were to their parents or grandparents—so universal that the exhausted mom or dad of a fourteen-year-old son or daughter is often tempted to dismiss whatever the teen may be complaining about with the same platitudes they got from their own parents: "Oh, you're just going through what we all went through," "You'll grow out of it," "Stop making mountains out of molehills."

Fortunately, many teens do "grow out of it." But some don't. Sometimes mountains really are mountains. We hear about kids bombing their own schools or shooting students and teachers in horrific rampages. We want to think: "Not my child. Couldn't ever happen to my child." We read stories of despondent teenagers who kill themselves and again think: "My child would never do that." Sex, drugs, alcohol: on some level, we know our teenage sons and daughters have to make decisions about these "demons" that they may never share with us, that some experimenting will go on that we won't know about. While we hope our children will make what we have tried to teach them are the "right" choices, deeper anxieties typically goad us: Should we administer "tough love," be our children's cops? Or should we "let go" and hope for the best?

Then there are the even more private and worrisome secrets—the stuff that "can't be talked about." Few families don't have stories of abnormal behavior in their teenaged kids, often feeling they're the only ones who have to deal with problems they never knew existed much less anticipated would ever surface in their lives. Sometimes it's cutting or some other form of self-injury. Sometimes it's taking life-threatening risks. Sometimes it's intransigent depression that clearly isn't just a passing mood. What is normal and what isn't?

Teen problems can be baffling. Families vacillate between being angry and appalled at their misbehaving teens and wanting desperately to understand and help them. Gender, age, and background obviously exert various different influences in who responds to what triggers (and how). However, increasingly, where teens live—country, city, or town—is less and less of a factor: there are few idyllic "safe" Mayberrys left. With the advent of the Internet and cable television, differences among rural, suburban, and urban family environments are increasingly leveled. The instantaneous access such media afford to a bewildering world of sexual practices and choices, images of violence and sadomasochism, and a general information overload can leave both teens and their parents dazed and gaping. The need for guidance that addresses this landscape comprehensively, shrewdly and calmly—and that enables families of teens and teenagers themselves to take immediate action to get guidance when they need it— has never been greater. This book will provide it.

First of all, some reassurance. Most teens are and will be just fine: there's a wide latitude of "normality" in teenagers, and in many cases their greater exposure to the media blitzes just described has resulted in greater sophistication—and new opportunities for them to apply common sense. In many if not most cases, parents can relax a good deal more than they think they can about the outcome of their children's adolescent years. The shoals teenagers must navigate may have become rockier, but often this has just sharpened the adolescent girl or boy's ability to navigate them. The most important point: whatever you or your teen's concerns or difficulties—and however legitimately worrisome they may be—you can learn to steer a steady course and come out on the other side of those challenges to you and your child's benefit.

Teen Problems Are Family Problems

Emphasizing the role the whole family plays in resolving teen emotional problems is particularly necessary because, as isolated and alone as the teenager may sometimes feel, no teen really is troubled in isolation. Teenagers affect and are affected by their families very deeply. Feelings often run as high in parents and siblings as they do in the teen, and although teenagers may go to great lengths to appear "cool" or otherwise hide their emotional reactions, you can be sure they're having them.

Unfortunately, the rest of the family can (however unwittingly) make the teen's perception of a problem worse; an unfeeling response (e.g., "Grow up!" or "Stop being stupid!") can make the teen feel hopeless about the prospect of ever overcoming it. A good example is the child with attention deficit hyperactivity disorder (ADHD), whose parents and sprawling clan of older and younger brothers and sisters may not have known that this was the cause of his short attention span, impulsivity, aggressiveness, and hyperactivity in pre-adolescence, and simply have accused the teen of being "bad." So much antisocial behavior, poor school performance, rude defiance of authority, self-hate, fighting, and other misbehaviors are ADHD-related and can become entrenched defenses by the time a child with ADHD is four-teen or fifteen if the disability is not treated in early childhood. For-tunately, while early treatment is the most effective way of curtailing such maladaptations, there is plenty that can be done to help the child in his teen years, too—even at his most rageful and defensive. But the whole family has to pitch in for the help to be effective: the child can't do it on his own.

Luckily, it's never too late to turn things around. In fact, teenagers who learn important lessons in their teens usually learn them very well, through the discipline of having had to overcome a lot of inner resistance to do so. These lessons learned later can have a good deal of power—indeed, can be life-changing. Many therapists who help teenagers deal with particularly painful or embarrassing symptoms like tics and stuttering have suffered from these symptoms themselves, only sometimes in their own adolescence learning to deal with and master them. Many emotional blocks and difficulties a teenager is able to overcome in adolescence similarly can turn from liabilities into considerable lifelong assets. The excessive stage fright that may keep a talented young dancer from attending dance school can, once she learns techniques to overcome it, provide her with tools to master many other fears in her life, teaching her that fears don't ever have to immobilize her. It might have been easier for her to have dealt with it in early childhood but the very difficulty of triumphing over it later on can give the lesson greater force and tenacity.

But any teenager's prospects of overcoming an emotional afflic-tion are immeasurably improved—indeed, sometimes only possible—when the whole family is involved in offering support. Virtually every entry in this book will take this into account. Parents may approach the book thinking they will learn how to "teach" their teens, but they will also learn to teach themselves. Emotional progress of any one family member almost always requires similar strides toward emotional health in every other family member. The good news: everyone gets better.

Format

The aim of this book is to offer on-the-spot help—accurate information and advice you can look up at a glance. The book is divided into eight different main sections: *Feelings* (depression, panic, stress, grief); *Behavior* (gangs, tattoos, bullying, self-injury); *Sex* (date rape, homosexuality, gender identity); *The Body* (eating disorders, obsessive working out at the gym, dealing with acute physical illness); *Drugs* (a primer on what to look out for in teen drug-taking and abuse); *Family Issues* (dealing with stepfamilies, divorce); *School Issues* (underachievement, learning disabilities, college anxiety); and a final section *Getting Help*, which outlines the kinds of psychotherapeutic help open to you in the event professional treatment is indicated.

Each chapter within these sections begins with a brief true-to-life vignette followed by a general overview of the problem, a "What to Do" section offering concrete suggestions, and "See also" cross-references to other related chapters so that you can attain the fullest possible view of whatever problem concerns you.

In other words, you have in your hands a guide to the most pressing concerns parents bring to the challenge of helping their teenaged sons and daughters through the sometimes perilous hurdles of adolescence. With the information you'll find in these pages, and your own compassion and determination, you can help your teen reach his or her full potential for a happy and productive life.

I

———◆———

Feelings

1. Anxiety

"Honey, it's only a little geometry homework. Please don't take it so seriously. Maybe I can help you with it. Honey? Come on, come out of your room. Come on, honey, talk to me. . . ."

LAST YEAR it was algebra. And feeling so anxious about her homeroom and the kids she was sure didn't like her, that she fled to the girls' room and wouldn't come out. The principal called Karen's mother that time. Every day seemed to be torture for Karen. This was something way beyond "normal," Karen's mother found herself fearing. What made her daughter so anxious? What could she possibly do to dispel Karen's anxiety?

All teenagers worry to some degree, but when the worrying becomes chronic and pervasive then the teenager is probably suffering from an anxiety disorder. It is not unusual, and certainly not pathological, for teenagers to worry about issues such as dating, performance at school or in athletics, approval from their parents, going off to college, sexual development, and other common concerns. But with chronically anxious teenagers these worries interfere with almost every aspect of living. The anxiety hits more frequently and completely consumes a teenager's life, sometimes interfering with performance to the degree that the teenager can't function. Teenagers with this degree of anxiety are said to have generalized anxiety disorder. And there is almost nothing that such a teenager will not worry about from time to time.

Anxiety disorders including generalized anxiety disorder, panic disorder, social phobia, obsessive-compulsive disorder, and post-traumatic states are the most common disorders in American psychiatry. Anxiety disorders affect femals more than males. Although sometimes the onset is in adulthood, up to 40 or 50 percent of the time it begins during the teenage years.

The specific diagnostic criteria used by the American Psychiatric Association for generalized anxiety disorder (GAD) are:

- Excessive anxiety and worry (apprehensive expectation) afflicts the teenager more days than not for a six-month period.

- The teenager finds it difficult to control the worry.

- The anxiety and worry are associated with three or more of the following symptoms (but sometimes in teenagers only one is required): restlessness or feeling keyed up or on edge, being easily fatigued, difficulty concentrating or mind going blank, irritability, muscle tension, and sleep disturbance.

Another criterion is that this anxiety is not associated with another psychiatric syndrome. Lastly, the anxiety has to have caused clinically significant distress in social, occupational, or other important areas of functioning. This anxiety is not due to the affects of a medical, disease drugs, or in light of a severe trauma.

Other symptoms that most anxious teenagers develop might include shortness of breath, rapid heartbeat, diarrhea, nausea, skin rashes, sweating, sleeplessness, dizziness, and increased urination. Often the chronically anxious teenager will appear nervous, restless, and tense. Sometimes a teenager feels unreal or as if the environment is unreal. Many teenagers with generalized anxiety disorder become depressed, housebound, overly attached to their parents, or scared to go out in the world. In addition, anxious teens have trouble concentrating, procrastinate, have an unrealistic assessment of their problems, and have poor problem-solving skills.

Many such teenagers come from uptight homes where perfectionist standards are expressed openly and expected to be met. They often feel pressured, their families often do not tolerate failure well, and there is little praise for accomplishment. Thus teenagers with this syndrome often have poor self-esteem and a poor self-image.

What to Do

- If your teenager manifests the symptoms of a generalized anxiety disorder, the first thing to do is make sure there is no medical disorder that might be causing it, such as neurological disease, or hormone disorders such as hyperthyroidism or Cushing's disease. A teenager also should be worked up for mitral valve prolapse, as well as carcinoid syndrome and pheochromocytoma, all conditions that can mimic this anxiety disorder. In addition some medications must be ruled out as the cause, such as steroids, over-the-counter cold medications, antidepressants, thyroid medication, and asthma medication.

- The child should be evaluated for substance abuse issues including the use of alcohol, caffeine, and nicotine.

- When these have been ruled out, the family should try to set limits and boundaries since teenagers with generalized anxiety disorder often rule the family through their symptomatology.

- A family with a child who has a generalized anxiety disorder has to look at itself and the standards that it might be imposing honestly, to make sure they are not too exacting for or harsh to the teenager.

- Finally a psychiatric evaluation by a child and adolescent psychiatrist may be necessary if this anxiety continues. This psychiatrist will rule out other syndromes such as major depression, manic disorder, or obsessive-compulsive disorder.

- There are two major forms of treatment for generalized anxiety disorder. One is psychological treatment including relaxation techniques and biofeedback, cognitive therapy, psychodynamic insight-oriented therapy, and family therapy, which may be most important. Pharmacological therapy is also available and this usually includes a benzodiazepine anxiolytic medication such as Xanax, Valium, Librium, Klonopin, or Ativan. BuSpar, another anti-anxiety drug of a different family, may also help. In addition, the antidepressant Imipramine has been used, as have Desyrel, Norpramin, and Pamelor. Drugs from other classes in the antidepressant realm that sometimes prove effective include Serzone, Paxil, and Zoloft. Some beta-adrenergic medications have also helped.

SEE ALSO:

Panic Disorder and Agoraphobia
Social Phobia and Shyness
Obsessive-Compulsive Disorder
Stress and PTSD
Depression
School Issues (for School Phobia)
Getting Help

2. Panic Disorder and Agoraphobia

"What do you mean you can't get Jimmy out of the nurse's office! Is he sick or isn't he? He's what? Scared? Scared of what?"

WHATEVER HAD just freaked out sixteen-year-old Jimmy, he wasn't able to tell the school nurse about it; he could only sit trembling on a chair in her office. He'd just fled there from the cafeteria in the middle of lunch. "Just call my mother!" was all he could rasp out, which, unable to get Jimmy to tell her what was going on herself, the nurse did. "Has this happened before?" the nurse asked Jimmy's mother. "Do you mean, has he ever gotten scared? What kid doesn't get scared?" She was sure they were making something out of nothing. "Just let him calm down!"

But Jimmy couldn't calm down. He wasn't just scared. He had suffered a full-fledged panic attack. For those who have not experienced one, it's often difficult to empathize and understand the phenomenon. A panic attack often seems to arise out of nowhere. Even if it is linked to events or situations the panicked teen may be able to name, say, embarrassment about schoolwork, a girlfriend, or gym class, the trigger probably won't seem adequate explanation for the severity of the reaction to anyone but the teen who experiences it. Panic attacks are terrifying and immobilizing. As with Jimmy, they usually result in a teen just freezing and becoming incapable of being reasoned or soothed out of the terror they feel.

Uncommon in young and preadolescent children, panic attacks become more common as the teen moves through adolescence, especially in the later teens. Defined as a discrete period of intense fear or discomfort, diagnosis is made, according to the American Psychiatric Association, when the teen manifests at least four of the following thirteen symptoms:

1. Palpitations, pounding heart, or accelerated heart rate
2. Sweating
3. Trembling or shaking
4. Sensations of shortness of breath or smothering
5. Feelings of choking
6. Chest pains or discomfort
7. Nausea or abdominal distress
8. Feeling dizzy, unsteady, lightheaded, or faint
9. Derealization (feelings of unreality) or depersonalization (being detached from oneself)
10. Period of fearing losing control or going crazy
11. Fear of dying
12. Paresthesia (numbness or tingling sensations)
13. Chills or hot flashes

It is extremely rare for anyone to experience all of these symptoms; however, in some cases what are called "limited-symptom panic attacks" may afflict teens suffering from fewer than four of these symptoms. Although Jimmy was too terrified to budge from the nurse's office, his having fled the cafeteria is typical: teens suffering panic attacks frequently will do anything to get away from whatever situation they feel threatens them. Panic attacks may be related to other anxiety-ridden issues such as separation anxiety, social phobia or performance anxiety, generalized anxiety disorder, and obsessive-compulsive disorder. However, a panic attack differs from these disorders in that it tends to be an isolated acute episode, while the others tend to be ongoing and persistent. Panic attacks may be triggered by just thinking about a threatening situation; for example, flying on a plane or imagining an animal that causes fear. Often panic attacks lead to agoraphobia, an anxiety about going to places that might be difficult to escape from (crowds, department stores, unfamiliar destinations), which keeps the agoraphobic from leaving the house.

If your teen suffers from a panic attack, it's important to rule out possible non-psychological causes. Some prescribed drugs, and recreational drugs such as cocaine, speed, alcohol, marijuana, and even caffeine, may trigger panic. Medical conditions may also need to be ruled out, including hormonal disorders such as an elevated functioning of the thyroid or parathyroid gland, a disturbance of the adrenal medulla producing high levels of epinephrine and norepinephrine, inner ear disorders, unusual seizure disorders, and even heart disease. More serious mental illnesses sometimes involve panic disorders as part of their symptomatology, including schizophrenia, borderline personality disorder, and bipolar disorder.

Causes

It is not fully known what causes panic disorder with or without agoraphobia. Some people appear to be predisposed to anxiety, nervousness, and shyness, often coming from families in which parents are the same. Some children never learn how to develop the tools to soothe themselves in anxious situations. Many teenagers who have panic disorder with or without agoraphobia experienced separation anxiety earlier in their lives and sometimes persist with it into adolescence, even though they may defend against it by acting independent in inappropriate ways, clowning, or taking risks. Problems at school sometimes induce panic disorder; sometimes panic disorder makes teens avoid school as well. Thus panic disorder may be related to an undiagnosed school-avoidance or school-phobic syndrome in the teenager.

What to Do

- As with teenagers who are anxious, compassion, patience, and support by the family constitute the number one defense.

- Try to be reassuring but not falsely so. Point out that it is natural to feel anxious sometimes, especially in adolescence, and help your teen by giving him or her specific techniques, encouragement, and role modeling that will help him overcome anxiety. Giving appropriate praise is important. However, if your child experiences a true panic attack, don't minimize it. Realize and have compassion for the fact that the experience is terrifying—more terrifying than you may be able to understand yourself.

- If panic anxiety and avoidance of situations takes over your child's life, professional advice is necessary.

- Treatment will include a full psychiatric and medical examination. This evaluation will determine what factors within the child, within the family, within the peer groups, and possibly at school might be precipitating this abnormal attack of anxiety. Other diagnoses will be ruled out such as those mentioned previously.

Also the mental-health professional will be able to diagnose if, due to demoralization, your child has become suicidal, self-destructive, or has started to use medication on his own, either legal or unprescribed, to quell his anxiety. In serious cases where suicidal symptomatology and other self-destructive aspects have occurred, hospitalization might be indicated. Therapy should include individual therapy, family therapy, and parent education. Cognitive-behavioral therapy also can be effective, as can long-term individual therapy. Medications combined with therapy often work best, including anxiety-reducing medications such as Xanax, Klonopin, and Ativan of the benzodiazepine family. As well certain antidepressant medications are found to be useful including Zoloft, Prozac, Paxil, Pamelor, and Tofranil.

SEE ALSO:

Anxiety Introduction (and GAD)
Social Phobia and Shyness
Obsessive-Compulsive Disorder
Bipolar Disorder
Suicide
Borderline Personality Disorder
Schizophrenia
Drugs
School Problems
Getting Help

3. Social Phobia and Shyness

"I know, honey—believe me, I was a wallflower too when I was in high school. But Arlene, you have *to get out of the house sometime!"*

ARLENE IS HER mother's daughter in more ways than one. Her mother remembers her own excruciating teenage years when she tried to "fit in" and never felt she could. She couldn't be more sympathetic to Arlene's terrible shyness at school—and how hard it is for her to make friends. But lately, now that she's fourteen and in high school, Arlene has become what her mother fears may be more than just "shy": she's gotten to the point where she won't leave the house on the weekends, and it's all her mother can do to get her on the school bus Monday mornings. "It's like she wants to fade into the wallpaper," Arlene's mother says. "Even when neighbors come over, she disappears. And it just seems to be getting worse, not better . . ."

Few people don't experience periods of shyness in adolescence: at no other period are we more concerned about appearances or more self-conscious about how we come across to peers. But sometimes shyness won't go away—and even seems to deepen. No amount of pep talk or sympathy or "tough love" seems to help the shyest teens, and parents are often stumped about how to encourage their withdrawn kids to engage with the world more happily and productively. "This will pass, won't it?" is the common parental plea. And the good news is that shyness usually does pass, and periods of excessive shyness are usually short-lived.

However, sometimes shyness doesn't just "pass." Sometimes— as, possibly, with Arlene—it signals a deeper and more serious intransigence. How do you tell if your teen is just shy—or socially phobic?

Adolescents who are socially phobic have an intense fear of being scrutinized or sometimes even observed casually by unfamiliar people. The great fear for socially phobic teens is that they will be humiliated. Having to speak in front of people, for example, giving a book report in English class, can induce anxiety to the point of panic. As a result, the socially phobic teen will avoid any situation in which there is even a remote possibility that he or she may suffer humiliation: gym class, dances, the cafeteria, getting on a bus or walking to or from school, and sometimes even answering the phone. Anticipatory anxiety defines the socially phobic teen: the world is a very frightening place, full of terrible minefields he or she is sure can't be navigated safely. As with Arlene, the socially phobic teen often withdraws and only leaves the safety of home under great duress.

Social phobia is marked by a hypersensitivity to criticism, rejection, or any kind of negative evaluation, problems with self-assertion, and feelings of inferiority. Problems range from not being able to take tests, academic difficulty, isolation from peers, and dropping out of school. Socially phobic teens experience a higher degree of depression, a greater tendency to abuse drugs and alcohol, agoraphobia, obsessive-compulsive disorder, and sleep disorders.

Causes of social phobia may include a genetic component, behavior learned in the family, or anxiety induced by anxious parents. In rare cases, there may be brain abnormalities, as studies of the section of the brain called the amygdala appear to indicate.

Onset is usually in the mid-teens, and there is usually a history of childhood shyness and social inhibition. In some cases, the duration of this phobia can be lifelong. At any given time, 3.7 percent of the population—5.3 million people—is socially phobic, with twice as many females as males suffering from it (males are more likely to seek help than females).

Fortunately there are effective treatments for social phobia, including antidepressants such as Paxil, MAOI, and anti-anxiety medications, along with cognitive-behavioral therapy.

What to Do About Shyness

- Don't criticize your teen for being shy.

- Prepare your teen for social events. Go over who will be there, whom your teen might want to talk to, and what activities she might enjoy and find relaxing.

- Encourage your teen to participate in small gatherings at home or with relatives or friends you know will be supportive and friendly.

- Lavish praise on your teen when she succeeds socially even in small ways.

- Encourage your teen to participate in noncompetitive sports, music, or other arts activities that will give her a sense of mastery that doesn't depend on "winning."

- For teens for whom the above measures are not helpful, or for teens whose shyness shows no signs of abatement or worsens over time, seek professional consultation. If social phobia is diagnosed, follow the course of treatment outlined by a health professional skilled in treating this disorder. And keep in mind the points that follow.

What to Do About Social Phobia

- Do not minimize or attempt to dismiss your teen's social phobia. Fears should be taken seriously.

- Remember anxiety and nervousness are contagious: don't react to your child's fears or complaints by becoming nervous yourself.

- Remember that the socially phobic teen will have criticized herself far more severely than you could probably imagine.

Don't add to this burden by being critical of your child's inability to interact socially.

- Group therapy can be helpful for socially phobic teens because they can meet others who are facing the same problems they are.

- More intensive psychiatric treatment may be indicated, including medications such as those already outlined.

SEE ALSO:

Anxiety
Panic Disorder and Agoraphobia
Obsessive-Compulsive Disorder
Depression
Drugs
Getting Help

4. Obsessive-Compulsive Disorder

"Damn it, Sammy, I told you not to touch that!
You're always messing up my stuff!"

SARAH'S OUTBURST at her eight-year-old brother Sammy sounds normal enough. Little brothers are always snooping around and getting into things, and older sisters have long felt exasperated by the intrusion. What Sammy just "messed up" was a meticulously ordered arrangement of tiny glass animal figurines Sarah has on the top of her dresser: carefully sorted according to size—big on the left, small on the right. Sammy had just picked up the kangaroo (the second biggest one) and put it back down—he thought exactly where it had been (he knew Sarah would yell at him if he didn't). But Sarah knew he'd touched it; it was a hair away from where it was supposed to be. (She can tell if anyone has touched anything in her room.) Glance around the rest of Sarah's bedroom and you'll see more evidence of her fastidious orderliness: everything has a "place." Books are organized alphabetically by author and pulled out on the shelves with their spines absolutely flush. (Woe be to Sammy if he touches one of those.) Open her drawers and marvel at her neatly folded, color-coordinated sets of T-shirts and shorts. Sarah, fifteen, won't let her mother put away her clothes. "She never does it right!" is her complaint.

Sarah's deeper and more silent complaint is aimed against herself: she knows her obsession with order has gotten out of hand, that it

16

isn't normal. But she can't help it. She can't bear anything being out of place in her room.

All of us—children, teens, and adults—at some point carry out ritualistic or repetitive behaviors as a way of lessening anxiety. From time to time all of us have silly, unrealistic, incomprehensible, and perplexing thoughts. As children grow older and acquire more appropriate behaviors, most childhood rituals and unrealistic thoughts die down. Unfortunately, in a group of very anxious teens they don't: these people develop what is known as obsessive-compulsive disorder (OCD) which, as its name implies, involves obsessional thoughts and compulsive behavior that come to dominate the teenager's mind. The disorder can start in late childhood but generally becomes more pronounced as the child moves through the teenage years.

Obsessions are persistent thoughts, feelings, mental pictures, and ideas that the teenager generally realizes are inappropriate, but that can't be "reasoned" away: they intrude on the person and cause great anxiety. A teenager usually understands that these obsessions are the product of her own mind, often admitting that they are weird and unwanted. Common obsessions involve feeling contaminated by germs, as well as feeling suspicion and doubt; over-scrupulous adherence to certain regimens or religious tenets; angry thoughts or impulses; sexual fixations; and acute distress when things are out of order. Bodily functions often become the object of obsessional thought. As hard as a teenager may try to overcome the obsessional thought, and understand its irrationality, she generally finds it impossible to keep it at bay for long.

Compulsions are repetitive behaviors and are often linked to obsessional thoughts; for example, an obsession with cleanliness or germs often goes along with obsessive hand washing. Compulsions such as hand washing often go with obsessions about dirt and germs. Checking that things are "right" or in order often has to do with the teenager's worry that she has done something that has caused harm or has been negligent, such as leaving a door unlocked or a gas jet on. Common compulsive behaviors include scrubbing all or part of the body, ordering, checking, praying, counting, touching things as many times with the right hand as with the left, or touching them a certain number of times every time they are encountered. The teen feels driven to pursue these activities despite the fact that they often know no decrease of anxiety is likely to occur. These compulsions are particularly baffling to people they afflict because they are rarely connected in any definable way to the issue, fear, or anxiety that they have been erected against.

Obsessions and compulsions not only cause marked distress, but they are also quite time-consuming. They often interfere in a teenager's general development, social adaptation, education, and ability to participate in family functions. Indeed, family anxieties often center around the teen's bizarre behavior and anxiety-provoking symptoms. The teenager may not be able to leave the house due to an elaborate ritual. Obsessive-compulsive disorder frequently consumes the teenager with an anxiety approaching dread. On the whole, this must be seen as a serious disorder—one that parents can't and shouldn't ignore or dismiss.

While the cause of obsessive-compulsive disorder is not known, it does appear to run in families and might be linked to some form of disorder involving neurotransmitters such as serotonin, dopamine, and norepinephrine. Some research indicates that it may be related to a brain disorder similar to that found in people with Parkinson's disease. In general, this disorder, though not intractable, is often difficult to treat. For many people, the natural history of the disorder is that it tends to get worse with time; for others, it waxes and wanes. In a smaller number of cases, there is remission over time.

What to Do

- As bizarre, intrusive, and troublesome as a teen's obsessive-compulsive symptoms might be, family members must remember that the teenager with OCD is experiencing enormous anxiety. Compassion is always the best initial approach.

- A full psychiatric evaluation by an adolescent psychiatrist is necessary in order to rule out other syndromes with obsessional and compulsive symptoms, such as phobias, post-traumatic stress disorder, schizophrenia, Tourette's syndrome, and psychosomatic disorders.

- Teenagers do best when families don't give in to the symptoms too much. Over-accommodating the obsession may reinforce obsessive and compulsive symptomatology. This may lead to a vicious cycle in which the family feels more anger, anxiety, and resentment, which in turn increases the child's anxiety.

- Treatment includes a combination of individual psychotherapy aimed at decreasing some of the anxiety that causes OCD and that OCD itself causes in the teen's life. Family and supportive therapy are also necessary to help educate parents. They need to know how to deal with their own distress about the disorder and how to handle their teen's problems more effectively. Lastly, psychotropic medication has become part of the approach to treatment. At the present time, effective medications include Anafranil, Luvox, Prozac, Paxil, Zoloft, Wellbutrin, Tofranil, and Effexor. These should be prescribed by a psychiatrist who specializes in treating adolescents and is skilled in prescribing psychotropic medication for teenagers.

- As with all teenage disorders, families should do what they can to keep teenagers on track in most areas of life. School attendance should be supported. Peer relations should continue. Hygiene issues should be addressed appropriately. Whatever increases a sense of unity in the family will help; families should resist giving in to conflict and fragmenting, or taking sides. A feeling of family connection is, as always, crucial to helping the teen with OCD overcome the problem.

SEE ALSO:

Stress and PTSD
Schizophrenia
Hypochondria and Body Dysmorphia
Psychosomatic Disorders (see Somatization Disorder)
Getting Help

5. Stress and PTSD

"Honey, it's been six months. And you still won't talk about it. Please, say something. It'll help, I promise! You're not sleeping—eating—this just can't go on. It wasn't your fault—it was an accident! I know it was terrible, but please, Jerry, don't keep it bottled up. Please let it out!"

SEVENTEEN-YEAR-OLD Jerry only dimly registers these words from his mother. They're a part of some distant fog that most of "reality" seems to him right now. Platitudes can't reach him; he doesn't see how talking about "it" could possibly help. He wants to forget it. He wishes people would quit pulling at him to "let it out." What do they know? How could they know what it was like to be sitting next to your best friend in a car you were driving and crash into a tree and see your friend's head smash through the windshield, then hear that horrible sound of him screaming and the glass shattering and then, suddenly, silence . . . and the blood. . . . The nightmares won't leave him alone. He wakes up in cold sweats, sometimes choking on a scream. If only people would stop trying to get him to talk about it! It would go away someday—it had to . . . "Just leave me alone!" is what he would howl at the world. If he could howl—or even talk.

"Stress" has become a buzzword. We are deluged with tips and products and advice designed to help us reduce stress. In fact, some stress is human and inevitable and even healthy, such as the stress involved in physical exercise and the rewarding exertions of getting something difficult achieved. But the stress Jerry is experiencing—and the stress to which psychiatry turns its primary focus—is devastating. Unfortunately, it is a stress with which, in the wake of 9/11 and war and other unforeseen disasters, we have become all too familiar. In Jerry's case it amounts to reacting to the trauma of having seen his best friend die horribly in a car accident. It has stained him with images and feelings he can't imagine how to shed. Well-meaning as his mother is—and even as accurate as she may be about the benefits of Jerry "letting it out"—dealing with this degree of traumatic stress requires the utmost care and understanding and attention.

In the teenage years there are many inherent stresses, including undergoing the physical changes of puberty, breaking away from parents, social involvements, academic pressures, leaving home, and the overall stress of passing from childhood to adulthood in a world as pressure-packed as ours. But the traumatic stress Jerry experiences, as we've suggested, is of a completely different order. Jerry is undergoing post-traumatic stress disorder, widely known by its acronym PTSD. It is a horrible experience. Sadly, it's not as uncommon as we would hope it would be in teens.

The focus on trauma has become one of great significance in our society, not only due to the recent horrific events having to do with the World Trade Center or international terrorist threats, but also, over the last twenty years, because of the attention paid to all sorts of traumatic events involving children and teenagers, including abductions, rapes, kidnappings, and murders. The effects of this focus have brought PTSD right up to center stage. Events that trigger PTSD, which used to be called shell shock or battle fatigue in times of war, break one's basic assumption about personal safety in the world. Due to a wide variety of causes, from terrorism threats to personal tragedies such as the one Jerry experienced, it is thought that the incidence of PTSD is now quite high in adolescents, ranging anywhere from 5 to 26 percent. In teens who use drugs, 20 percent have been found to have experienced PTSD earlier; indeed, PTSD is one of the major reasons they turn to drugs. Types of trauma that are included as "stressors" leading to PTSD are physical abuse, sexual abuse, violence in the home, rape, kidnapping, ritual abuse, sexual molestation, accidents, disasters like floods and earthquakes, and being tortured or bullied, assaulted, or mugged, or even witnessing these acts. Of course not everyone who experiences a stressor will develop PTSD. It depends considerably on how severe the trauma was, how long it lasted, and if it recurred repeatedly, as in the case of sexual and emotional abuse. Also, one's biological strength, individual temperament, and pre-existing capacity to deal with and overcome severe stress have a lot to do with overprotecting a child from post-traumatic stress. Lastly, the emotional and family support the child gets often make a great difference in who does or doesn't develop PTSD.

PTSD is officially diagnosed as one of the anxiety disorders. Like Jerry, teenagers with PTSD often have frightening thoughts and are hounded by the memory of the stresses that occurred. Sometimes they even feel that the stressor is re-occurring—seeing, smelling, or otherwise sensing things that make them feel as if they are actually reexperiencing the event (known as a flashback). Often teenagers with PTSD feel detached and alienated from people. They habitually avoid anything or any person who may remind them of the trauma. Not surprisingly, they often have nightmares and are depressed. Teenagers with PTSD tend to be startled easily and are quite irritable. Sometimes they act immaturely and sometimes they develop physical symptoms as well. Generally teenagers with PTSD lose interest in things that once engaged them. Their school functioning falls off. Some teenagers become very self-conscious. Sometimes they may even reenact the trauma (or some aspect of it) and engage in very risky behavior. They often feel revengeful, talking about vindictive feelings and fantasies they have either toward people who traumatize others or generally against everyone. They are often withdrawn and focus entirely on themselves. They tend to push people away, feeling that any contact is over-involvement. Often due to feelings of shame, guilt, and humiliation, they have to distance themselves from those emotions in any way they can. This may involve becoming sexually promiscuous, taking reckless risks, or taking drugs to quell the enormous anxiety that teenagers with PTSD experience

What to Do

- It is very important that family members and other people whom the teen turns to for support create a safe environment for the child and provide some degree of consistency. A familiar environment decreases anxiety.

- Parents should reassure their children and give them extra emotional support during the time after a trauma.

- It is best not to cover up what has happened to the child or minimize what he or she might be experiencing.

- Compassionate listening and talking to your teenager about his or her experiences very soon after the evident have been known to cut down on PTSD. This type of attention should be given within twenty-four to forty-eight hours following the crisis in the best-case scenario.

- Teenagers should immediately be told that they in no way caused the trauma. This is especially important in cases of abuse, sexual abuse, divorce, death of family members, accidents, or being victims of a crime.

- If full-blown PTSD has erupted, it is best to get professional treatment. There are various treatments that are known to help alleviate PTSD, including the use of various psychotropic medications (Zoloft, an antidepressant for example) and other anxiolytics, Clonidine, and beta blockers combined with talk therapy. Family therapy, group therapy, and counseling therapy also help.

- If there has been a natural disaster or a disaster that has affected many people, there are usually many support groups that parents should join along with their child.

■ Children and teenagers should be encouraged to participate in
  physical activities such as sports and also be given opportunities where they can experience mastery and control over some
  aspect of their environments.

SEE ALSO:

Anxiety
Self-Injurious Behavior
Bullying
Sexual Development
Sexual Abuse
Drugs
Getting Help

6. Depression

"Jane?"

Silence.

"JANE?"

"Yeah?"

"It's almost eight o'clock. You'll be late
for school again!"

Silence.

"Jane!"

"Yeah?"

"What's gotten into you? You've been late getting
up every day for months now..."

Silence.

JANE'S SILENCES and monosyllabic responses to her mother may seem
to identify her as an all-too-typical fifteen year old who just doesn't
want to go to school. But her reluctance to get up in the morning is
only one symptom of many that have begun to worry her parents.
For many months she's been listless in general. When she does
emerge from bed in the morning, she doesn't seem to care about
what she wears, eats almost nothing at breakfast, and ignores her
brothers and sisters. When she finally gets to school, she sits in the
back of her classes and doodles aimlessly in her notebook, paying
little or no attention.

Adolescence has long been known to involve pain and angst. Most teenagers have a hard time getting out of bed or bringing much enthusiasm to the day's activities occasionally. However, while some degree of transient moodiness is normal in adolescents, depression of the kind that afflicts Jane is not.

Teenagers suffer from major depression just as adults do. There are two basic types of depression: major depression and dysthymic disorder. Characteristics of each are:

- **Major depression:** Symptoms usually involve sad or irritable moods, diminished interest or pleasure in activities, sleeping too much or too little, weight loss or gain, slowness or agitation in movement, and fatigue or loss of energy, as well as feelings of worthlessness, inappropriate guilt, and a diminished ability to concentrate or make decisions. The teenager may also have recurring thoughts of death and suicide, sometimes involving plans and even attempts to carry it out. Anger, social withdrawal, and feelings of helplessness and hopelessness also commonly characterize depression, as do physical symptoms such as headaches and abdominal pain. The ability to function in school generally decreases; cutting school is common. Some teenagers act out their problems by developing disruptive behavior disorder, school refusal syndromes, or substance abuse problems. Eating disorders are sometimes linked with depression. Often, depressed teenagers look withdrawn, sad, tearful, and listless. Major depression is indicated by the teenager evincing at least five symptoms of those mentioned above for a two-week period.

- **Dysthymic disorder:** Depression is called dsythymic disorder when a depressed mood persists for two years with no abatement. These teens present at least two of the following symptoms: (1) poor appetite or overeating; (2) insomnia or hypersomnia; (3) low energy or fatigue; (4) low self-esteem; (5) poor concentration or difficulty making decisions; (6) feelings of hopelessness.

Causes

It is not yet certain why teenagers—or others—get depressed. There is some evidence that there may be a genetic tendency to inherit depression. Other biological tendencies, including hormonal changes in puberty, may also be indicated. Stress, early traumas, or other serious losses such as the death of a parent or sibling, sexual or physical abuse, witnessing domestic violence, or being the object of chronic aggression or teasing at school have all been considered as possible causes. However, it is my opinion that depression is a symptom resulting from unresolved inner conflicts, feelings of perplexity, and confusion about the environment and oneself. Depression is a symptom picture that should lead concerned parents to try to understand what is truly troubling their teenagers. Patience and compassion are key.

Treatment for depression should include a complete psychiatric and physical evaluation, administered by a mental-health professional trained in the area of adolescent psychiatric disorders. Effective treatment includes dynamically oriented individual psychotherapy, interpersonal or cognitive-behavioral therapy, and group and family therapy. In addition, antidepressant medication is quite commonly indicated, including the use of tricyclic antidepressants, selective serotonin reuptake inhibitors, and occasionally MAOIs. Sometimes, in the case of an emergency, a short-term hospitalization is necessary, especially if suicide is the issue. It should be noted that depression is more common in teenage girls than boys.

What to Do

- If you think your teenager is depressed, the most important first step is to talk to her. That in itself—the genuine desire to reach out and understand—can give hope to a hopeless adolescent.
- If the depression does not seem to lift within several weeks, consultation with a child and adolescent mental-health professional is indicated.

- Don't be scared to ask about suicide. There is no truth to the worry that discussing it causes it.

- However worried or frustrated you may feel, be patient and compassionate in any communication with your teen.

SEE ALSO:

Bipolar Disorder
Suicide
Anger
Behavior Disorders
Anorexia, Bulimia, and Overeating
Psychosomatic Disorders (Somatization Disorder)
Drugs
School Problems
Getting Help

7. Bipolar Disorder

*"You know any teen who isn't ecstatic one
minute, sulky the next? So maybe Joey did sort of
go to extremes sometimes. Sure, there were times
I thought he'd bounce off the walls he had so
much energy. And other times he'd mope around
like a slug. I was that way too when I was
sixteen. But then his principal called . . ."*

MOOD SWINGS are often regarded as normal phenomena in adolescence, and for good reason. Given the tumultuous physical and social changes and pressures any teen has to deal with, alternating feelings of sadness and happiness, anger and elation are virtually inevitable. But when Joey's principal called his parents, she called to alert them to the probability that Joey wasn't just swinging on a normal teenage pendulum. Joey had developed an exasperating reputation as a "class clown"—cutting up in class, throwing spitballs, firing out sarcastic ripostes whenever anyone else spoke. But the morning his principal called his parents, Joey had clearly gotten out of hand. When his geometry teacher had had enough of his pranks, and sharply told him to stop it or Joey would end up in detention, Joey blew up. He jumped out of his seat, hauled back a fist, aiming at his teacher's face, and didn't land the blow only because two other students quickly leapt up and restrained him in time. "We had to get one of the guards to take him, yelling curses, to my office," the principal said. "And now he's sitting in the waiting room completely shut down. Won't say a word." The principal—who fortunately had encountered symptoms of bipolar disorder before—gently but firmly informed Joey's parents that she thought their son might need professional help.

Not all adolescent mood swings are normal. When they are severe enough to indicate bipolar disorder, which can begin to manifest as early as middle childhood, they need prompt attention. Diagnosed in an increasing number of teenagers, bipolar disorder (formerly known as manic depression) usually involves periods of deep depression alternating with episodes of mania, which can range from over-the-top high spirits to irritable and violent outbursts like the one Joey had in his geometry class. Once again, it is fortunate that Joey's principal recognized what she realized was probably an illness, not a bout of bad behavior to be punished.

You'll find a full discussion of the depression end of the bipolar spectrum in "Depression." Here we'll concentrate on the other pole: mania. Its symptoms devolve into two general categories:

- **Mood symptoms:** Moods may be elevated, expansive, or irritable, sometimes manifesting as being excessively silly or funny, or laughing and joking obsessively. Ecstatic and exuberant feelings can quickly flip, as they did with Jerry, to irritable displays of anger, frustration, and hostility that are clearly out of proportion to whatever situations triggered them and may escalate into physical violence.

- **Associated symptoms:** At least three out of the following seven associated symptoms are necessary to make the diagnosis of a manic episode: 1) inflated self-esteem/grandiosity or inappropriate bragging about various abilities and talents; 2) decreased need for sleep; 3) rapidly changing racing thoughts and ideas (often described as a tape in a tape recorder playing at high speed; as a result teens with bipolar disorder tend to talk excessively and dominate or push others out of a conversation); 4) poor judgment or hypersexuality; 5) an excessive number of goal-directed activities taken on simultaneously; 6) distractibility; attention is too easily drawn to unimportant or irrelevant things; 7) excessive involvement in pleasurable activities that have destructive consequences (e.g., spending too much, sexual promiscuity, using drugs or alcohol).

Bipolar teens will have had at least one episode of depression and some degree of hypomania, which can be described as a consistently elevated, expansive, or irritable mood lasting for at least four days, clearly distinct from a normal non-depressed mood. (Hypomania is indicated when the teen exhibits three or more of the symptoms just described.)

There seem to be two types of juvenile bipolar disorder: that which has its onset in early childhood and early adolescence, and that which begins in adolescence. Perhaps the greatest difficulty in diagnosing either category is that many of their symptoms overlap with those of attention deficit disorder, and even oppositional defiant disorder, one of the behavior disorders; consult this book's entries for both.

Suicidal behavior is not only a threat in depressive disorders—up to 20 to 25 percent of children and adolescents who suffer from bipolar disorder also evince this behavior. As in depressive disorders, bipolar teens also sometimes present a break with reality severe enough to be diagnosed as psychosis, involving delusional feelings of worthlessness, guilt, disaster, and other varieties of doom, which may include visual or auditory hallucinations.

Causes

Strong evidence suggests that there is some degree of genetic transmission of bipolar disorder in families. (It may be that Joey's father, who said he'd behaved similarly to his son, suffered and may have suffered from a milder and undiagnosed version of the illness.) It appears that there is approximately a 1 percent chance that anyone may develop the disorder some time in her lifetime.

Unlike earlier descriptions of bipolar disorder, which focused on discrete episodes of mania or hypomania followed by an interval of normality followed by another manic episode, bipolar disorder, especially in children and adolescents, is now known often to involve an intermixing of mania and depression, sometimes in the same episode. This is often referred to as "mixed and rapid cycling bipolar disorder" in youngsters.

What to Do

- If you feel your teen might be exhibiting symptoms of bipolar disorder, be careful not to gloss over them or imagine they are transient "normal mood swings" that will disappear in time.

- Bipolar disorder requires treatment, and will not go away on its own, so it is important that you get your teen an immediate evaluation. Treatment aims first at stabilizing whatever episode your teenager is currently undergoing, and then at preventing future episodes from occurring. This is accomplished through a combination of individual supportive psychotherapy, behavioral therapy, group therapy, and family therapy, as well as with medication and, if necessary, hospitalization. A combination of medications geared to your teenager's particular symptoms are generally prescribed in addition to psychotherapeutic intervention.

- Medications include mood stabilizers such as Lithium, Valproate, and Carbamazepine. More recent medications include Lamictal and Neurontin. These drugs are also administered during the acute phase of mania. (Risperdal as well as some other newer and atypical antipsychotic drugs may also be indicated.) It is important to point out that sometimes antidepressants used for depressive disorders and stimulants used for attention deficit hyperactivity can exacerbate bipolar symptoms, although these can be employed after your teen has been stabilized. This is one of the reasons it is essential that you consult a mental-health practitioner with experience specifically treating bipolar disorder.

- Hospitalization is only considered in the event of suicidal or aggressive behaviors that cannot be controlled on an outpatient basis, as well as to protect the teen's safety during otherwise intractable episodes of mania.

SEE ALSO:

Depression
Suicide
Violence
Attention Deficit Disorder
Behavior Disorders
Getting Help

8. Suicide

"I'm scared. Jeremy's best friend Paul hanged
himself in the basement. His parents found him
and we're all devastated. We just can't understand
how a sixteen year old could possibly do this. But
worse is, Jeremy isn't mourning Paul; he doesn't
even seem sad. He just keeps defending him, saying
how 'brave' he was to do it. As if Paul were some
kind of hero. It's almost as if he envies him ..."

SUICIDE IS NEVER more devastating than when a teenager makes the decision to end his or her life. How worried do we have to be that our own teens may make this terrible choice? What are the warning signs? How can Jeremy's mother reach him with the message that suicide does not make anyone a hero?

Jeremy's mother is right to be concerned. The appalling news is that suicide is now the third leading cause of death in fifteen to twenty-four year olds. Some statistics: whites tend to commit suicide more than blacks, although the number of black teenage suicides is rising. Girls attempt suicide twice as often as boys, but boys successfully achieve it more than twice as much as girls. (This is thought to be because girls tend to use pills, from which there is a greater chance of saving them; boys tend to use firearms.)

Many theories have been put forth in the attempt to understand in a general way why teenagers commit suicide, focusing on stress and family turmoil; confusion, self-doubt, the impact of recent humiliations; and the effects of alcohol and drugs. Moving, feeling isolated, sexual or physical abuse, and divorce and family breakup have also been implicated as triggers. Family history may also play a role: teenagers with relatives who have committed suicide may be more likely to consider it themselves.

But perhaps the most plausible overall reason for teenage suicide is simply this: the teenager feels hopeless. This is often coupled with, or is the product of, major depression, as well as feeling caught in inner conflicts and/or environmental constraints or difficulties from which the teenager feels there is no escape. Because the most common psychiatric diagnosis associated with suicide is depression, it is crucial for parents to watch for symptoms that commonly indicate this condition. If your child is suffering from a recent onset of eating or sleeping disorders, seems to have undergone an abrupt personality change, is withdrawing socially, engages in alcohol or drug use or other risky behaviors, has shown a marked decline in school performance, can't concentrate, is fixating on a particularly painful experience of humiliation, or is afflicted by headaches or gastrointestinal complaints, regard it as an urgent "heads up."

Often teenagers who are suicidal give verbal hints: Jeremy, in his praise of his friend Paul's "bravery," is an example. Teens may betray suicidal intentions by "cleaning house," writing about death and dying, or in other ways becoming absorbed in morbid subjects (movies, books, videos, Internet sites, or music). "I can't take it anymore" or "you'd be better off without me" are the kinds of warning statements a suicidal teenager often makes—warnings that are too frequently dismissed as evidence of passing adolescent mood swings. Obviously if your teen has ever attempted suicide before, you need to be particularly alert: seek professional help. Sometimes, after a period of depression, the teen may exhibit a sudden burst of cheerfulness which may indicate he or she has decided to end his depression with death. Teens at highest risk have withdrawn from their friends and family and are sometimes rigid, supercilious, and aloof. Often, they also have a history of behaving impulsively.

Of course, teens end their lives in other ways without intending to: often through drunk driving or drug overdose. These teens may not be overtly suicidal, but clearly if your teen engages in any self-destructive behavior, you need to take it seriously. No teen should die by his own hand, whether voluntarily or involuntarily. Parents need to be vigilant in detecting any warning signs of self-destructive behavior and take immediate measures to deal with them.

What to Do

- Always take seriously any mention or discussion of death, dying, suicide, self-destruction or other evidence of morbid thinking that your teenager may manifest.

- Talk to your teen, listen, don't lecture, express love and reassurance, and realize that suicide and depression are usually temporary and treatable states.

- If you are worried that your teenager may be contemplating suicide, remove any weapons, pills, or other objects or substances in the house to which he or she may have access to achieve the act.

- Get professional help *now*. Remember that depression is almost always indicated in suicidal teenagers and that a combination of "talk therapy" and medication can turn things around.

- Get the numbers and/or websites of suicide hotlines both to report any fears or concerns you may have and to learn more about the likelihood of your teen carrying through any suicide attempt.

- Note changes in behavior mentioned previously (including dressing in black) and take them seriously. Engage your teen in conversation about what's going on with him in his life and what he intends by the changes in dress or behavior you have noticed.

- Don't judge. Family supportiveness is crucial. The point is always to get your teen to talk, not to lecture or try to persuade him or her out of feelings.

- Be especially alert if your family has had a history of suicide or suicide attempts.

■ Understand that in a minority of cases, if the depression or other underlying reasons for your teen's suicidal thoughts and/or behavior indicate it, your teen may need hospitalization and a combination of therapy and medications.

SEE ALSO:

Stress and PTSD
Depression
Bipolar Disorder
Self-Injurious Behavior
Drugs
School Problems
Getting Help

9. Grief

"Grandma was different. I could talk to her. She never judged me. I can't imagine her not being here. Sometimes—to tell the truth, Mom, sometimes—I wanna go wherever she is. What will I do without her in the world?"

WHILE MOST CALLS to me about young children who have lost someone through death have to do mostly with whether they should attend funerals, and be talked to about death and the process of dying, most calls about teenagers who are grieving are from parents who are worried that their child might suffer serious depression or other pathologies during their teenage years. Certainly fifteen-year-old Angela worried her mother in this way. How seriously did Angela "wanna go wherever" her recently deceased grandmother had gone? Was it something to worry about or a normal expression of grief?

The question can be answered simply: Adolescent grief or bereavement is normal and natural. Teenagers who are grieving have many characteristics of adults who are grieving; thus it is not unusual to see a grieving adolescent be somewhat withdrawn and isolated, and to feel anger, guilt, and helplessness. As with adults, they often yearn for the return of the loved one. We want to allow our grieving teenagers to experience this stage in life normally, without interfering in the process they must undergo to get through it.

I sometimes think that it is not the death of a loved one that causes problems as much as the mishandling of the teen's grieving by his or her family members. In other words, normal grief does not cause pathology, but grief that is interfered with may. Grief is not an illness; it is a normal reaction to loss. It only becomes pathological if it becomes what is called complicated grief, which will be discussed lated in the chapter. Healthy grieving is more probable if there had been a secure relationship with the dead person prior to the death. (This bodes well for Angela who loved and felt loved by her grandmother.) It is important that teenagers be allowed to ask any questions that occur to them and receive prompt and correct information, to express every concern, to participate in all rituals having to do with the death and the grieving, and be comforted by those who are still alive.

Teenagers should not be kept from going to funerals; parents should encourage and support them to do so. Unlike very young children, teenagers can be given details about how a loved one died. Keeping a scrapbook or other mementos having to do with the deceased loved one and talking about the person who has died are very important. Grieving involves many complicated feelings, such as anger, guilt, shame, conflict, and even rage. Teenagers may sometimes feel, as Angela did, that they want to join the dead loved one, even sometimes feeling that they see or hear the image or voice of the dead person—all of which teenagers should be encouraged to talk about. Of course, if the wish to join the deceased is accompanied by suicidal plans or behavior, this is another story and needs immediate professional attention. But emphasizing the positive relationship the teen had with the dead person—going through old pictures, telling old stories, and answering all questions about the deceased—will go a long way to allowing the teen to vent his or her distress. Regularly visiting a cemetery where a loved one is buried will depend somewhat on one's cultural and religious traditions, but this should be encouraged as well if the teenager wants it.

Parental honesty, availability, and support are the key to helping the teenager work through grief. Harm is done not from honest confrontation and discussion of death but rather from misguidedly trying to protect the teenager through hypocrisy, duplicity, and misinformation. These are what could make death a more traumatic situation for a teenager. Not only should surviving family members be honest and open but they should tend to their own grief as well, which will free them to provide the emotional availability and lack of anxiety necessary to help teenagers in the family and also give the teen implicit support. Shared grief ultimately becomes less of a burden to all.

If the teen's grief proves to be intransigent, support can be sought in groups devoted to dealing with grieving—groups that may involve only peers or the whole family. A sense of belonging to a group that provides a safe place to talk about feelings will lessen the sense of isolation and sadness that are normal parts of the grieving process. Whatever the means of achieving it, keeping communication open always remains the key.

Of course, teenagers' experiences and expressions of grief vary greatly. Some teenagers will experience shock and denial, even disbelieving that the death has occurred. These teenagers might show very few signs of grieving. They experience a kind of numbness, which might be necessary for them to go through; it should, however, wane within several months. Many teenagers feel guilt after the death of a parent and even more so after the death of a sibling. This is because the teenage years have been filled with such opposition or rebelliousness that, unconsciously, the teenager feels as though he might have caused the death, even though he knows the facts are otherwise. Family members should be open to hearing about this guilt and not rush to correct it: the key, as always, is listening without jumping in to contradict or dismiss what the teen is expressing. As with Angela, thoughts of wanting to die are not uncommon. If the teenager expresses such thoughts, he or she should be told they're normal. Again, however, if these ideas prove intransigent and involve a suicidal plan, professional help should be pursued immediately. Some teenagers look to drugs and alcohol to numb their feelings, which is why teenagers are sometimes at risk of self-destructive behavior after a death. Sexual activity may also be resorted to, not only to feel close to someone in the fresh wake of the loss but also to numb emotional pain. Not all teens cry openly; some may cry to themselves in private. This should be respected as well.

Complicated grief is when a grief reaction has become pathological. Symptoms include profound depression, severe withdrawal, loss of interest in the outside world, and excessive preoccupation with thoughts of the dead person. Complicated grief is a high-risk factor for a teen having problems, including behavior problems and a desire to commit suicide. Depression is also part of a complicated grief reaction. Remember that depression is different from mourning because during depression self-esteem decreases. This commonly means the teen cannot function well in the outside world—socially, athletically, or academically. Overwhelming feelings of guilt, shame, and self-hate flood the teen suffering from complicated grief. Although some guilt is often experienced during normal bereavement, guilt about things having nothing to do with the survivor can be a symptom of major depression. Thoughts of death that are unconnected to the deceased are also symptoms of depression, not normal grief. Feeling worthless, tired, or impaired in various areas, and experiencing hallucinations of anything or anyone unconnected to the dead person, are also symptoms of depression, not normal bereavement.

What to Do

Although we have already discussed what to do in some detail in the foregoing overview, keep the following points in mind as you help your teen deal with grief:

- Respect the form and time that your teen takes to grieve.

- Assist your teen in expressing thoughts openly, on the teen's terms not yours. Encourage your teen to share feelings, even if they are scary, unusual, and frightening. Listen to your teen's dreams and even hallucinations.

- Help your teen by letting him gather articles, old pictures, and old stories about the dead person. Some people even suggest making a collage as a way of helping the healing process.

- Be as present and available as you can to your teen. Many teenagers feel rejected when people, especially parents and close family members, aren't physically and emotionally there for them. (This sometimes happens because the teen's grief may make others feel anxiety about death and thus may give in to the desire to avoid the teenager.) This adds to the sense that somehow they didn't love the deceased person as much as the teen did, which increases the teen's sense of isolation and aloneness.

- Look for signs of hypersexuality, drug abuse, risky behavior, depression, suicidal thoughts or plans, and other symptoms of major depression in order to intervene with professional help if necessary.

- Involvement in a grief support group can be very important for the teenager and surviving relatives.

- Lastly, we should be sure that our attitudes about death are as healthy as possible to set a good example for the teenager. As always, we affect teens more by what we do and how we act than by what we say.

SEE ALSO:

Depression
Suicide
Anger
Self-Injurious Behavior
Behavior Problems
Sexual Development
Drugs
Getting Help

10. Anger

*"Leave me alone, dammit! What, I can't talk to
you like this cause you're my father? Big deal! I'll
talk to you any damned way I feel like! You don't
like it? Tough! Do something about it!"*

TIMMY'S ANGER is frightening to his parents. He has such a short fuse
that they don't know what to do with him. Worse, Timmy's anger
sometimes inflames his father so much that he feels like he might
someday indeed "do something about it"—something he'll regret.
"Timmy was always a feisty kid," his father says. "But ever since
he hit his teens, he's been impossible. I can't tell you how close I've
come to just hauling off and hitting him. We try to punish him, we
try reasoning with him. Nothing works. He just keeps blowing up. Is
this normal? Is Timmy the kind of kid who, you know, has real problems later on?"

"Real problems" is the dad's nervous code for: Is he a sociopath?
Might he really go off the handle and turn into one of those kids
who starts shooting up their high school? Is this kind of anger
normal or abnormal?

Anger is a difficult feeling for parents to understand. Should it be
expressed, repressed, or displaced into other areas? Part of why it's so
baffling is that most parents themselves haven't been educated about
anger—what it means, and how to handle it effectively themselves.
Most parents don't know how to make sense of the confusing messages in the media that bombard them about kids and anger, worrying even when their youngest children get angry that it might mean

they're destined to become criminals later on. Parents worry that angry teens might hurt somebody, hurt themselves, join gangs, deteriorate academically and socially, and end up in prison.

First, some reassurance: although a majority of teenagers commit at least one anti-social act during adolescence, it is rare that they become criminals later in life. More fundamentally reassuring: anger is a perfectly normal feeling. Defined as a sense of displeasure or distress caused by feelings of powerlessness and helplessness, it runs the gamut from mild annoyance and crankiness to actual rage and fury, all of which can be normal reactions. Along with guilt, love, passion, joy, sorrow, and excitement, feeling and expressing anger are part of being human. Indeed, without the ability to express anger, children and teenagers would be badly endangered. Anger is a great communicator. It signals a sense of distress or helplessness that enables parents to know when and how to help their child. Angry feelings are reactions to frustration, helplessness, and vulnerability— an alarm that the child needs aid.

There are two main sources of anger in children and teens: one is the anger that occurs as a result of facing new daily challenges. For teenagers this may result from dealing with the bodily changes of puberty, sexuality, increased independence from parents, new social situations that are baffling and demanding, school and peer pressures, anxiety about getting into and going off to college, and all the other awkward and anxiety-provoking challenges that the passage through adolescence entails. Another is interpersonal relations, which can also induce anger in a host of ways. Not only the often tumultuous relationship between teens and parents but social stresses with peers. Indeed, anger is triggered by anything that induces a sense of feeling unwanted or being treated unfairly—neglect, breaking promises, inconsistency, hypocrisy, double messages, overprotection, teasing, disparagement, the arbitrary exercise of power, intimidation, humiliation, bullying, excessive demands from authority figures, unjust comparisons, and reacting to a generally angry household.

The most important thing to remember about anger is that it is a response to feeling helpless. It usually can be understood if parents take the time to try. Anger usually disappears when the sense of helplessness underlying it is taken care of. Anger leaves no damage when it passes. Since feelings of helplessness are usually temporary and anger, freely expressed, can elicit help, parents are best advised to see it as a constructive feeling, even a helpful and life-enhancing one.

Not that every teen's expression of anger is the same. Like Timmy, some teenagers have shorter fuses than others. The degree of a teenager's anger varies according to certain influences, all of which are experienced differently by different teens: (a) tolerance for stress; (b) age; (c) gender (most males tend to act out their anger aggressively, while females—although more willing to express it outwardly than in the past—tend to subsume it in other feelings such as depression); (d) temperament (a set of biological characteristics that we are born with that mold how we respond emotionally); and (e) role model(s) for the expression of anger teens had growing up.

Because they so often misunderstand anger, parents frequently mishandle it in their teens. This may include denying that the teen is angry at all, ignoring it, attempting to eradicate it by abuse or punishment, complying with it, resorting to bribery, or refusing to set limits. All of these responses result in impeding anger from serving its function: to communicate to the parent what's bothering the teen.

Therefore, parents need to examine their own motives and styles of anger management. Questions parents should ask themselves: Are you confused about your own anger? Are you trying to exercise excessive control over your teenager? Do you feel an unconscious identification with your child that interferes with good judgment? Are you afraid of your teenager's anger, or applying a standard of "perfection" in which anger is not permissible? Dependency, egocentricity, martyrdom, vengefulness—these are all personality traits that parents need to address in themselves before they can clear the way to reacting to their teenagers' anger more productively.

Thus, while most anger is normal, when parents mishandle their teens' anger because of their own incomprehension of it, they can cause problems that otherwise wouldn't ensue: they effect what I call an anger metamorphosis, in which the child begins to see his anger as a bad, threatening, and disruptive feeling and therefore goes to great lengths to repress it. When anger is repressed it evolves into many symptoms that we especially see in teenage years. It can become the fuel for generalized anxiety states, depression, school failure, conduct disorder and other behavior disorders, criminal-type behavior, drug addiction, and a host of other problems. These legacies of mishandled anger will only grow if parents don't realize that the original anger was healthy to begin with—that it carries a message of need that must and can be addressed directly, without fear.

What to Do

- If your teenager truly gets so angry that he is violent or imminently violent so that you are threatened with an "anger emergency," do all you can to stay with your child and restrain him in whatever way you must. At that point, the teen should not be criticized, although you should employ whatever means necessary to protect yourself, the environment, and any others present. You may need to call in extra help, such as another parent or family member, or, in rare cases, the police. Remember, you do your teenager no good by allowing him to rant and rave uncontrollably, especially if he is physically violent. Restrain him but do not berate him.

- Fortunately, most teenagers don't reach the "anger emergency" point. With most teenagers, the aim should be to understand what message the teen's anger seeks to convey. This cannot be achieved by lecturing, chastising, or intimidating, but rather by compassionate listening and questioning. Once again, you want to find out what is troubling your teenager and to locate the trigger for the anger. Some teens will be able to tell you, while with others you may need to play detective, trying to piece together what you know from your child's actions, activities, and friends. Try to come up with a working theory to present to your child about why he might be angry. Observing, listening, and questioning your child are key.

- Your primary goal should be to relieve the teenager, to ease whatever situation has induced the anger in the first place.

You might suggest a solution to his problem, or offer direct assistance; you might have to look at your own behavior and how you might be able to keep from triggering your teen yourself. You may have to intervene at school or at local clubs or wherever else your child may have been unfairly or poorly treated.

- Lastly, if your teenager's anger just won't go away despite your hard work in trying to detect the cause and/or ameliorate the underlying causes, then professional consultation is warranted.

SEE ALSO:

Violence
Behavior Disorders
Discipline
Getting Help

11. Borderline Personality Disorder

"Sometimes I look into her eyes, Doctor, and it scares me. I mean, I know it's normal for teenagers to be anxious sometimes, but what happens to Darlene . . . it's like she's lost in there. And she has such exaggerated reactions to things, more than I ever saw in her older sister, or than I remember when I was a teen. I just have this nagging feeling something's really, really wrong."

DARLENE'S MOTHER intuits that something is "really, really wrong" with her daughter—but what? She knows that the teenage years are rarely a picnic either for the teen or for the teen's parents. Is her intuition something she should worry about?

It's a hard question to answer. We see teenagers grappling with important issues and showing signs of stress and strain, often through the entire period of adolescence. All teenagers struggle frantically with issues having to do with separation and individuation and worry whether they will be able to stand on their own two feet, even if such struggle and worry are sometimes masked by opposition and defiance. We see teenagers profoundly absorbed by their images, how they look, how macho or "cool" they are, and especially by what other people think of them. We see teenagers expend great and intense anxiety over their sexual and physical development, interpersonal relations, school, and athletic performance. We see teenagers experimenting, doing risky things, sometimes hurting themselves, often by accident, in their efforts to establish themselves as whole and separate from their families of origin. We often see intense mood swings in adolescence from day to day, week to week. We see changes of heart and impulse-ridden decisions such as changing interests, boyfriends or girlfriends, friends, hobbies, and life goals. Teenagers, lacking expertise and experience in life, overreact and sometimes even underreact. We often see anger quickly followed by happiness.

Thus it is not always easy for the mental-health professional (never mind the parent) to differentiate the normal or usual swings in feelings, thinking, and behavior of teenagers from a more serious psychiatric behavior, the borderline personality disorder. A teenager with a borderline personality disorder seems often to be in extreme exaggeration of some of the aforementioned traits. Core to the borderline personality disorder is an intense anxiety. This anxiety is more intense than the anxiety normally associated with the developmental stresses and strains of teenage years and even more intense than the anxiety found in other psychiatric disorders, such as in phobias, anxiety disorders, mood disorders, post-traumatic stress disorder, attention deficit disorder, eating disorders, and obsessive-compulsive disorder.

Often the anxiety of a borderline teenager has to do with a loss of her relationship with someone. These rejection-sensitive teenagers experience intense abandonment fears and they often get rageful if they sense that their attachment to someone is being threatened. If the borderline teen doesn't feel rage, she often feels crippling despair, a sense of emptiness and loneliness, and sometimes a haunting feeling or of wishing to be dead, at what might appear to be a relatively normal social setback. Borderline teenagers are unstable teenagers and often in contrast to the typically impulse-ridden decisions of teenagers, have massive shifts in their ideas about who they are, what they want to be, their sexual orientations, who their friends are, and even in regard to their family relations. The borderline teenager tends to idealize some and devalue others. Often the one person who is idealized today is devalued tomorrow. This split in the teenager's image of the outside world as being idealized or devalued reflects her own self-perception—some days feeling wonderful, happy, even euphoric and the next day plunged into despair and suicidal depression. In addition, impulsivity is sometimes expressed by being irresponsible; eating self-destructively even to the point of bulimia; using drugs; engaging in reckless activities including promiscuous sex; attempting suicide (and sometimes succeeding); injuring themselves on purpose, such as cutting or burning themselves; and in general, leading a reckless and deteriorating life. The borderline teenager typically feels bored with almost all aspects of life or simply empty inside. These teens often engage in massive verbal and sometimes physical battles with their closest relatives and friends. Borderline teenagers are unpredictable.

However, one thing is predictable: a key issue that upsets the borderline teenager is the fact that she feels abandoned, that someone was disloyal, or that she has not succeeded in successfully manipulating someone into her corner.

As a result of the above, life for borderline teenagers is one of intense pain. Not only are they in pain from their psychiatric status, but as a result of the problem, often do not succeed in life. They alienate people, they do not finish school, and they cannot concentrate. They may deteriorate to the point of having what appear to be psychotic symptoms such as hallucinations, delusions, and sometimes drug-induced states of psychiatric disturbance. They may commit suicide.

It is hard for a parent to differentiate this disorder from commonly co-occurring disorders such as drug-induced problems, bulimia; post-traumatic stress disorder; sexual or physical abuse, or neglect, which may be common in their family background); attention deficit hyperactivity disorder; and mood disturbances. The cause of borderline personality disorder is not known but difficult childhoods with high degrees of interpersonal stress within the family are a factor. Being physically or sexually abused, or neglected, is also associated with the disorder. There is some research that shows that there might be a genetic component and there is also a link in families between borderline personality disorder, substance abuse disorders, antisocial personality of adulthood, and mood disorders, in general.

Usually by the time parents consult me about their borderline teenagers, much has been attempted including vacations, changes of schools, changes of neighborhoods, visits to medical doctors or to emergency rooms for self-induced injuries, special tutors and remediation, and even various medications. Most important is that parents recognize that the borderline personality disorder is a serious condition that carries a mortality risk of somewhat under 10 percent but a risk of deterioration far greater if untreated. Many of the symptoms of borderline personality seem to occur in normal adolescence and the diagnosis should be made only by a trained mental-health professional. The good news is that many borderline adolescents tend to get better by the time they are through their twenties and recent studies have shown that sometimes even without treatment, an increase in stability can occur by the time they are in their thirties. But this should not be taken as an excuse to avoid treatment because of the many secondary effects that borderline personality has on the functioning of the individual as mentioned above.

What to Do

- If the teenager manifests any of the above symptoms, she should receive a complete psychiatric and physical evaluation.

- The psychiatrist should be certain of the diagnosis and rule out other conditions that often appear the same symptomatically, including other personality disorders, attention deficit disorder, mood disorders, substance abuse, PTSD, eating disorders, obsessive-compulsive disorder, and anxiety disorders.

- Appropriate treatment involves individual psychotherapy, including cognitive-behavioral therapy, dialectic behavior therapy, and dynamically oriented insight therapy.

- Family therapy is important both for psycho-educational reasons and also to heal some of the rifts that might be present—rifts which may be the cause or result of the borderline teenager's psychiatric disorder.

- Various medications are useful in the treatment of the border-line adolescent and depend on whatever major symptomatology needs attention; for example, mood instability can be treated with mood stabilizers while depression can often be treated with antidepressants. In the case of violent, angry, and aggressive behavior some of the anti-aggression medications, including the use of the new atypical antipsychotic medications such as Risperdal, Seroquel, Zyprexa and others, might be indicated.

- Substance-abuse treatment might also be necessary.

- Sexual counseling is also necessary to avoid reckless sexuality, which often results in pregnancies and sexually transmitted diseases.

- Hospitalization is sometimes indicated for the borderline adolescent due to out-of-control behavior, suicidal acting out, and/or psychotic deterioration that often occurs under stress.

SEE ALSO:

Anxiety
Obsessive-Compulsive Disorder
Stress and PTSD
Depression
Bipolar Disorder
Suicide
Anger
Self-Injurious Behavior
Violence
Attention Deficit Disorder
Sexual Abuse
Anorexia, Bulimia, and Overeating
Drugs

12. Schizophrenia

"Is there any hope? Did I do something wrong to him? WHY IS HE LIKE THIS?"

THESE ARE the kinds of anguished questions the parent of a schizophrenic teen asks. It is a devastating mental illness. Fortunately it is rare, afflicting approximately 1 percent of the population.

It is most rare in children and relatively uncommon in the early and middle teenage years. However, as late adolescence approaches, schizophrenia becomes more common, and even more common by the third decade of life. Despite the fact that full-blown schizophrenia is uncommon during the teenage years, there are a number of signs during this time that are considered prodromal markers of the disease—indications of the disease that is to come later.

Schizophrenia affects teenage boys and girls equally. It begins to appear slowly in adolescence and has many signs and symptoms, usually associated with a serious inability to function in the social and occupational spheres of life. It is considered a psychosis in that the teenager with schizophrenia often loses touch with reality. All areas of mental functioning can be involved including thinking, feeling, language, behavior, and the ability to function successfully in society.

There are two general categories of symptoms. The first are so-called positive symptoms, which include delusions that often have a bizarre quality to them. Also, there are often hallucinations, or pseudo-perceptions, involving any of the five senses, such as hearing voices, and seeing, tasting, smelling, and feeling things that don't exist. In addition, communication is impaired, most frequently manifested by disorganized speech. The last positive symptom is grossly disorganized behavior.

There are also the so-called negative symptoms, which include a flattening out of feeling states called "affective flattening," decrease in the fluency and amount of thinking and speaking, and a decrease in the ability to initiate goal-directed behavior. These are called negative because they manifest loss of mental functions.

Delusions are varied and often cause the teenager to believe that he can read thoughts, predict the future, manipulate events beyond his control, and to sense he is being persecuted when in fact he cannot. Delusions may include thinking that he is someone famous, of a particular high order of religiosity, or in fact anyone in world. Schizophrenic teenagers often have trouble communicating and carrying on understandable conversations. In other words, their associations are often "loosened," making it difficult for others to follow the teenager's train of thought. Incoherence is common. Behaviors such as gesturing or walking around in circles also contribute to the sense of disorganization that schizophrenic teens evince. Therefore delusions; hallucinations; disorganized speech, including frequent derailment and incoherence; grossly disorganized or even catatonic behavior; and negative symptoms are often considered among the diagnostic criteria of schizophrenia. Most characteristics of true schizophrenia are bizarre, such as hearing voices talking about the teenager or talking with one another, or the feeling that thoughts are being inserted into or withdrawn from their minds.

The inability to perform well in one or more areas of functioning, or not ever reaching the capacities or standards of other teenagers of the same age, are characteristic of schizophrenia. Thus, education is often interrupted, and the ability to hold a job and social adaptation are impaired. The schizophrenic teenager is unable to take care of himself in any appropriate fashion.

Often parents will state that prior to the outbreak of full-blown schizophrenia they noticed that their teenager had been withdrawn, had expressed unusual thoughts, was socially isolated, was "obsessed" with irrelevant or strange ideas, showed compulsive behaviors beyond that found in typical obsessive-compulsive disorder, and was "slipping away" into "another world." Confusing television, daydreams, and night dreams with reality is often common. Schizophrenic teenagers appear confused, are very moody, and often appear depressed and sometimes paranoid as well. Teenagers often act younger than they really are and show severe anxiety, panic attacks, and phobias. The schizophrenic teenager dresses and grooms poorly. Numerous fears and inappropriate ideas pop up. The schizophrenic teenager often appears to be in a world of his own.

There are no physical symptoms of schizophrenia and thus the diagnosis is made on the basis of symptoms as well as on a psychiatric examination of the teenager. Schizophrenia is a complex illness and often is misdiagnosed early on and confused with other syndromes. Schizophrenic changes in personality are slow and often are confused with normal teenage rebellious behavior. Also, since teenagers undergo so many emotional swings normally, the ups and downs of the pre-schizophrenic teenager are often considered normal. However, the schizophrenic teenager often manifests many symptoms that will perplex parents: thinking that is difficult to understand, bizarre sleep and wake patterns, acting "strange" in general, and losing friends. Rarely does schizophrenia start suddenly, but sometimes it does.

No one knows what causes schizophrenia. To some degree it is inherited, but the exact contribution that genes make is unknown. It tends to run in families. Brain chemistry is thought to be important, specifically neurotransmitters, which are considered the agents that cause this mental illness. There are other factors as well. In particular, the neurotransmitter dopamine is considered one of the major causes of the positive symptoms of schizophrenia. Having too much dopamine circulating in the brain's synapses is thought to cause this. The evidence for this is based on the fact that some drugs that lower dopamine help schizophrenic teens and some that increase dopamine, such as amphetamines, tend to make it worse. Also, some people feel that structural changes in the brain such as enlarged ventricles— spaces in the brain—might be responsible. Some feel that the different sides in the brain of the schizophrenic are uneven. Environmental factors are also thought to be contributive, such as stress, problems in the family, and other psychological phenomena. On the whole, however, no one knows for sure what causes schizophrenia at this point.

The psychiatrist making a diagnosis of schizophrenia has to rule out other conditions that might be similar, such as drug-induced psychotic states—especially those caused by drugs like amphetamines, LSD, and hallucinogens. Sometimes depression or other mood disorders present with psychotic features and sometimes even medical conditions or brain tumors can present with psychotic inhibitions that mimic schizophrenia. The doctor will also rule out pervasive developmental disorder, also called autistic disorder, that was perhaps diagnosed earlier in childhood, as well as severe communication disorders that might be present and that might lead some diagnosticians to the wrong conclusion if the history isn't known. There is treatment for schizophrenia although no cure. The good news is that some schizophrenic teenagers have one psychotic breakdown and recover completely. The earlier treatment is received for the first breakdown, the better the prognosis is thought to be. Unfortunately, receiving appropriate early treatment happens in a minority of cases.

Despite the fact that schizophrenia presents as a chronic disease, there are many treatments that do help, including the use of medication—specifically antipsychotic medications (see Getting Help chapter and section on psychotropic medication). Old-line antipsychotics include medications such as Thorazine, Stelazine, Mellaril, Haldol, and other drugs. Many of these medications are called neuroleptic drugs because they induce neurological syndromes, including disturbances of movement such as dystonia (stiffness and twitching), Parkinsonism (symptoms similar to Parkinson's disease), akathisia (such as restlessness, foot tapping, anxiety, and hyperactivity), and tardive dyskinesia (involuntary movements around the mouth and tongue area such that the patient often looks like he is chewing or rolling his tongue). The set of atypical antipsychotic medications help quell the symptoms of schizophrenia but do not induce such serious neurological side effects. These are being discovered and manufactured quickly; at the present time, the most common ones are Risperdal, Zyprexa, Geodon, Moban, Abilify, Seroquel, and Clozapine. There are side effects to these medications as well and patients have to be followed quite closely. Some of these drugs also are considered to have some effect on the negative symptoms, which the earlier neuroleptic generation of antipsychotics did not.

Other therapeutic interventions that are known to help include:

- Hospitalization when necessary. Hospitalization protects the patient and others from bizarre, violent, and anxiety-producing behaviors, especially during the acute psychotic phase of the illness. Often hospitalization allows a patient to receive medication and to be monitored closely for side effects and therapeutic effects as well.

- Supportive psychotherapy. This often helps people learn how to live independently, get various forms of therapy, and comply with taking medication.

- Individual psychotherapy, family therapy, and specialized day treatment programs both in schools and hospitals, which are often used to help patients with their illness.

- Group therapy and group activities, which help decrease isolation, despair, and depression, and make a person better able to live with his illness in society.

- Psychosocial rehabilitation, often found in the community, which helps people get out of the hospital and live independently. Many of these programs are twenty-four-hour-a-day, seven-day-a-week programs.

What to Do

- If you notice that your teen is developing any of the prodromal signs or more acute signs of schizophrenia, immediate consultation with a mental-health professional, preferably a teenage psychiatrist, is mandatory. Also, a complete physical examination to rule out organic illness is done at or around the same time.

- Your psychiatrist might recommend hospitalization for your teenager. This is often difficult and painful as the teenager might resist, partially due to just being a teenager and partially due to delusions or beliefs that nothing is wrong with him. It is important that parents who are quite anxious and devastated by recognition of this illness in their teenager go along with the doctor's suggestion if hospitalization is indicated.

- It is important that you stay in contact with your child through his hospitalization and stay as close as possible—and be as compassionate as possible—during that time and after he leaves the hospital and goes back into the community. Your involvement in parent groups, support groups, psycho-educational groups, and any other community support is very necessary, not only to give you support but also as a message to your child as a sign of hope.

- It is important that you make sure your child takes his medication. There will often be resistance to taking medication because the teenager does not want to think he is crazy but despite this resistance, it is important that you recognize the help that medication will give.

- On the whole, the earlier the treatment the better for the prognosis. This is why it is important to pursue the help that is needed the first time you notice something unusual that persists for more than several days or weeks.

SEE ALSO:

Anxiety
Social Phobia and Shyness
Obsessive-Compulsive Disorder
Depression
Drugs
Getting Help

II

Behavior

13. Self-Injurious Behavior

"I told you, Mom, it was an accident! I was opening a can of soda, and, you know, the pop-top? Well, uh, it cut into my arm . . . Yeah, okay, it's happened before. So, I'm clumsy, okay? Leave me alone!"

ISABEL IS A JUNIOR in high school and she's been carefully, secretly slicing her arms with a thin razor blade at regular intervals for the past three years. Not all the time—just at moments of higher than usual anxiety. And not as a suicide attempt. The cuts are superficial; she's learned how to inflict them so that she just bleeds a little. Tiny lines of blood per careful draw of the blade are produced, after which she carefully dabs them with rubbing alcohol. It satisfies her in a way she can't explain. Indeed, she doesn't have any idea why she does it. She's ashamed even to think about it, much less admit it to anyone. It's like a compulsion—she knows that. For some reason, when she feels anxious only this behavior helps her to calm down, distract her. If her mother hadn't noticed the thin scabbed slits on her forearm more than once, she would never have talked about it even as much as she has here. All she knows, is that when she's anxious, she reaches for the blade . . .

Cutting and other forms of self-injurious behavior—hitting one's own limbs or head, picking at skin lesions and hair, purposely bruising or biting oneself—constitute deeply baffling and troubling behaviors both to the teenagers who perform them and family members who can't imagine why they're doing it, or even how the idea to do

61

it ever came into their heads. "Why would Isabel even think of cutting herself?" Isabel's mother asked me when she came to my office. "I mean, it's not something she's ever seen anyone else do! Is she losing her mind?"

Usually teenagers who harm themselves are experiencing enormous and uncomfortable anxiety, tension, or anger; this causes them to feel an irresistible urge to hurt themselves. People who don't resort to these behaviors tend to be baffled by why anyone would want to self-inflict physical pain; in fact, teenagers who regularly injure themselves often self-induce a kind of anesthesia or dissociation that allows them to escape pain. Through the distraction of "acting out"—turning amorphous, painful emotions into a concrete, nameable physical sensation—the teenager finds at least momentary relief. It is no wonder teens who've discovered this means of self-induced "anesthesia" so regularly return to it. For them, it's the only means of reducing anxiety that works.

As with Isabel, self-injurious behavior usually is done secretly and is a source of shame. Often the behavior is part of a larger ritual (for example, involving a carefully prescribed preparation for the self-cutting and caretaking of the wound, such as dabbing it with a medication after it is inflicted). The self-injury is usually repeated in the same manner, although sometimes teenagers do vary their behavior, for example, alternating sticking needles into their skin with burning themselves with cigarette lighters.

Alarming as this behavior is, the relatively reassuring news is that self-injurious behavior generally does not involve a suicidal motive, nor is it usually life-threatening. (Isabel's great care in causing only superficial wounds that can heal quickly is typical.) However, the behavior needs careful and compassionate attention nonetheless. Sometimes self-injurious behavior can be permanently disfiguring or accidentally cause more serious damage. The shame and revulsion the teenager may feel about her own self-mutilation may be far worse than the momentary relief the behavior affords them, an emotional pain that may adversely affect every area of life. Whatever can be done to encourage the teen to talk about this compulsion with a mental-health professional who understands its nature ought to be pursued.

Psychiatric diagnoses of self-injuring teenagers include depression, conduct disorder, and anxiety syndromes; often self-injuring adolescents also engage in alcohol or drug use, may suffer from an eating disorder such as bulimia, or are otherwise antisocial. It usually begins (as it did with Isabel) in early adolescence and, if untreated, tends slowly to decrease over time, sometimes not disappearing until well into adulthood (the twenties and thirties). Again, the most important thing to remember is that the motive behind self-injurious behavior is to soothe and alleviate intolerable feelings.

Girls are much more likely to harm themselves than boys. Most self-injuring behaviors occur in upper-middle- and middle-class females, in often intelligent and educated young women. There is some thought that there may be a link to having been physically or sexually abused, or being the child of an alcoholic. Eating disorders are also common to self-injuring teenagers.

The common denominator found in most families of self-injuring adolescents is a pattern of poor communication among family members. Various contributory stressors may be parental substance abuse, violence, neglect, and physical or emotional abuse of the teen. These kinds of family or parental behaviors make teenagers feel there is no one in the family available to talk with or confide in. In this kind of environment they learn that words have little value and that certain feelings are taboo. Increasingly, they feel that there is little empathy to be had from anyone; as their sense of isolation intensifies the need for an "escape" becomes more urgent. In addition to the general family-induced depression and anxiety described above, the self-injuring teen may be suffering from post-traumatic stress disorder as a result of having been physically traumatized or abused.

As peculiar as it might seem to the outsider, self-injuring teens hurt themselves as a means to gain mastery over their bodies at a time when they feel they have no control over their minds, their inner worlds, or their lives as a whole. In this way, hurting themselves may be the only time when they feel they get any care. In addition, self-injurious behavior is thought by some to express rage or to re-enact past traumatic events. However, whatever the complex of motives gives rise to it, self-injurious behavior is always a cry for help from teenagers who feel that their real cries, their real yearnings, and their real words evoke no response.

What to Do

- Most important is that parents create an atmosphere in which they listen attentively to the teen and acknowledge the teen's feelings. Parents should learn to validate teenagers' feelings rather than diminish their importance or scold teens for having these feelings. This in itself will set the stage for communication and obviate the need to "act out" self-injuriously.

- If a child is cutting or committing other self-injurious acts, a mental-health professional should be called in to diagnose the underlying cause of the behavior. Diagnosis will determine the course of treatment.

- Although self-injurious behavior is not suicidal per se, there does seem to be some increased risk of suicide among those who injure themselves compulsively (and non-suicidally). This is another reason fostering good communication in the family and seeking appropriate professional help are indicated.

- In addition to psychotherapy and family therapy, some anti-depressant medications, especially within the category of selective serotonin reuptake inhibitors, have been found to be helpful.

SEE ALSO:

Anxiety
Stress and PTSD
Depression
Suicide
Behavior Disorders
Anorexia, Bulimia, and Overeating
Drugs
Teens of Alcoholics and Substance Abusers
Getting Help

14. Bullying

"Jason, I told you I can't drive you to school every day. What's the problem? One of the reasons we moved here was that we were within walking distance of school. What are you afraid of?"

WHAT FOURTEEN-YEAR-OLD JASON is afraid of is a fifteen-year-old big, rough guy Ken, who has taken to waiting for him around the corner every morning before school—waiting to kick Jason's books out of his hands, push him down on the ground, make fun of him, and call him names Jason couldn't ever bring himself to repeat to anyone, certainly not his exasperated mother. What Jason is afraid of, to the point where it's interfered with his concentration in school, shamefully obsessing as he does almost constantly about how to avoid Ken (and what a wuss he is for not being able to stand up to him), is being mercilessly bullied.

Bullying is seen in all age groups, starting even in the preschool years, increasing during the elementary school years, and peaking in middle school and junior high before declining only somewhat in high school. It is estimated that 25 to 35 percent of all children are involved in bullying, either as perpetrators or victims. Both boys and girls bully but differently. Boys tend to intimidate physically, while girls bully more through gossip and inducing rejection of other girls. By definition, bullying consists of behaviors such as hitting, teasing, threatening, humiliating, intimidating, pushing, taking personal belongings, name-calling, making threats, manipulating, and engaging in social exclusion, extortion, and other behaviors. The key issue in bullying is that intimidation occurs repeatedly and becomes a form of harassment and abuse of other children.

The teenaged bully usually was a bully earlier in life and has a higher propensity to become an adult criminal—and even smoke and drink. Although for many, bullying decreases over time, for others it becomes an ongoing characteristic, leading to diagnoses of teenage oppositional-defiant disorder and conduct disorder, an adult diagnosis of antisocial behavior, and problems with the law.

Bullies derive a feeling of power and control by bullying, by inflicting their tactics on victims. Sometimes they rationalize or lie, claiming that the victim provoked them. Bullies enjoy physical aggression and violence. They usually have poor impulse control, have trouble tolerating frustration, and are often angry and prone to temper tantrums. Bullying is not an insignificant issue. It can cause great harm, disrupting other people's lives in negative ways. It also signals that the bully is in trouble: the bully's antisocial and violent traits do not bode well for his own future. Lacking empathy for other people, the bully may be destined to be as miserable as he wants his victims to be.

Bullies often come from homes where they receive very little emotional empathy themselves—little involvement in their lives from their parents, poor or no monitoring of their behavior, and, in general, a broken home that is either too permissive or too harsh. As a result of poor parenting, these children do not know how to handle problems in a mature fashion and often repetitively resort to impulsive and physically and emotionally destructive ways of handling developmental issues. These include vandalism, shoplifting, truancy, fighting, and substance abuse.

Victims of bullies often possess certain common characteristics too. They are typically nervous, have poor self-views, are often depressed, and have trouble defending themselves when they are bullied. Sometimes they are overly close to their parents. Therefore they often have little experience with separation and individuation, and an inability to fend for themselves, especially when attacked. They experience themselves as weak and communicate this to bullies, who readily pounce on them. Often bullies target victims who have certain physical characteristics that make them unpopular or set them apart, from being overweight to suffering from some physical anomaly or wearing glasses. Victims of bullies often don't have many friends; the friends they do have tend to be victims of bullies as well. Bullies seem to have radar for finding "easy marks"—people who are predisposed to being victims. If bullying continues, it can make these children even worse; as with Jason, affecting their concentration in school and even causing them to miss school in order to avoid being bullied. Bullying increases depression, anxiety, and social isolation. In some cases, victims of bullies have even committed suicide, one instance of which brought major media attention to the issues of bullying not many years ago. Even when these victims grow up, long-term studies have implicated their childhood victimization as factors leading to adult depression. Other mental-health problems, including schizophrenia, have been connected to the effects of bullying.

What to Do

If your teenager is a victim of a bully you should do the following:

- Notice if he is suffering from signs of depression, low grades, loss of appetite, trouble sleeping, refusal to go to school, or obsessing about (and possibly obtaining) certain weapons or defensive tools to stop bullies from bothering him. This fortifies the diagnosis of depression in general, but more specifically may indicate that a child is having trouble with a bully. These symptoms don't automatically indicate bullying but they may.

- Take time to talk in an empathetic way with your child. Do not criticize your child if he is a victim of a bully and don't bully him yourself.

- If your child is being bullied you should notify the organization or place where the bullying is taking place, such as the school, camp, or venue for an after-school activity.

- Help your children with social skills and teach him how to make friends. This can decrease the feeling of victimization.

- Parents should become active in in their community in order to avoid bullying issues. For instance: there are effective intervention programs across the country that parents should get involved with in their children's schools. Schools should be encouraged to create and enforce anti-bullying policies and to have class discussions about bullies. Conflict-resolution classes have also helped.

- Parents should make other parents aware of these issues, especially since many parents tend to overlook bullying as if it were a normal rite of passage in a child's growth.

- Role-playing exercises that give teenagers the experience of bullying or being bullied have become very popular in many school systems and can be illuminating and helpful.

- Schools and other places where children congregate also should have increased supervision at free time, as this is known to decrease bullying behaviors.

- If your child obviously is suffering from a major mental problem having to do with bullying, professional help might be necessary.

If your teenager is a bully you should:

- Be sure to view the bullying behavior as part of an overall behavior problem.

- Be sure you are not a bully yourself.

- Explain the effects of being bullied in the hopes of inducing a degree of empathy.

- Empower your teenager by directing him toward activities that will increase his self-esteem.

- Seek professional help, if necessary, in an effort to insure that a bully does not continue to take advantage of others, since this can easily lead to the intervention of other authorities.

- Try to teach your child other modes of conflict resolution. This effort can probably be helped by any of the numerous anti-bullying campaigns that have been established in educational systems across the nation.

Keep in mind that bullying is a major problem in this country. Teenagers should be able to live and learn in a safe environment. Chronic bullying or victimization erodes the chances of successful life adaptation and is not a normal rite of passage.

SEE ALSO:

Anxiety
Depression
Suicide
Schizophrenia
Violence
Behavior Disorders

15. Violence

"Yeah, I kicked him, so what?"

AT SEVENTEEN, Danny is a big guy, obviously tough, and naturally athletic. The football coach in the new high school to which Danny had transferred thought so, too. He got in touch with Danny's previous school when he found out Danny had played ball there. He asked the head of the physical education department what the scoop was. "Stay away from him," the man said. "He's bad news, a real loose cannon. We had to kick him off the team. Couldn't control him; kept getting into fights." Apparently one of the reasons Danny's family had moved to a new town was because Danny was on the verge of getting expelled; he had been in so many fights and vandalized so much school property that no one in the town would have anything to do with him. Even his parents were afraid of him. Danny had recently gotten drunk at a party and wrecked a friend's car. When the friend got angry at him, Danny kicked him in the stomach. Danny's mother finally voiced her deepest worry: "Is my son going to be like this all his life? Is there no hope of turning him around?"

A deeper worry: Is Danny the kind of kid you hear about who suddenly flips out and starts gunning down people at a shopping mall? The reassuring news is, there is no reason to assume this. While Danny's actions are certainly dangerous to himself and others, the likelihood of him "snapping" and indiscriminately mowing down innocent people in a parking lot or a school yard is very remote. Like most other "loose cannon" teens, Danny can be helped. However, it's no wonder we fear he can't be. The specter of extreme teenage violence has haunted us for a number of years through highly publicized shootings, murders of kids and teachers and passersby by a few clearly disturbed teens. Violent rock-music lyrics, the Internet, television, and movies have been implicated by some in causing this "flipping out," often making it seem like not only the culture but the kids it affects have gone dangerously out of control.

Ranking with fears of suicide and drug abuse, violence in teens is one of the most pressing concerns of parents who come to me for help. I can't count the number of times I've been asked by parents if I think their children are likely to commit heinous crimes. The truth is, despite what the media have led us to believe, there is no epidemic of teenage violence in this country. Although there was some increase in the number of violent acts committed by teenagers up until the early nineties, there has been a decrease since 1993. This does not mean that there aren't still many thousands of teenagers like Danny who commit violent acts, but the attention focused on isolated acts of extreme teenage violence has led to unwarranted fears that every teen is at risk, either as perpetrator or victim of a violent act.

This is also not to suggest that violence in teens isn't a problem. A wide range of violent behavior is committed by teenagers, from fighting to vandalism, and felonies such as rape, robbery, assault, and even homicide. However, although about 85 to 90 percent of teenagers commit an antisocial act at some point in their lives, a very small percentage (probably under 1 percent) will ever go on to become hardened violent criminals. It's important to note that it's rare to find a teenager who commits a violent crime without also having committed many other antisocial acts as well. Most violent teenagers also have problems such as substance abuse, academic failure, truancy, suspension, and expulsion. A high percentage of violent offenders have been victims of physical violence themselves.

Causes

The causes of teen violence are hard to pin down, but there appear to be a number of predictors of it. A child who exhibits violent or aggressive behavior will tend to do so in his teens as well. Long-standing learning or emotional disabilities can exacerbate the tendency to act out violently in adolescence, such as performing poorly in school and exhibiting symptoms of inattention, hyperactivity, and impulsivity, all of which may indicate the presence of attention deficit disorder. Related problems such as the inability to sit still, restlessness, and difficulty concentrating also increase the odds of a teen turning to violent behavior. Children often learn violence at home: a teen used to a family mode of fighting and physical abuse is more likely to continue that legacy in his own life. Parental neglect, inconsistent discipline, and emotional abuse also make it more likely that a teen will express himself aggressively. Large families and single-parent families may also predict difficulties in this area. Peer pressure from antisocial friends or gang members goads many teens to act out violently as well. Violence in the media, and exposure to guns and other weapons, also play a role.

While it is difficult to diagnostically link violence to psychiatric disorders, some appear to be related. The most common is conduct disorder, which for unknown reasons seems more likely to lead to chronic violent behavior when its onset occurs in childhood than when it first appears in adolescence. Teens diagnosed with a mood disorder such as depression and especially those prone to suicide attempts, are at high risk. So are those with mania or hypomania typical of bipolar disorder, and attention deficit disorder or oppositional defiant disorder. Some teens are violent under the influence of psychosis, when they may be experiencing hallucinations or hearing voices instructing them to cause hurt or damage. Teens prone to paranoia or suspiciousness, who feel habitually abused or insulted, or who are under the influence of drugs and alcohol are more likely to be violent. Some drugs in particular tend to induce violence, including "angel dust" (PCP), methamphetamines, and crack cocaine. Any mind-altering substance that lowers the threshold of awareness may unleash the potential for out-of-control aggression. Abused children who develop dissociative symptoms may, during a dissociative episode, commit violent acts.

Studies of anatomical or functional brain disorders also have indicated a greater probability of violent behavior in teens. These disorders include learning disabilities; the inability of brain function to aid good judgment, decision-making, or a feeling of self-control; certain brain lesions resulting from trauma or head injury, which lessen impulse control. Frontal lobe impairment also has been related to violence. Remember that these are theories, meant to give a context of possibilities, not to suggest any definitive connections.

Warning Signs

What should alert you that violence may be more than a transient problem with your teen? The most frequent warning signs are the boy or girl's increasing inability to control anger, which leads to frequent tantrums and chronic irritability. Teens who don't think before they act or who have a very low tolerance for frustration are also more likely to become violent. Some teens resort to anger because they know of no other way to express frustration; some use it to manipulate others. Both motives can fuel aggressive or hurtful acts. Teens who can't let go of powerful resentments or grudges, who seek revenge for any perceived slight, or who are especially susceptible to peer pressure are also often prone to act out violently. Sometimes violence expresses a need for attention that teens don't get elsewhere.

Immediate warning signs include frequent physical fighting, significant increase in vandalism, use of drugs or alcohol, dangerous risk-taking, gang involvement, and bragging about specific plans to hurt or injure others or making frequent threats. A teen who enjoys hurting animals or carries a weapon is an obvious candidate for violence. People who have been victimized by bullies also may act out violently.

What to Do

- If you are worried about your teen being or becoming violent, the most important concern should be your own safety or the safety of anyone else who might possibly be subjected to the teen's violent behavior. Take measures to protect yourself first.

- Do all you can to encourage your child to talk about his feelings rather than use anger to express them. Discuss the early signs of oncoming violence; ask your teen to describe for you the progression from anger to violent action, and see what you can both come up with to short-circuit the process so that violence can be averted. Signs of rage that lead to violence may include: faster breathing, shaking, heart rate increases, the face flushing, and increased tension in the chest or other area of the body. Suggest that the teen note his own progressive reactions and practice deciding not to give in to them. This will help the teen to think before acting out.

- If anger leading to violence is chronic and intractable, make sure your teen undergoes a full physical and neurological examination, and seek professional help from a mental-health practitioner experienced in treating emotional distress in teenagers.

- Specific forms of treatment that have proven to be effective include parent-management training, where parents are taught how to help their child contain and deal with anger, cognitive problem-solving skills, and systemic therapy geared to altering the systems from which violent behavior emanates. Although no specific medication exists to treat anger per se, pharmacological interventions may be indicated if an underlying and possibly contributory problem such as ADD or depression is diagnosed. Stimulants, mood stabilizers, antipsychotics, and drugs that calm the sympathetic nervous system may, if appropriate, be of help.

- Confinement in specialized residential treatment centers, or employing probationary measures with psychiatric hospitalization, will rarely be indicated but may be necessary if the problem is severe.

- Make sure that the teen has no access to any weapons or other dangerous objects.

- Remember the power of example: if you and other family members demonstrate that you can manage anger in a healthy way, you'll go a long way to helping your teen learn to do the same thing.

See also:

Depression
Bipolar Disorder
Suicide
Bullying
Attention Deficit Disorder
Behavior Disorders
Drugs
The Media
School Problems

16. Gangs

*"Hey, Tony? Yeah, it's Bill. Yeah, I can get out
okay tonight. I'll tell her I'm goin' to the library
or somethin'. She's workin' the night shift; she
won't know I ain't comin' home. What, we
breakin' in some new guys tonight? Hot damn,
I'm up for somethin' nasty. Gonna give those guys
an initiation. You get the beer?"*

TONY AND BILL are whispering on the phone. Bill's mother is in the
next room, and if there's one requirement for being a gang member,
it's secrecy. Tony's the head of "The War Lords," a gang Billy has
been part of now for two years. He remembers his own initiation
and how he nearly got caught holding up a local bodega, which he
had to do to be admitted. "Man's gotta prove himself before we'll let
him in," they told him back then. Another requirement: selling dope.
"Proceeds pay for the beer. Plus, we get to do some too if we want."
Sure it got dangerous sometimes, but the payoff, Bill thinks, is worth
it. "Gangs'll take care of ya if you don't wuss out," Tony told Bill
back then. Bill was determined to meet their requirements when he
joined and he still is, even though he's gotten into some bad fights,
had some close calls with the cops, and, well, his friend Jeff did get
gunned down. He missed Jeff on the rare occasions he let himself
think about it. But he keeps telling himself nothing bad is going to
happen to him, not if he keeps watching his back and hanging with

the War Lords and doing what Tony, the leader, tells him. Anyway, where else could he get the kind of thrills—and acceptance—he gets with these guys?

The craving to find some sort of group identity is usually strong in adolescence. Generally, this urge starts to take hold earlier in childhood, during what is known as the "latency" period (roughly ages six to twelve). It's normal and healthy for boys and girls to seek participation in groups and to achieve some degree of identification with their peers. By the time they become teenagers, they frequently find or have found nurturing group acceptance in sports teams, rock bands, or any number of special-interest organizations that offer the opportunity to bond with like-minded teens. But the tendency to bond "tribally" in adolescence is never more frightening than when the "tribe" is a gang. While gangs offer their members a powerful sense of belonging, almost inevitably, they also lead to disaster for virtually every member. Untold numbers of teens have gotten into drugs, and committed violent acts, crimes, and felonies—sometimes to the point of murder or being murdered themselves—directly as the result of being gang members. Prisons are full of gang members.

A gang, as usefully defined in the Northeast Communities Against Substance Abuse (NECASA) Web site, is "any group of people who engage in socially disruptive behavior usually within a defined territory and operate by creating an atmosphere of fear and intimidation in a community." Many gangs are loosely defined, although some use a logo and name or sport a certain color or particular article of clothing as identification. Common characteristics, say NECASA, are "intimidation, extortion, vandalism, assault, 'swarming,' drug-trafficking, stabbings, shootings, and sometimes murder." Hand signals, nicknames, and other symbols—and, of course, graffiti on buildings, telephone booths, and other public places—are ways that gangs "mark" their territory and identify themselves. Wherever young people congregate—transit stops, malls, parks, schools, and streets—gangs congregate. And they have become more violent than ever before. It's not an exaggeration to say that an unprecedented tribal youth subculture has emerged and shows no signs of abating.

Teens who join gangs often turn to gang leaders—as Bill turns to Tony—out of the powerful need to find some authority they can "believe" in. Often these teens come from broken homes—single-parent households where supervision is either lax or erratic—and don't receive anywhere near adequate attention or care. (Bill's situation falls into this category: his mother, a nurse's aide, spends her nights working at the hospital and her days sleeping; she's virtually never awake when Bill is.) Because so little support is found at home, the craving for it becomes particularly acute in many teens who join gangs. But the support gangs offer can be lethal. Gang violence is responsible for up to 50 percent of murders in Los Angeles and 40 percent in other states. Street gangs now operate in over 90 percent of all major cities. Gang crime has increased even in smaller cities with populations of twenty-five thousand or less.

While gang members frequently don't advertise their membership too blatantly—doing so would alert authorities that they're involved in drugs and crime—they do, as mentioned above, signal to each other and rival gangs their particular "affiliations" in various ways: with colored bandannas, sometimes stuffed into a back pocket, tied around the arm, or worn under a cap; with tattoos—sometimes painfully and meticulously administered burn marks (the result of what can be very brutal and dangerous initiations)—flashed as a sign of their gang affiliations. However, many parents have no clue that their sons or daughters belong to gangs: as Bill's whispered phone conversation with Tony attests, secrecy is paramount.

Teens join gangs for a host of reasons: prestige and status, excitement, selling (and doing) drugs, the prospect of making more money than they feel they can via legitimate means, and seeking to boost self-esteem (particularly true of minorities who feel neglected or abused or otherwise dismissed). Risk factors in the community abound and peer pressure and growing up in neighborhoods in which social attachment tends to be low are high on the list. Poor adjustment to school (inability to relate to teachers and/or performing poorly in academics), unsupervised hanging out with delinquent friends, easy access to drugs (drugs in and of themselves make it more likely that a teen will join a gang), traumatic life events, and episodes of depression are all implicated. Early sexual activity and being male can factor in as well.

Common misapprehensions about gangs are that only boys join them (there are plenty of "girl gangs"), that they are only an inner-city problem, that they are only made up of black or Hispanic youths, or that gang members come from families who don't care about them.

What to Do

- A teenager can refuse to join a gang: talk with your teen about resisting any intimidation tactics he may be experiencing from other gang members.

- Encourage your teen to go to police, parents, teachers, and other authority figures for help. Gang activity can and should be reported.

- Getting involved in other activities—both group (sports and other special interest) and solo (hobbies, playing an instrument, and so on) options abound—can give your teen a healthy sense of purpose and belonging.

- Increase parenting skills by attending parent-education groups—and especially any that address the dangers of gangs, so that you'll know what to watch for in your teenager.

- Set a good example: show, in your own life and dealings with other people, that there are healthy and satisfying modes of interaction your teen can pursue. This is the most powerful help you can give.

- Know what your teen is doing and where he is, and make sure he is involved in supervised activities.

- Praise your teen. Do what you can to bolster his self-esteem, the lack of which is a frequent motive for joining gangs and committing other antisocial acts.

- Be very clear about your disapproval of gang activities.

- As in virtually every other dilemma or potential problem your teen faces, family communication is essential. When you're able to talk to and listen to your teen on a regular basis, the odds go down that your teen will turn to a "new" family for guidance, identity, a sense of belonging, or other support.

SEE ALSO:

Depression
Bipolar Disorder
Violence
Discipline
Drugs
School Problems

17. Risk Taking

"Are you crazy? And after we grounded you for
six months! Do you realize you might have killed
yourself, not to mention everybody else in the car?"

KEITH, EIGHTEEN, has just stumbled in, reeking of beer, at three a.m.
on a Sunday morning, three hours past the Saturday-night curfew
his parents had set for him. The front end of the car in which he'd
driven six of his friends back from a party is smashed, the result of
careening over a highway divider and into a tree. He'd barely man-
aged to skid back onto the highway, narrowly missing oncoming traffic, and get away before the cops came. It would have infuriated his
father further to know that Keith and his friends felt they'd just had
the time of their lives.

Some degree of risk taking in teenage years is inevitable, and
much risk taking is healthy, such as taking the risk of pushing oneself to accomplish something new or difficult, or risking making new
friends at an unfamiliar school. At such times it constitutes an important step from childhood to adulthood. Healthy risks aid the teenager
in developing and consolidating his identity. Risk taking also helps
teens to develop values; for example, taking the social risk of not
going along with the crowd if the activity is dangerous, illegal, or
unappealing. In fact, it's not only impossible to stop teenagers from
taking risks, but inadvisable. Encouraging healthy risk taking is an
important part of parenting a teen.

However, the risks Keith has taken are obviously of a different
order. Under peer pressure from his friends—and out of his own need

to "prove" himself as fearless—the behaviors Keith has engaged in are dangerous to the point of possibly being fatal. What Keith's dad doesn't realize is that his son's desire to "prove himself" partly comes from wanting to get his emotionally distant dad's attention, possibly by becoming the cutup his dad had often boasted about being in college.

The fact that Keith's dad doesn't realize there's more going on in his son than mere willful misbehavior is key. Parents not only need to be clear with their teens about what are acceptable and unhealthy risks but to be alert to the reasons teens may resort to unhealthy risk taking. If, like Keith, your teen regularly resorts to behaviors that endanger his own safety or well-being, see it as a signal that you need to pay much closer attention to him. Dangerous risks repetitively engaged in are red flags: messages from your teen that all is not well. Merely punishing a risk-taking teen for behaving badly won't help either your teen or you to get at the root of what is really causing the problem.

Many surveys over the years have indicated the most prevalent risky behaviors that should worry parents: smoking cigarettes, drinking alcohol, and taking illegal drugs; fighting and risky sexual activity; and, of course, any expression of suicidal or violent intentions. Eating disorders also constitute dangerous risk taking, such as extreme dieting, anorexia, or bulimia. Getting involved in gangs, scapegoating, shoplifting, and stealing comprise other dangerous risks. While studies have indicated that teenage risk taking has generally decreased over the past decade, the above are all risks to whose signs parents must be alert. Studies indicate that teens who take dangerous risks in one area tend to take risks in others.

Helping the teen to differentiate between healthy experimentation and dangerous risk taking is important because teens often lack the maturity and judgment to do so on their own; for example, sometimes it is difficult for teenagers to understand long-term risks, such as those involved in smoking, since there is no immediate harm. Teenagers often feel invincible, immortal, and invulnerable. They feel "this can't happen to me." Feeling good at the moment even if it means drinking and driving or having dangerous unprotected sex often supersedes any thought that these behaviors are life threatening. Parents need to balance allowing teens to make appropriate decisions for themselves and setting guidelines about unacceptable behavior.

Statistics make the need for this balance urgent. The most common causes of death in teenagers are accidents, suicide, and homicide. These most commonly involve reckless and risky driving. Judgment, decision-making, driving skills, and ability to respond to hazards are less reliable in teens than adults. The fatal and non-fatal accident rates for teenagers between the ages of sixteen and twenty are twenty times higher than for the general population. Especially dangerous is the combined use of alcohol and other drugs when driving. Nighttime driving also constitutes a risk, as does not wearing a seatbelt (the concept of a seatbelt may be seen by the teen as a symbol of parental restriction).

The largest and most comprehensive studies of teenagers have concluded that enhancing a teenager's feeling of positive connection to his home, his family, and his school is most crucial in protecting him from getting involved in risky behaviors. It is now known that the example set by parents is an extremely important factor in preventing teenage risk taking; for example, teens whose parents smoke, drink alcohol, or use drugs are more likely to engage in these behaviors themselves. Similarly, violent homes beget violent teenagers. Statistically, where there are weapons in the home, teenagers tend to be more involved in violent behaviors as well as experiencing suicidal ideation at some point in their lives. Parents who are regularly present in the home and expect excellence from their teenagers help reduce the odds of their taking unhealthy risks.

How common are risky behaviors in teens? Statistics paint a varied picture: 25 percent of teens smoke; 17.5 percent reported drinking during any single month; 12 percent had smoked marijuana; sexual intercourse was reported at a rate of 16 percent in seventh and eighth graders and at about 50 percent in ninth to twelfth graders; 3.5 percent of teenagers reported suicide attempts in the past year. Clearly, these indicate reasons for concern—and reasons for parents to find ways to stay connected to their teens. In all studies, feeling connected was found to decrease the incidence of unhealthy teenage risk taking. Teenagers who resist these behaviors feel cared for by their parents and other family members. A part of expressing this caring means simply being present in the home: teenagers want to see their parents in the morning, after school or at dinner, and at bedtime—and regularly share activities with them.

What to Do

- Set healthy limits for teens that do not squelch constructive risk taking but also don't allow teens too much room to hurt themselves.

- Stay in constant communication not only with your teenager but with his friends, teachers, and other parents.

- Be a regular daily presence in your teenager's life.

- Hold open discussions about risky subjects without fear of making your teenager angry or rebellious (don't walk on eggshells with your teen or avoid topics like sex or drugs that you think might be too sensitive).

- Never be violent with teenagers emotionally, verbally, or physically.

- Ensure that there are no weapons in the house.

- Be good role models, particularly in your own use of alcohol or drugs.

- Talk to your teen about risky things you may have done in the past without glamorizing or overstating particularly dangerous behaviors; assure your teen that everyone is faced with the choice to become involved in them and that your own experience—learned the hard way—is that the best choice is not to.

- Encourage your teen to become involved in extracurricular arts-, team sports-, or other athletics-related activities.

- Unstructured "hanging out time" should be decreased as much as possible.

Finally, parents should be aware that whatever risky behaviors their children may occasionally engage in, the great majority of teenagers become healthy adults. Fortunately, the incidence of unhealthy risk-taking behavior has decreased over the last decade, and even if he gets involved in an antisocial activity (85 percent of teenagers do at one point or another), the odds of your child becoming a serious antisocial personality are well under 1 percent. In general, most teenagers will push the envelope but most stay on track. Parents' close involvement and connectedness with their teenagers constitute the most important factors in determining happy outcomes.

SEE ALSO:

Suicide
Violence
Gangs
Behavior Disorders
Discipline
Sexual Development
Anorexia, Bulimia, and Overeating
Drugs

18. Runaways

"Honey? I'm sorry. I know I got you out of an important meeting. But would you please just forget about your job for a moment? Please, just listen. Peter's gone. No, it's not like last time. We can't just ignore this! His school called and said he hadn't been in all day. And I checked his room—most of his clothes are gone. Should I call the police? I don't know what to do."

PETER IS SIXTEEN and as we hear from his mother's end of her anxious telephone call to her husband, this is not the first time he's run away from home. However, before he'd just cut a half day of school and stayed out late. Before he hadn't packed a bag. His mother worries now that this new exit might be more serious—and more permanent. We can deduce from what we hear that Peter's father wants to downplay what's happened. In fact, work consumes Peter's dad; his job has kept him from relating to his family members or their problems. All of which probably are reasons Peter runs away so often in the first place.

The problem of runaway teenagers constitutes a growing and urgent problem in this country. Some estimates indicate that up to five hundred thousand teenagers run away from home each year. Although most return home within several days, many don't, and many of those teenagers are at very high risk of becoming involved in an unnerving array of dangerous activities: crime, gangs, drugs, violence, and prostitution.

Not all teenagers run away from home because of problems interacting or communicating with their parents but most do. A child who runs away typically does not feel heard; does not feel his or her essential needs are being met. If ever a teenage "problem" were a family problem, it is here. This isn't to suggest that there is usually any easy blame: a child may feel dictated to, or misunderstood, or otherwise treated unjustly when in fact he hasn't been. But even if the teen's feelings of alienation seem irrational or unfounded to his parents, those feelings need to be acknowledged and addressed. Too often for the potential runaway the family has long been an armed camp; the teen feels an intolerable sense of "them against me." He may feel such a degree of hopelessness or frustration that the only solution seems to be to get away completely.

Runaway teens may also be running toward the hope of acceptance—hoping to find a new world of contacts and friends to whom they can relate and with whom they can feel more comfortable or simply have more fun. Unfortunately, many of the environments to which they run are filled with people who can only mean disaster—antisocial and rule-breaking acquaintances, or sometimes even religious groups or cults. Some teenagers run away to avoid punishment by their parents, to avoid restrictions they find intolerable, to avoid physical or sexual abuse, or sometimes just to provide an exciting distraction in their lives. Teens may also run away after the death of a family member or because of an unwanted move to a new home. Predictably, teens who are oppositional and defiant tend to run away more than others.

Signs Your Teen Might Be Planning to Bolt

There are usually signs from a teen that he or she is preparing to run away from home. These include arguing more than usual, angry complaints about feeling abused, disagreeing with parents at every opportunity, accumulating money secretly, and/or expressing wild and rageful feelings. Potential runaways may make no bones about the fact that they want to run away, announcing it frequently to the family or telling friends at school they plan to leave. Performance at school generally takes a downturn. The teen may isolate himself and become markedly antisocial. There may be evidence of a mood disorder, with symptoms like eating or sleeping less, withdrawing from activities formerly found pleasurable, and, above all, clearly wanting to have as little to do with the family as possible.

What to Do

- Most important for parents is to try to prevent the teen from running away in the first place. This means doing everything possible to keep the channels of communication open. Avoid reacting to your teen's increasing isolation tactics and negativity by punishing or scolding him for it. Remember the old adage: "When you're talking, you can't listen." In other words, keep your ears open. Allow your teen to feel safer about letting you know what's bugging him. This doesn't mean you have to agree with your teenager's point of view, but it's important to let him know that you're listening. The point is to show that you understand and perhaps even sympathize with what he is feeling or going through, without necessarily giving in to the teen's demands. Opening these channels of communication constitutes the most effective tactic you can employ to keep a family from fracturing. In fact, in just about every case, a teen runs away only when the family has already fractured: his exit gives evidence of a split that probably happened a long time before he left the house. Sarcasm or screaming will only widen this divide. Remaining calm, or taking a break when you feel you can't keep your cool, is essential.

- If your child runs away, use as much common sense as possible in your attempt to locate him. Call his friends; call the school; contact anyone with whom you know your teen has regular contact. Go to your child's room to see if he has left any clues or a note. Normally your son or daughter's diary is none of your business, but in this instance, all bets are off. If there is one to consult, do so for any clues it might give you about where he may have gone and perhaps also to get a sense of the reasons he left. Some parents have checked cellphone bills and even computer sites their teens recently accessed to pick up further clues. E-mail and recently visited chat rooms may provide leads. If you've combed the more obvious possibilities with no success, contact the police and tell them anything you know. This is the time to contact local area hospitals and bus terminals as well.

Fortunately, most children return within several days, but that doesn't mean the problem is solved. The family's prevailing aim must be to investigate why the teen left in the first place. Although some families are able to explore this painful territory without help, it's a good idea to engage a mental-health professional to enable you and your teen to find a model of communication that works for you, and perhaps to embark on ongoing individual or family therapy as well. Individual therapy for the teen may help to investigate whether mood disorders, behavior disorders of various types, academic or learning problems, or romantic problems (typically kept very quiet) might be at the root of your teen's urge to bolt.

SEE ALSO:

Depression
Grief
Behavior Disorders
Discipline
Drugs
School Problems

19. Tattoos and Body Piercings

"No, Dad, it doesn't mean I've joined a gang. Yes, Mom, I know it's permanent. Yeah, it was safe! Don't worry, the guy who did it used clean stuff. No, mom, I don't care what Grandma will think! Why'd I get it? I like it. That's the reason I got it. Period."

STEVEN, FIFTEEN, knew his parents would blow their tops at the sight of the tattoo he just got on his shoulder. If only his mother hadn't caught him coming out of the bathroom shirtless after his shower. Usually he was more careful. But now that the secret is out, his parents are more than angry—they're frightened about what else Steven might be doing and not telling them. They've heard that gang members typically signal their gang affiliation by displaying tattoos. And they know gangs get involved in drugs and crime. With the secrecy and Steven's sullen responses—and the possible unhygienic procedure of getting a tattoo—they don't know how worried to be.

Tattoos are permanent marks in the form of a design in which pigment is injected into an underlying layer of skin with a small needle. Body piercings are created with plierlike devices that press a removable piece of jewelry (such as an earring) through the skin. While men usually get an ear pierced, women often enjoy piercing navels and the upper part of the ear as well. However, almost every part of the body can and has been pierced, including the tongue, genitals, nipples, eye brows, and lips. Both tattoos and body piercings are common in teenagers. Some studies report that over 12 percent of teens have tattoos and slightly less than 50 percent of teens are considering acquiring them. Other studies show that close to 50 percent of college students have had body piercings and 22 percent have tattoos.

Tattoos and piercings are nothing new: human beings have subjected themselves to such markings for thousands of years. Various cultures throughout history have countenanced them for ritual or aesthetic reasons. For today's teenagers, they tend to be an expression of individuality and sometimes of rebellion. Steven's father was right to be concerned that his son's tattoo might be evidence that he'd joined a gang: tattoos and piercings do often identify gang members. Health considerations (such as whether tattoos or piercings been administered hygienically), the possible permanence of such markings, and messages of rebellion the teen may be expressing with them are of understandable concern to parents. Indeed, the dangers of tattoos and body piercings go beyond the physical: they can signal deeper issues your teen may be facing. The kinds of pictures drawn in tattoos often tell a good deal about the distress your teen may be feeling. Somewhat like a Rorschach Test, the tattooed teenager sometimes wears his insides on his outsides: he may be signaling quite blatantly the turmoil he's undergoing internally.

Possible physical dangers must also be heeded. One of the most common risks of breaking the skin surface is inducing infection, especially with hepatitis C, but also hepatitis B and HIV. Re-use or improper cleaning of needles in the process of tattooing makes contamination more likely. Tetanus and tuberculosis may also be contracted. As far as permanence, piercings are relatively easy to remove (often the hole, as in the ear lobe, will close on its own), but removing tattoos may require possibly complicated procedures such as laser surgery, dermabrasion, or surgical incision. There is also no guarantee that colors other than black and blue can be removed completely.

What to Do

- If your teen is considering getting a tattoo—or if, like Steven, he's already gone out and done it—let this be an invitation to open a dialogue. First of all, give your teen the facts about the dangers and possible permanence of body markings. While you should be alert to possible deeper meanings or turmoil in the teen that tattoos or body piercings may represent, and talk to your teen about them, there's no need to overreact, especially if he is considering a small tattoo or earring. You may want to suggest that your teen "try out" a press-on tattoo or body paint, which will give the same effect but be removable. However, if you and your teen come to an agreement about getting the marking or piercing, make sure the place your teen chooses to have it done is clean, and that gloves and disinfectants are used. Jewelry inserted in piercings should be hypoallergenic. Because piercing enterprises and tattoo parlors are not controlled by most states or localities, your judgment and participation in deciding where your teen goes are important.

- After application, tattoos generally heal in one to three weeks with no special intervention. However, with piercings, it is very important to keep the site clean with antibacterial soap and water. The most common complication is redness, but sometimes swelling and infection can develop. Some people use Vaseline to help the healing process.

- On the whole there is no reason to be overly concerned about tattoos and body piercings; once again, they are a common means of expressing individuality. However, the risks do need to be pointed out and precautions taken. Threats are not the answer: calm and informed discussion is. Use this episode in your teen's life to increase communication.

SEE ALSO:

Gangs

20. Attention Deficit Disorder

"Okay, maybe we were wrong not to be worried
before. I mean some kids just don't pay attention
in school. What kid likes school? And yes, Johnny
never did well in grade school and junior high—
teachers could never keep him in his seat. I just
thought this meant he was high-spirited. I was a
wild kid too when I was his age. But now, hell,
he's fourteen and he's reading at the level of a
second grader. What do we do about it?"

WHAT JOHNNY'S FATHER doesn't realize is that his son suffers from a syndrome called attention deficit disorder (ADD) or attention deficit hyperactivity disorder (ADHD). While it is not unusual for a teenager to have AD(H)D, it is unusual for it to have gone undiagnosed for as long as it went undetected in Johnny, especially given the great attention this disorder has received in schools and in the media over the past decade. For some teenagers, the initial diagnosis is made in the teenage years; for most others, the syndrome is diagnosed when they were younger. Anywhere from two to three million American children have a diagnosis of attention deficit disorder of some sort. Boys have it more often than girls.

The three symptoms of ADD or ADHD consist of:

1. **Inattention:** People who are inattentive get bored easily and sometimes have trouble attending to certain tasks. They find it difficult to focus and organize, and have trouble finishing things they start.

2. **Hyperactivity:** Teenagers with hyperactivity always seem to be in constant motion. Often they can't sit still or they talk too much. Hyperactive teenagers squirm, fidget, pick at things, find it hard to be calm, and always seem to create some degree of chaos in their environment. They often feel restless and seem scattered.

3. **Impulsivity:** Impulsive teenagers can't control their emotions and especially can't juxtapose thinking between a feeling and an action. They might grab things, hit other teenagers, blurt out certain inappropriate sentences or words, and in general have a lowered frustration tolerance.

Because temperament differs in each of us, a parent should not conclude that a teen has attention deficit disorder if the child occasionally shows one of the aforementioned symptoms. In other words, to make this diagnosis these behaviors have to be excessive and have persisted for quite a long time. The diagnosis also depends on determining that these behaviors occur in more than one setting (at home as much as at school) and are not just being created by particular stresses in one area.

In general, the inability to sustain attention, listen, follow through, or engage in quiet leisure activities; chronic disorganization and being distracted; losing things, fidgeting, running, and climbing; and talking too much are all signs a parent should look for to investigate the possibility that the child might have attention deficit disorder. Keep in mind that underachievement at school; attention difficulty due to other causes such as chronic anxiety, seizures, major stress, chronic infections, or tumultuous and chaotic family situations; and chronic or acute depression, can all mimic attention deficit disorder.

Teens with AD(H)D often have accompanying problems such as learning disorders, tics, positional defiant disorder, anxiety, worry, depression, and sleeping and eating problems. In addition, conduct disorder, which is a more severe behavioral disturbance, may affect those with ADHD.

At this point we are not sure what causes AD(H)D. While some people feel it is a disorder of brain functions, others feel that it is a sign of stress, especially the stress caused by parental chaos and confusion. There seems to be a genetic influence operating in some children as well. Although it appears that as society, and specifically the psychiatric community, moves more and more toward a chemical understanding of all psychiatric syndromes, there is less focus on the other possible causes of AD(H)D at this time. While it may relieve parents to know that the causes of this syndrome may be chemical or inherited, and not caused by any psychiatric problem with their children, the responsible parent will want to investigate if there is something going on in the family situation that may contribute to AD(H)D. The final word is not yet in on this and we have to await further research. (Although some have claimed that diet, especially an excess of sugar, causes children to become "hyper," this has never been shown to be the case.)

What to Do

- If you feel that your teenager may be suffering from attention deficit disorder a consultation with a child and adolescent psychiatrist is indicated. Although psychologists, neurologists, and other doctors might be able to make a diagnosis of this syndrome, it would be a child and adolescent psychiatrist who would have the most experience with AD(H)D and thus be most likely to make an accurate assessment. The psychiatrist will also be able to rule out other syndromes that appear similar to AD(H)D and be able to diagnose what are called co-morbid states; in other words, other syndromes that the child may have.

- Parents should be careful never to accuse the teen with AD(H)D of being "stupid," "retarded," to be merely acting up or refusing to learn, or in other ways "doing it on purpose." Most children with AD(H)D are of normal intelligence and are not "bad kids." Secondary rejection, humiliation, and eventually self-hatred often ensue in children who have not been diagnosed correctly or who have been berated, neglected, and not appreciated for who they are: children with a specific syndrome.

- If the diagnosis is made there are many forms of treatment available at this time including stimulant medications (Ritalin,

Concerta, Adderall, Dexedrine, Metadate and others) and non-stimulant medications as well (Strattera is a new non-stimulant compound that is being used). Some antidepressants and other medications have been found to be effective as well. In addition to stimulant medication, parent counseling, family therapy, cognitive-behavioral therapy, special remediation, and skills training all help the child.

- Many parents question the use of medication in the child because of their fears that the child may become a substance abuser; the opposite is true. Although there is some evidence that children with untreated ADHD or ADD have a higher risk of becoming substance abusers, those who were treated with stimulant medication actually have a decreased risk.

- There has been much in the media that has scared parents including the worry that children are being over-diagnosed and over-treated with ADHD drugs. It has been my experience that not enough children have received the diagnosis of ADHD and most children who do rarely get treated with the appropriate medication and therapy. While there might be cases where children were wrongly diagnosed and over-treated, in my experience the proper diagnosis made by a child and adolescent psychiatrist and proper treatment with medication and various forms of therapy, including help from the school, often result in the teen feeling normal, happy, and well-adjusted despite the fact that he has the aforementioned problems. As usual, the family's positive and supportive attitude toward the teen and ensuring that the teen receives treatment in a compassionate way make all the difference.

SEE ALSO:

Anxiety
Stress and PTSD
Depression
Behavior Disorders
Drugs
School Problems
Getting Help

21. Behavior Disorders

*"You did WHAT to Bobby? And they had to call
an ambulance? This is the last straw, Ted. I can't
take this anymore. You're headed for prison the
way you're going. Get out of the house right now!
I don't even want to look at you!"*

TED'S FATHER has reached the end of his rope. His son Ted has gotten
in trouble too often for beating up kids at school and in the neighborhood, even once trashing the biology lab in his high school
(because, in his words, "I didn't like the way the teacher was looking at me"). Ted has been suspended so many times from school the
principal has threatened expulsion if he acts up again. And now he's
seriously hurt Bobby, a little kid next door. "He bothered me," is all
Ted says about it. All his father can think right now is that his son is
a "bad seed." He's a hairsbreadth away from giving up on him completely.

Ted's appalling behavior certainly goes far beyond normal adolescent rebellion. He is clearly a danger to himself and to others. But
he is not a "bad seed." He has a number of behavioral disorders
that need care and treatment. Unfortunately, because teens like Ted
alienate so many people—especially anyone in authority, even if that
authority wants to help—getting Ted to accept treatment is an enormous challenge. Nobody has to tell Ted's father just how big a challenge that is.

Although the major behavior disorders afflicting adolescents—
attention deficit disorder (see previous chapter), conduct disorder,

and oppositional defiant disorder—are defined as separate disorders in the *American Psychiatric Association Diagnostic and Statistical Manual, Fourth Edition,* there is almost always much overlap between these three diagnostic syndromes. Teens rarely manifest one of these behavior disorders in isolation. Despite this overlap, these behavior-disorder categories do deserve separate attention—attention which (in addition to ADD), has been paid in separate chapters (bullying, violence, gangs, runaways, risk taking, and tattoos and body piercing). This chapter will focus on conduct disorder and oppositional defiant disorder.

It's normal for parents of teens to worry about their behavior, concerned that episodes of "acting up" may be harbingers of future antisocial, sociopathic development, or that their teens are on the road to violent criminality, substance abuse, living on the "edge," and ending up in jail or prison. Most normal teenagers do act up from time to time, sometimes in very disturbing and destructive ways. Adolescence is a time of testing limits and few teens don't push the envelope in this realm. A great many teenagers do commit minor antisocial acts. However, although a small minority, probably less than 1 percent, ever develops true antisocial personality, this reassurance remains cold comfort to parents who are faced with teens talking back; driving recklessly; committing violent acts; experimenting with sex, drugs, and alcohol; and cutting school, among other defiant behaviors. What do you do when a teen's behavior has gotten out of hand? When does a teen need special help with behavioral problems and what help is available?

First of all, parents should remember that while they are often the best judges of their children's personalities and behavior (no one else is in closer contact with them, or has more of an investment in their well-being), they can also be their worst judges. Teens considered to behave inappropriately or indulge in "bad behavior" basically receive these labels from their parents. Sometimes parents' own fears, temperaments, negative expectations, childhoods, and alienation from cultures and subcultural trends that engage their teens lead them to make unduly pessimistic conclusions about their sons and daughters. Many parents don't take into account that each individual teenager has his own temperament that affects the way he behaves. Thus an active, outgoing, somewhat assertive child is some-times misconstrued as being a bully or having some type of behavior disorder. Mistakes are made on the other side, too; for example, when a child is seen to be somewhat passive, shy, and slow to warm up and parents misdiagnose this as a teenager who has depression or social phobic disorder.

Parents tend to hold one of two assumptions about how teenagers behave: Some parents believe that children behave based on inborn reflexes or temperaments while other parents believe that a child's behavior just happens to be a result of how the child is feel-ing at the particular moment. If you subscribe to the former view, your method of dealing with your teen is probably "behavioral"; that is, you employ rewards and punishments, rules and strict disci-pline to control your child's behavior. If you subscribe to the latter view, you may be a parent who is extremely flexible and perhaps softer than necessary, seeking only to understand the teen's feeling state rather than imposing any boundaries on his behavior. Parents must be clear about which approach they tend to adopt. They must balance out any extremes so that they develop an appreciation both for the teen's inborn temperament and the necessity for setting firm but compassionate rules that will help the teen effectively rein in any excessive negative behavior without crushing her spirit.

If your teen's behavioral problems have proven to be intransi-gent, he may suffer from a behavioral disorder that requires greater attention and more specific help. Read through the following descrip-tions of conduct disorder and oppositional defiant disorder and con-sult the chapter on attention deficit disorder. If any of them seems to describe your teen, be assured that there are ways to help your teen deal with and overcome it.

Conduct Disorder

Teenagers with conduct disorder don't like following rules and rarely appreciate society's standards. These are the children often labeled "juvenile delinquents." Some are wrongly labeled "bad seeds." Please know that there is no such thing as a bad seed. No child is born antisocial or prone to criminal behavior. These are learned behaviors based on a complex series of influences and events, including role modeling and family, and the subculture and culture in which the teenager is raised. However, teenagers with a conduct disorder exhibit behaviors that are very upsetting even if they are not evidence that the teen is inherently "bad." These teens are very aggressive, often fighting, and bullying. They can be cold and cruel, both to people and animals. They may commit crimes like assault and rape. They commonly commit vandalism of other people's property. They break laws, commit burglary, lie, steal, run away, cut school, and often stay out late at night despite the fact that parents may have rules against doing so. Some teens will have developed this disorder when they were young children; some only in adolescence. The prognosis for improvement is worse for the former group.

Oppositional Defiant Disorder

Teenagers with oppositional defiant disorder are somewhat different from those with a conduct disorder. While most teenagers, especially in early adolescence, occasionally are rebellious and don't like bowing to authority, those with oppositional defiant disorder persist in these characteristics far more deeply and dramatically, and for a much longer time. Their defiance and hostility toward authority figures is pronounced. They rarely cooperate; they say no as a reflex. They refuse to live by the rules of the family. They often get very angry when asked to do things and argue unendingly. They are quite irritable, tend to blame anyone other than themselves, and are often anxious, angry, resentful, and arrogant. They tend to use foul language and hold grudges as well.

While we do not know the causes of these behavior disorders, the teen afflicted by one or the other of them usually exhibits them in every area of life: in the home and at school, as well as outside the home or school.

In my view, behavioral disorders are common final pathways for a host of difficulties that a teen more than likely has experienced throughout his life, including early inadequate parenting, being traumatized, feeling alienated, and/or being neglected or abused. Biological factors, the specifics of which are unknown at this time, may contribute to the development of behavior disorders as well. Brain damage and school failure may also be implicated. Teens with these disorders often have learning disabilities.

Many children with behavior disorders have what are called co-morbid disorders—other psychiatric disorders that commonly include disorders of mood, such as depression or bipolar disorder; substance abuse; stress-related disorders like post-traumatic stress disorder; learning disorders; psychotic disorders like schizophrenia; and anxiety disorders such as phobias or generalized anxiety disorder. These conditions must be treated as well as the behavior disorder for the teen to have the best chance of recovering. Not only do these conditions coexist but, in reality, often cause the behavioral disturbances as well. Although sometimes a behavior disorder has to be treated directly, it is often only by getting to the teen's underlying issues that a lasting cure is achieved.

Unfortunately, behavior-disordered teenagers often discourage those who want to help, resist verbal psychotherapy, and end up alienating even the most valiant of health-care professionals, all of which perpetuate their own deteriorating courses of behavior. It is therefore crucial to seek help from mental-health practitioners who have had extensive experience in treating teens with behavioral disorders.

What to Do

- Be reassured that a teenager manifesting typical disruptive behavior rarely goes on to become an adult criminal, or violent, abusive, or antisocial. Most teenagers grow up okay.

- Know who your teenager is hanging around with and be sure he is not under the influence of severely misbehaving or violent peers.

- Try to understand your misbehaving teen's underlying issues. Focus on where and when he misbehaves, and attempt to see what triggers it. If you pay close attention to the stresses in your teen's life and how he reacts to them, you can become an effective diagnostician and may be able to help your teen on the spot at home.

- Be a good role model, and don't misbehave yourself.

- If violence is part of your child's behavior, be sure you know how to handle anger appropriately. If it is out of hand, be prepared to call in a third party so that everyone is safe and protected.

- If you have tried to understand your teen and intervene appropriately and still cannot figure out the triggers for your teen's misbehavior or can't reverse it, professional consultation is necessary.

- Professional consultation by a mental-health professional experienced in adolescent behaviors is often enough if it involves treatment for other likely disorders or disabilities your teen may face. Therefore it is important that your teen be tested for learning disabilities, organic brain disease, psychosis, and all of the co-morbid disorders as well.

- Therapy for a child with a behavior disorder usually involves psychotherapy on an individual basis, as well as family therapy and parent work. Schools and community centers often get involved in treatment as well. One way family therapy can help parents is by teaching them how to interact with their teens differently to break cycles of negative reinforcement that may exist. Behavior disorders are a family affair.

- The use of psychotropic medication with behavior disordered children is not particularly beneficial, although sometimes in treatment for co-morbid states (particularly a proneness to violence) medication has proven helpful.

- Some children with resistant disorders do better living out of the house. There are various residential centers and facilities and other housing options about which an experienced therapist or social worker can inform parents. This decreases stress for the rest of the family as well.

SEE ALSO:

Anxiety
Stress and PTSD
Depression
Bipolar Disorder
Anger
Schizophrenia
Bullying
Violence
Gangs
Attention Deficit Disorder
Drugs
School Problems
Getting Help

22. Discipline

"My son Ed made me so mad I almost hit him. How'm I supposed to discipline him when he acts up like this?"

ED'S FATHER is in a quandary. His own father beat the tar out of him when he acted up. But something in him doesn't want to treat his own son that way, even though Ed can really rile him up. His anxiety is very common. In fact, questions about how or whether to discipline teenaged sons and daughters rank second in frequency and importance to questions about teens and sex. Of course, a minority of parents have no question about discipline—generally those who are strict authoritarians, with stringently enforced rules, who believe that meting out forceful punishments is the correct way to keep their children in line. They are wrong.

The goal of disciplining teenagers isn't to punish them, but to guide them toward the development of responsibility, morals, and ethics. Unfortunately, discipline is too often confused with punishment—actions that parents take when teenagers break rules but that are not geared to helping the teenager learn. One of the reasons that parents are so anxious about discipline is because of the conflicting messages that society sends to parents and teenagers both about what appropriate discipline ought to be. "Spare the rod, spoil the child" may seem old-fashioned, but unfortunately it's still a common paradigm. Parents question how much "rope" to give a child, worrying that there might be too much, and the child will "hang himself." Other parents worry that being too strict will result in adolescents rebelling, losing respect, and not loving them. Still others worry that even the least bit of discipline or punishment will crush their teenagers and ruin their lives. Others consider rebellion and defiance to be "normal" in teenagers and thus may rarely take a teen's misbehavior seriously. While to some degree rebellion and defiance are natural, it has been found that excessive rebellion and excessive defiance are usual indicators of an oppositional defiant behavior disorder and are not necessarily associated with health. Parents should not accept high and compulsive degrees of opposition and defiance.

The problem is that most parents only have the model of discipline that was meted out to them as children and teens. For many, identification with the normal rebellious and defiant aspects of teenage years has never been normalized by mature growth; thus they either subtly (or not so subtly) stimulate "bad behavior," only to follow it, in their own anxiety and confusion, by administering punishment to the adolescent. Not surprisingly, this causes the teen perplexity, anxiety, and confusion.

On the other hand, constructive discipline tends to result in the development of a mature young adult by the end of the adolescent passage. It helps a teenager control his impulses, cooperate with other people, and be patient. The aim of discipline should not be to develop a homogenized and completely socialized teenager; parents should always stress the uniqueness of their teenage sons and daughters. Rather, discipline should result in a teen taking a wholehearted and responsible approach to life. Disciplining a teenager is different from disciplining a younger child since the teenager is more mature, more reflective, and more able to enter into discussions and negotiations. This means that discipline can and should always be enlightening to teenagers, never a means of deriding, shaming, or making them feel as if they are "bad."

What to Do

- Don't be a cruel parent. Don't humiliate, criticize destructively, physically attack, or try to cripple your teenager's will just in order to make him conform to certain rules.

- Expectations and rules should be made clear to your teenager but not impossible to live up to. When setting a rule or articulating an expectation, explain your reasons for it. Each teenager has a different level of understanding, so parents should be sure that he understands clearly both the rule and the reason. This may be more challenging to explain to some teens than others. Each teenager has a different level of competence and ability to conform, based on his unique set of characteristics, strengths, and vulnerabilities.

- Don't be scared of setting limits. Limits are very important, not only to protect the teen against dangers that he might create or to which he might be vulnerable in the outside world, but also because limits are part of life and learning how to live within limits is an important life lesson.

- Rules shouldn't be laid down arbitrarily, even if you feel strongly about them; they should involve some give and take, a two-way street. In this manner, parents will be able to teach, teenagers will be able to learn, and there will be respectful interaction and negotiation.

- Understand that whatever teaching and disciplining you do, most teenagers will mature through trial and error. Don't try to overprotect your teenager from learning the consequences of his or her actions.

- Rewarding constructive aspects of a teenager's behavior is more important that criticizing negative aspects of behavior.

- Be a good role model for your teenager. Avoid yelling, brinksmanship, and especially destructive violence.

- Give your teenager compassionate, patient attention when it comes to discussion of family rules and responsibilities. Make your teenager feel useful, important, and powerful. Listen carefully to your teenager's reasoning about any issue having to do with discipline.

- When punishment of a teenager is called for, it is best to withdraw privileges rather than use some techniques that are used with your children like time-outs. When meting out punishment, the rule that was violated should be explained so the punishment makes more sense. Don't over-punish because you are angry; for example, grounding the teen for six months or for the rest of the semester. Not only will you probably take back the punishment but this will create a perception in your teenager's mind that you overreact and that punishment is somewhat arbitrary.

- Never use corporal punishment or physical torture. The lesson learned from physical violence is that out-of-control anger is a consequence of not behaving correctly. This will be internalized by the teenager and he will learn to do the same to others. There is rarely a bully who hasn't been bullied himself. If you are so angry that you are on the verge of acting out destructively leave the room and call for another family member to deal with the teen. This goes for verbal abuse as well, since words can sometimes be as harmful as, or more harmful than, physical violence.

- Try to inject humor into disciplining. Humor sometimes lessens the tension; sarcasm doesn't.

- Teenagers can be loud, intimidating, and even destructively threatening when they throw a tantrum. Don't give in to tantrums. If your teenager is out of control, a third party may be necessary. This may sometimes include the police, if the teenager is violent.

- Don't let guilt induction by your teenager manipulate you into not meting out a punishment or lowering your expectations. This is very difficult, as many parents want their children to stay bonded to them. The problem: this does not allow teens to separate from parents in a natural way and is often fueled by parents' particular hang-ups. Try to resist this. Don't bribe your teenager but encourage with incentives.

- Remember, all teenagers test limits in one way or another. This is important in developing maturity in decision making. It is a parent's job to be sure that the teenager doesn't go too far while on the other hand assuring that your teenager does test and letting him know that, from time to time, it's okay that he does.

- Always remain compassionate, empathetic, and identified somewhat with the struggles a teenager has growing up. Always keep in mind that a parent's greatest influence does not come through punishment but through appropriate role modeling, guidance, attentiveness, and sympathy for the sufferings inherent in normal adolescent development.

SEE ALSO:

Behavior Disorders
Sexual Development

III

Sex

23. Sexual Development

"You are not leaving this house in that outfit!"

FIFTEEN-YEAR-OLD Melissa has a Britney Spears fixation. She knows she looks as good in a short tight halter top and hot pants as her idol does and so do the boys in the mall. She "blossomed" a little later than her friends (who all seemed to fill out at thirteen), and she is determined to make up for lost time. If you've got it, flaunt it, right? Parental disapproval was predictable, but she'd find ways to get around it. Maybe she'd do what she did the last time: put a sweatsuit over her "outfit" and take it off when she got into her boyfriend's car. . . .

Sex and teens constitutes a very charged topic. Although it is well known that even young children have many sexual feelings and impulses, the physical changes that come with puberty bring sex to center stage. Many parents, like Melissa's, sometimes just wish it would go away. Plus, there's the onerous task of talking to teens about sex. Many parents hope that school and sex-education classes will teach their children so they won't have to. However, teens are learning from peers and the provocative sexual messages in all aspects of the media.

Some parents still cling to religious and moral beliefs about the immorality of premarital sex; some inhibited parents just shy away due to anxiety. Other parents give conflicting messages about sex based on the inner ambivalence and conflict generated by their parents. One thing is for certain: sexual impulses that begin in early childhood soar during adolescence. In fact, a teenager without sexual impulses, thoughts, and fantasies is unusual and is a greater source of concern than a teenager with sex on her mind.

The onset of adolescence begins with the physical changes of puberty. Girls usually begin puberty somewhere around ten or eleven years old while boys enter a bit later, usually around twelve. A fairly reliable predictor of when puberty will start is when it started for the teen's parents because the age at which the onset of puberty occurs is usually passed down through generations. For girls, body fat begins to increase as breasts enlarge. Pubic hair appears and height and weight increase. Menstruation begins, hips get wider, hair begins growing in the axillae (underarms), skin and hair become a bit oilier, and early acne can start. In addition a clear or white vaginal secretion may occur earlier in puberty before the onset of menstruation.

The first signs of puberty in boys often are enlarging testicles and darkening of the scrotum. The penis grows longer and fuller, and pubic hair develops. Sometimes, interestingly, breasts can become somewhat enlarged as a passing phenomenon. Sometimes the lumps in the boy's breasts can even become tender. As with girls, boys grow, weight increases, and muscles develop. Wet dreams or nocturnal emissions (sexual dreams that occur with ejaculation during the night) sometimes occur as well. The voice changes, sometimes cracking or getting deeper, and, as with girls, the skin and hair become oily. Hair grows in other areas such as on the face and under the arms and acne may occur.

It is important that parents and other family members not criticize, tease, or make fun of the pubertal changes, which are a source of great anxiety and shyness in many teenagers. Educational discussions, including a rundown of adequate hygiene, are measures every parent should take. For girls, a discussion of the female reproductive cycle (inner anatomy as well as reproductive facts) is an important one to have. With boys, discussions about erections and ejaculations are important. We should always remember that we are out to reduce confusion with information and lessen anxiety by creating an acceptance of one's bodily functions. We should also point out that no two teenagers are the same and that each develops at her own unique rate.

For most parents, concerns about teen sexuality commonly include teens having sex early, becoming pregnant, or getting a sexually transmitted disease. It is a known fact that sex is occurring earlier and earlier as time passes. The sexual revolution of the sixties did in fact change sexual mores. As adolescence begins, parents are more concerned than ever about such issues as kissing, petting, oral/genital sexual contact, mutual masturbation, and intercourse.

We should remember that sexual experimentation is normal. But parents worry because we now know that by the time a teen is fifteen (Melissa's age), the majority of boys and girls have had sexual contact. Even under fifteen, about 20 percent of girls have had intercourse. Many adolescents do not use birth control early on; many never do. Often those who start having sex early have multiple partners. The great concern about teenage pregnancy is appropriate: about a million girls get pregnant each year. However, none of this means that everyone wants to have sex or likes to have sex. There is an enormous amount of peer pressure in this realm. In fact, studies of boys and girls show that after having sex many boys and girls did not enjoy it and sometimes feel guilty or anxious. (Girls tend to feel that way more than boys do.) Again, many teenagers feel shy about sex and guilty or shameful. Although society has made sex more open and has therefore tended to decrease guilt, we shouldn't believe that guilt has been eradicated. Because peer pressure is the main reason teenagers have sex, often it is difficult for teens to stay friends with other teenagers who are having sex when they are not. Of course, curiosity compels teens toward sex as well. Sexual stereotypes still hold sway in this country, with boys tending to focus more on the sex act and sexual gratification and girls generally tending to equate sex with intimacy and emotional relations. This division seems to go on even through adulthood.

Masturbation is a perfectly normal phenomenon, for both teens and younger children. In fact the stimulation of one's own genitals for sexual pleasure is a necessary part of development. Through masturbation, teenagers (and for that matter, all people) release sexual tension. In teenage years boys tend to masturbate more than girls, but one should not think that girls do not masturbate. The fantasies that accompany masturbation seem to be somewhat different in boys and girls. While most boys' fantasies have to do with performing the sex act aggressively, girls' fantasies tend, as mentioned above, to focus more on relationships. Girls usually are more romantic. Masturbation should not be seen as abnormal unless the teenager is consumed with it; if masturbation is so frequent that it interferes with normal educational and social activities, and if it is done in public.

We should never forget that the family is very important in helping teenagers make their way through the sexual morass that occurs during the teenage years. Open discussions about masturbation, contraception, sexually transmitted disease, pregnancy, date rape, and sexual abuse are very important. We should remember that sexuality in and of itself does not hurt teenagers. But we also should remember that unprotected sex and sex without contraception can lead to teenage pregnancy and all the problems associated with it such as the issue of abortion, adoption, and teenage parenthood, as well as sexually transmitted diseases, which can be fatal.

Lastly, the issue of promiscuity is one that concerns many parents. Sexual promiscuity is quite dangerous. It is like playing Russian roulette with one's life. Engaging in sexual relations with more than one partner on a frequent basis is risky. Chances of becoming pregnant or, even worse, getting a fatal sexually transmitted disease are increased with promiscuous behavior. Alcohol is a powerful influence in engendering promiscuous behavior. Sexual promiscuity can also damage self-esteem and the emotional health of a teenager. Promiscuous teenagers often feel invulnerable to risks, but they are not. Often promiscuity is associated with emotional difficulties in teenagers. Children with a borderline personality, those who have been sexually abused, those who are impoverished, those who crave attention, and those who are angry and seeking to rebel often use promiscuity to vent their anger and frustration or achieve contact they don't feel they can get in any other way. Some teenagers who feel depressed and some who use drugs also get involved in promiscuous behavior.

What to Do

- Most important is to see teenage sexuality as a normal, healthy, life-enhancing phenomenon not only for teenagers but for all of us.

- Parents should know their own hang-ups and prejudices, as well as religious values—sort out what they feel, know, and believe about sex before they sit down and talk to a teenager. In this way, parents can be as clear and helpful to their teens as possible.

- Parents should delineate what their values are but also see their teenagers as individuals and not try to impose or inculcate values into their teenagers. Parents should know the facts about sexuality that are going to come up—issues like masturbation, sexually transmitted disease, rape, date rape, pregnancy, homosexuality, anatomy, sexual acts—and should be as open to discussing them as possible. The timing of these discussions should be based on the teenager's development and receptivity.

- If parents shy away from sexuality or criticize or make the teenager feel guilty or shameful, odds are the teenager might use sexuality as a weapon against the parent.

- Teaching a young woman that she can say no is very important. One can teach a girl how to talk to her partner and to understand that sexual intercourse is not mandatory. Girls do not have to explain, they can simply say that they've decided to wait or that they are not ready to get involved in that way. Girls should be encouraged to respect themselves. Boys need education as well about forcing themselves on girls aggressively in order to measure up to what they see as cultural or peer "standards."

- Teenagers should be taught that sex is not an "answer"; intercourse will not solve their problems. Sex will not enable them to hold on to relationships, make them better or more socially acceptable people, or more feminine or masculine. What it might do is lead to pregnancy or sexually transmitted diseases or greater anxiety.

- The dangers of mixing alcohol/drugs and having sex are paramount and these dangers should be discussed.

- If a child is having intercourse, proper protection against sexually transmitted diseases and pregnancy must be discussed.

- Teenagers should be told that masturbation does not adversely affect a person's health (many teenagers believe this). Neither should there be any taboo on other ways of enjoying physical pleasure without intercourse, such as through what some people call "outercourse": kissing, petting, holding hands, and so on.

- Teenagers should be told that if they have engaged in some mutual homosexual activity in early adolescence this does not necessarily indicate that they are homosexuals. Many young teenagers in our society worry that if this occurs they are gay.

- We should remember that teenagers want to hear accurate information from their parents and studies have shown that the more information they get from their parents the longer they generally wait to have intercourse. In general, where academics and family values are stressed, the onset of having sex is delayed. Parents should make themselves available, be honest, use correct names for body parts, and admit when they do not know something. One should not worry that too much education will increase sexual activity. In order to reassure and inform, sometimes sex has to be talked about repeatedly.

- Methods of contraception vary and it can be safely said that condoms used with contraceptive foam, jelly, or cream are 99 percent effective while being only about 90 percent effective if used without them. Foam, jelly, or creams used alone are less effective. The birth control pill is 98 percent effective and IUD is 99 percent effective, a diaphragm with jelly is 82 to 98 percent effective, a surgical cap or sponge is 82 to 94 percent effective. Thus, no form of birth control is 100 percent effective. Withdrawal mechanisms should not be used as this is very ineffective.

- The most important thing we can do to avoid promiscuous behavior and all the dangers that ensue is provide appropriate education for our teenagers. It has been reported that there is not enough discussion about the connection between the use of drugs and alcohol and promiscuity and it is important that parents do this. Most important to remember is that promiscuity usually is a symptom of other issues in the teenager's life.

See also:

Depression
Borderline Personality Disorder
Behavior Disorders
Pregnancy
Abortion
Date Rape
Homosexuality
STDs and Safe Sex
Drugs

24. Pregnancy

"You were only sixteen when you had me, Mom!"

LOREN, SIXTEEN HERSELF, has just dropped the bombshell to her parents that she's pregnant. Loren's mother is especially devastated. "How could you have been so stupid?" she keeps asking. "Don't you know how this is going to affect your life?" Loren's mother knows; she was, as her daughter reminds her, the same age when she gave birth to Loren. It was and still is against her religious beliefs even to consider abortion. And she can't say if she'd had it to do over that she wouldn't have had her daughter, whom she loves. But, yes, she wishes with all her heart she could spare her daughter the difficulties she knows Loren now faces as a teenage mother.

Despite all the focus that institutions and media have placed on adolescent sexuality and the perils of teenage pregnancy, the problem remains. The issues involved in teen sexuality remain complex, confusing, and perplexing for many of us. Teens have sex earlier than ever. The old indicators that a teen is more likely to have sex at an early age remain, including a history of being abused, poor and inattentive parenting, socioeconomic problems such as poverty, poor academic involvement, and living with a role model who in one way or another promotes early sexual activity or, like Loren's mother, herself had a child in her teens.

Pregnancy tends to happen shortly after the teenage girl first has sex. Although information about contraceptive use is far more accessible today than ever, methods of contraception are not reliable and teens often risk not using any. Being pregnant as a teenager results in higher rates of poor prenatal care, miscarriage, and stillbirth. About a third end up having induced abortions. Being pregnant as a teenager is often associated with serious medical complications including a higher death rate (of mother and/or child) and getting pregnant again while still a teenager, as well as poverty, never finishing school, and ending up with low-wage jobs. Teenage fathers rarely get involved in helping their children. Many babies from these pregnancies end up in foster care. Many teenage mothers become homeless.

Although birthrates for teenage parents decreased when abortion became legal in the early seventies, they rose again in the eighties and only started decreasing again in the nineties. But the rate is still quite high, especially among younger mothers who have not shown the decrease in pregancies that older teens have. While the great majority of teenage pregnancies are unintended, some teenagers get pregnant because of an inner feeling of emptiness and a need to be needed, to keep a boyfriend, or to get more attention. There are many medical risks of teenage pregnancy: underweight children, premature births, stillbirths, and a higher mortality rate. While it is not clear what factors contribute to all the medical problems that teenagers have, it seems to be a combination of inherent biological immaturity as well as psychosocial factors. The children of teenage parents have more difficulties than other children, including academic, behavioral, and substance abuse, as well as a host of developmental problems.

What to Do

- Parents should encourage their teenagers to participate in the many pregnancy-prevention programs for adolescents that have popped up throughout the country. These include contraception availability, sex education, promotion of sexual abstinence, and helping children stay involved in afterschool activities, school, and jobs.

- If you discover that your daughter is pregnant it is normal to become anxious, exasperated, and even angry. Parents must control this initial reaction and be as compassionate as possible. Accusing the girl of stupidity or immorality won't help. The teenager who comes to her parents about the pregnancy is herself quite anxious—possibly guilty or shameful—and needs her parents' help.

- An adequate medical examination is crucial, as is determining that the teen is pregnant.

- The teenager has to come to her own decision about what to do, including carrying the child to term, having an abortion, or giving up the child for adoption after birth. This is not easy and cannot be determined over night, but as she grapples with the decision, the teen needs her parents' care, love, and support probably more than at any other time in her life. Whatever her decision, parents should be as supportive as possible, even if the teen's decision goes against their wishes, thoughts, and religious beliefs.

- Parents can and should help their daughter understand the consequences of whatever course of action she may decide to take. Discussion of what her future will be with the child, the finances involved, educational interruption, and the change it will mean in the family picture should be discussed.

- Remember that if abortion is chosen, the procedure should be done as quickly as possible. The decision may be complicated, however, if your daughter reveals her pregnancy late in the first trimester when abortions become a more difficult medical procedure.

- Counseling is advisable for all teenage parents (including teen fathers) and their families. Teenage boys often report that they have gotten a girl pregnant and they deserve the same compassion as teenage daughters who come home and announce a pregnancy. Often the teen father is in a panic, feels guilty, and is as worried about his whole life going down the drain. Although boys sometimes are considered to be the "perpetrators" or aggressors in a teenage pregnancy, this is not always the case, and deserves the same fair, educated, and rational approach to dealing with this crisis as the teen mother.

SEE ALSO:

Sexual Development
Abortion

25. Abortion

"You think this is easy for me?"

Note: This chapter does not explore the relevant religious, political, or moral dimensions of the abortion issue. The purpose of this chapter is to simply supply information regarding abortion.

ABORTION is an extremely emotion-laden issue for the pregnant teenager, the biological father of the fetus, and family members. The decision to have an abortion is a complex one and involves many emotions, including anxiety, guilt, shame, disappointment, and often fears of repercussion. This decision is never made lightly. The effect of abortion on a teenager, and on anyone, is monumental. Although having an abortion might be treated as just a medical or surgical procedure, in fact abortion often has a lifelong impact on those who decide to go that route. At different times, the experience is often relived later in life, such as when trying to conceive, when the woman experiences other losses, or at the time of birth of other children. I am continually struck by how often and how deeply the "underground" effects of abortion shape many people's ideas about life. Afflicted by silent shame, guilt, and the trauma of having had an abortion can lead to lifelong adjustment problems—especially to chronic mood disorders, relationship difficulties, long-lasting guilt, and shame, although not always.

The decision to have an abortion is an important one and demands that as family members we be as supportive as possible, even if we disagree on religious and moral grounds. Parents should

121

be sure that their teenage daughter has adequate access to the appropriate health care in determining whether she actually is pregnant and then in supplying her with appropriate information on which to base a decision.

About one million unwanted pregnancies occur annually, 40 percent of which occur in girls under eighteen years old. Approximately 40 percent are terminated by elective abortion. The number of abortions among teenagers is decreasing but is still high. Mandatory parental involvement in a teenager's abortion is an issue that is somewhat controversial at this time. As of 1992 there were thirty-eight states with some form of specific legislation regarding abortion on record, but a Supreme Court decision has questioned the validity of many of these state laws. One problematic issue is that laws mandating parental involvement sometimes make it difficult for teenagers to get abortions because they do not want their parents to know; as a result, often they do not receive good care, which may force them to resort to later abortions that are riskier. Fortunately, most teenagers, especially younger teens, voluntarily seek out the help of parents when considering abortion. But some teens do not, for fear that knowledge of the pregnancy will damage their relationships with their parents (they are usually correct in predicting increased family problems). The worry about involuntary parental notification is that irreparable family crises may occur.

It is important that teenage girls make their own decisions about abortion, after consultation with parents and their doctors about options. This will add to their feelings of competence and sense of taking responsibility for their lives, which may reduce future negative emotional repercussions.

Although many reports have stated that there are no negative emotional and medical effects of having legal first-term elective abortions—even that people experience relief and reduced depression and distress—my own personal finding is that the emotional effects often tend to be buried but surface later in life causing pain. (For some teens, abortion is a great stressor at the time of the event and leads to major psychopathology). Generally, the more religious the person, the greater her experience of guilt will be. However, it is interesting that there is less psychiatric illness after an abortion than after childbirth.

Most people think that psychiatric illness that emerges after abortion is due to pre-existing psychiatric problems. Despite the results of these mass studies, individual anecdotal experience reported by psychiatrists and those of us who do long-term therapy reveal the more delicate and intricate details of post-abortion remorse, guilt, and, sometimes, lifelong grief.

The American Academy of Pediatrics strongly suggests that adolescents involve their parents in these decisions, and that concerned pediatricians and other doctors make sure that involvement with the family is supported. However, in the event that parental support would not be forthcoming, the Academy also feels that adolescents should be allowed confidential care and that parental consent not be mandatory. The Academy also is opposed to legislation that limits or delays access to care.

There are two general types of abortion:

1. **Medical abortion:** Medical abortion relies on a combination of drugs rather than surgery to achieve an abortion early in a woman's pregnancy. The drugs Mifepristone or Methotrexate (the former taken orally and the latter by injection) combined with a second medication, Misoprostol, are used to induce a medical abortion. These can be safely administered up until nine weeks after the last menstrual period. Mifepristone, formally known as RU-486, was approved in the year 2000 to use up to forty-nine days after the last menstrual period, although further studies have shown that up to sixty-three days is safe. This drug blocks progesterone, which is necessary to sustain pregnancy. It is taken in the form of three pills. Two days later the woman takes Misoprostol orally as a vaginal suppository. This procedure is 90 to 97 percent effective. In the second form of medical abortion, Methotrexate is administered as an injection into the muscle and five to seven days after this Misoprostol is given orally as a vaginal suppository. This regimen is approximately 88 to 90 percent effective. In general, medical abortions are induced by women in their homes although follow-up visits to the doctor are necessary. The

most common side effects are cramping, bleeding, and fatigue. Some women experience headaches, nausea, vomiting, diarrhea, and dizziness as well. Early medical abortions are safe. Most women who undergo them are satisfied with the procedure.

2. **Surgical abortion:** The second form of abortion is surgical abortion. This is when pregnancy is ended by removing the contents of conception from the uterus. Various methods are used:

   ▪ Manual and vacuum aspiration is done in the first trimester as well as dilatation and curettage. In the second trimester, dilatation and evacuation is done as well as inducing labor. Medical society regulations prohibit abortion after the twenty or twenty-first week but exceptions do occur, especially if the life of the woman is at risk or to avoid serious disabling health consequences.

   ▪ Partial birth abortions, also known as DNX abortions, are when the cervix is dilated and the fetus is delivered feet first and its brain removed. The terms partial birth abortion and DNX were originally coined by pro-life groups when this became a political hotbed for debate. This usually is performed during the fifth month or later. Abortions in general and DNX in particular are extremely emotional topics. Laws have been passed to bar partial birth abortions.

What to Do

▪ Should the issue of abortion come up with your teenage daughter, it is important that you respect her independence and keep her confidences private, and ensure she has access to good health care. At no time in teenage life is a child more vulnerable to parental criticism, rejection, and anger.

▪ There is no time when parents are made more anxious and sometimes angry, and are more critical of their teenagers. This volatile combination of emotions and events is fraught with a higher than normal possibility of creating psychopathological responses, and should be handled as carefully as possible by parents. Outside counseling, seeking help at family planning centers, and consultation with the teen's doctor are essential. Parents should undergo counseling themselves if they are having particular difficulties understanding and accepting the crisis.

■ Keep in mind that any psychological damage due to abortion can be minimized by a supportive family response and appropriate counseling.

SEE ALSO:

Sexual Development
Pregnancy
Getting Help

26. Date Rape

"So how did it go with Tom?"

"Oh, Janey . . ."

"What happened?"

"It was—awful. I tried to—I couldn't get him to—
he wouldn't stop, Janey . . ."

"You mean he—?"

"It was so awful. He forced me! I kept saying no, but . . . I
mean, sure, I kissed him, but I never wanted him to—"

"Barbara, you have to tell someone about this! The animal
should be locked up. It's not the first time. I've heard from
other kids—"

"I can't, Janey! Don't you tell anyone! Please don't breathe
a word of this!"

BARBARA AND JANEY, both sixteen, know each other so well they almost talk in code. Janey could hear something was wrong the moment she heard her best friend's voice. And she knew from Barbara that Tom, eighteen, had been pushing to have sex with Barbara in previous dates—pushing way too hard. Janey warned her to be careful. Tom was a football player with a temper. She'd heard of other girls he'd treated badly. But Barbara liked him—and kept saying she could handle him. Only this night she couldn't.

Date rape is also called acquaintance rape or hidden rape.

Increased awareness of it has pretty much kept pace with growing awareness of domestic violence and women's rights generally. (While some teenage boys are date-raped, the incidence of male date-rape victims is very low compared to female victims, who will therefore be our focus here.) Date rape occurs when a teenage girl is subjected to sexual intercourse, oral or anal sex, or any other sexual act against her will through the use or threat of force. For teenagers, rape by a stranger is less common than rape by an acquaintance.

Date rape has become more publicized through television coverage of famous date-rape or acquaintance-rape cases. Although it is impossible to know the exact frequency of date rape, in some surveys up to 20 or 30 percent of young women have stated that they have been date raped or been victims of attempted date rape. Most of them knew their attacker and most of this sexual coercion occurred on dates. About 5 to 10 percent of young males have stated that they have attempted date rape. Often girls who have been date raped do not tell anybody. It is rarely reported to the police. As a result, date-rape victims rarely get help, despite the fact that they have been seriously traumatized.

The typical scenario for date rape involves a young girl who, at a club, bar, party, or other recreational gathering, feels social and sexual pressure to meet a boy. Drinking is also often involved and sometimes sexual provocations are made by both girl and boy. Eventually the two end up alone in a car, in an isolated area, or in the home of either the date raper or victim. It is at that point that the male often overpowers, threatens, and forces the rape victim to give in and have sexual intercourse. Increased risk factors for getting date raped are "traditional" assumptions among some teenage girls that they should be passive or submissive and the boy is "supposed" to be dominant. The use of alcohol or drugs occurred in up to 65 percent of victims, generally consumed just before the rape occurred. The rapist often picks out victims who he feels, based on their personalities, would be unlikely to turn them in. The teenage boys or young men who commit date rape are often influenced by a powerful version of "machismo"— an assumption that it is the male's prerogative to be dominant and take what he wants sexually. Sexual aggression in this context is not only acceptable but often idealized. The use of drugs or alcohol by the aggressor is very common.

After date rape the victim often tries to rationalize what happened. She will often blame herself. Despite these attempts at rationalization, she often suffers some degree of post-traumatic stress symptomatology and depression, and may even contemplate or attempt suicide. A very small number of date rapes are reported to the police. Because of her guilt (her sense that somehow she may have caused it), her acquaintance with the date raper, and sometimes even the dismissive way she may be treated by family, a date-rape victim is usually unlikely to report the rape to authorities. Sometimes the victim's family members or friends look for reasons to accuse her, such as claiming she drank too much, dressed too provocatively, or in some other way "brought it on herself." Other effects of having been date raped include promiscuity, social withdrawal, chronic anxiety, and persistent mistrust.

What to Do

- If you are the parent of a teenage boy, particularly if you are the father, it is important to let him know what date rape is, to tell him the importance of respecting teenage girls, and that if the girl says stop, he must. Say this with the understanding that his attraction to a girl and urges to have sex are perfectly normal, but that restraint must be employed, not only for moral reasons but because he would be breaking the law if he did otherwise. This could result in various forms of punishment. Above all, reinforce the notion that being a man does not mean being indiscriminately or insensitively dominant.

- Girls should be told that rape is a violent crime, whatever may have led up to it, and that she has a right to stop anytime she wants to during a sexual encounter.

- Without overstating the case—the point here is not to make your teenage daughter paranoid—make it clear that even when she doesn't feel sexually provocative or flirtatious, and thus may not be aware she is "leading a boy on," that a potential date raper may be misreading her intentions. In other words, encourage your daughter to be clear about her limits with any boy she dates and to be careful not to send out sexual messages she doesn't intend.

- Great care must be taken about alcohol or the use of other drugs, especially at social gatherings.

- If she has been raped, your daughter should know that it is not her fault in any way.

- Certain drugs have been used in date rape, and your daughter must know about them and steer clear of any possibility of being given them; specifically, Rohypnol, generically called flunitrazepam, which is normally prescribed for short-term treatment of insomnia. These are white tablets that easily dissolve in drinks and are undetectable. Sold illegally in the United States, the drug creates a high in combination with alcohol, impairs judgment and motor skills, and makes it impossible to prevent a sexual attack. It affects memory, starts to work within thirty minutes, and peaks at two hours. Also called "the forget pill" or "the mind eraser," it causes a blackout during which nothing is remembered by whomever ingests the drug. Women have reported being raped after being given this drug involuntarily, usually slipped into one of their drinks. Its first effects present as dizziness, disorientation, and often nausea. Many victims have trouble speaking or moving. Common sense should prevail: Girls should be told never to accept drinks from anyone they do not know. Also, they should not leave their drinks unattended, and they and their group of friends should know the effects of the drug so that they can recognize if it may have been given to someone manifesting any of these symptoms. Another date rape drug is GHB, gamma hydroxybutrate, which is also called liquid ecstasy or scoop. Overdosing on this drug can be fatal. (See chapter on Club Drugs.)

- Anyone who has been date raped should receive a mental-health consultation to rule out any residual serious psychiatric effect. Sometimes short-term follow-up counseling can prevent far greater psychic harm in the future.

S<small>EE ALSO</small>:

Anxiety
Stress and PTSD
Depression
Suicide
Behavior Disorders
Drugs
Getting Help

27. Homosexuality

*"Uh, Mom and Dad? I think I have something
to tell you. . . ."*

DESPITE INCREASED societal acceptance of homosexuality, evidenced by the success of TV programs such as *Will and Grace*, for example, coming out for gay and lesbian teens is rarely an easy task. The notion of being "different" is anathema to teens generally, but the "differentness" of being gay can have an especially heavy impact on a teen. Parents are advised to employ much compassion and patience toward their homosexual adolescent sons and daughters, as well as examine their own resistance to the possibility that their children might be gay. Dealing with this issue always involves the whole family.

Many gay and lesbian youths first become aware of being homosexual during adolescence. The American Academy of Pediatrics defines homosexuality as the persistent sexual and emotional attraction to one's own gender and is part of the continuum of sexual expression. While the American Psychiatric Association for many years considered homosexuality an illness, it changed its position in 1973 and reclassified homosexuality as a psychologically viable sexual orientation/expression.

The cause of homosexuality is unclear at this time. Not all homosexual behavior, especially in early adolescence, is a predictor of future homosexuality. It is common for adult heterosexual males and females to report having had homosexual contact during their adolescent years. The exact percentage of adolescents who are homosexual is not known. Many people view homosexuality as a choice, while others feel that it is not. This debate rages on in many circles. What is a choice for all teenagers, regardless of their sexual orientations, is the expression of sexual behavior and lifestyle. This is emphasized in education that all teens should receive. Sex education is extremely important, especially due to the serious and often fatal aspects of sexually transmitted diseases.

In our culture homosexual youths have a higher suicide/mortality rate than heterosexuals. Studies of gay youths reveal that as many as one in three has attempted suicide; they may comprise as much as 30 percent of youth suicides. As a whole, increased societal acceptance of homosexuality has led to some increased comfort with their sexual orientation for homosexual youths.

Many gay teens feel guilty about their sexuality and painfully different from their peers; they worry about the response from their families, are often teased and bullied, worry about AIDS infection and other STDs, feel discrimination when joining various clubs and other activities, and often are rejected and harassed by other teenagers. This leads to isolation and withdrawal, low self-esteem, depression, and sometimes trouble concentrating or other performance difficulties in school. Adding to the gay teens' distress, many parents have tremendous difficulty accepting the reality of a homosexual son or daughter, sometimes withdrawing from and rejecting their child.

Often when teenagers become aware of homosexual stirrings, they feel great confusion and attempt to deny and repress them. This leads to anxiety, sometimes causing teens to run for treatment to get the problem "fixed" and sometimes even to make religious commitments to overcome homosexual feelings held to be bad or "sinful." Other teens decide to "come out" if they are asked about their sexuality; others may decide to proclaim their homosexuality from the start. Over time, increased socialization with other gays tends to solidify the sexual identity of a homosexual teenager. This decreases the sense of loneliness and isolation. Some pride in being gay often develops. Validation, acceptance, and support by others leads to affirming the gay teen's identity. Eventually, positive relationships with other gays and lesbians result in positive self-identification and ultimate integration and acceptance. This encourages teens to be open about their sexual orientations without defensiveness. Increased awareness of homosexuality, and gay teens' own growing self-acceptance and self-expression, hopefully will continue to reduce societal prejudice against being gay.

It should be remembered that a gay person is not less worthy or fundamentally any different from anyone else in society. Gays have no measurable differences in physical or intellectual spheres from non-gay people. Unfortunately, however, there is still much prejudice and discrimination against gays, which recently has become worse due to the association with homosexual transmission of AIDS, even though AIDS is not a "gay" disease.

"Coming out" is a controversial issue. Who should the teen tell about his or her sexuality? Friends? Parents? Siblings? Most concur that gay teens should tell people whom they know will be supportive. Regarding parents, most studies show that telling both parents at the same time is best, but in many families, due to emotional instability or because of greater closeness to one particular parent, gay teens may decide to tell one parent before the other. In most cases, it is best for siblings to be told after parents, although in cases where the gay teen is extremely close to a sibling, this might not be the case. Interestingly, studies show that sometimes coming out casually is more effective than a more serious and dramatic coming out. Also, strong family ties lead to a more positive experience during the disclosure. The bottom line is homosexual teenagers have to decide whom they are going to tell and how they are going to tell them based on their particular and unique families, friendships, and social adaptation. Most parents love their children sufficiently to survive what might be the initial shock of hearing that their son or daughter is gay; after a period of disbelief or denial, most parents can be counted on to come around and accept the news.

What to Do

- If your teen is gay or lesbian you should provide emotional support, despite the fact that you may have trouble accepting it.
- Counseling and/or psychotherapy are suggested for teens who are uncomfortable with or uncertain about their sexual

orientation. Therapy can also help with adjusting to society at large. According to studies, conversion psychotherapy is not considered helpful at this time. In other words, sending your child to a therapist to change sexual orientation usually does not work.

- There are many local and national gay support groups that can help your teenager overcome some of the stigmatization and negative feedback that he or she gets. This includes the National Counsel for Gays, Lesbians, and Transgender Youths.

- It is extremely important that sexually transmitted disease information be given to your teen as soon as possible in the fullest and most open way. Homosexual transmission of HIV is common and knowing the importance of condoms and other protection against such transmission is essential for your teen.

- A very large percentage, up to 95 percent, of gay, lesbian, bisexual, or transgender teenagers report that they are often called names or threatened. As a result, they often skip school because they feel unsafe. They are three times as likely to be assaulted than their heterosexual peers. In addition, they are threatened more and injured with weapons more. Lesbian and bisexual teens are more likely than heterosexual girls to be victims of rape or attempted rape. For these reasons and others, specific legislation may be passed that protects gay and lesbian youths as well as bisexual and transgender youths. On the other side of the argument, some say this would offer special treatment for this group.

SEE ALSO:

Anxiety
Depression
Bullying
Sexual Development
STDs
School Problems
Getting Help

28. STDs and Safe Sex

*"I don't know what to do, Carol. I have a
discharge and it's just gotten so itchy and burning
down there. Tell my parents? What? Are you
crazy?"*

So WHISPERS seventeen-year-old Annette to her best friend Carol on
the phone. Getting "itchy down there" may indicate the presence of
a sexually transmitted disease, for which Annette is afraid to seek
treatment because of what she fears her parents' reaction will be. Let
this be a warning: one of the most important services parents can
offer teens is the open and nonjudgmental invitation to talk about
whatever happens to them sexually. This is important for many reasons but paramount among them is the potential danger of sexually
transmitted diseases, which is too great to be ignored.

About 25 percent of sexually active teenagers are infected with a
sexually transmitted disease (STD) under the age of eighteen; therefore
sexually transmitted diseases are of great concern. Sexually transmitted diseases are extremely common. Thirteen million people in the
country each year are diagnosed with STDs, which are most common
in teenagers and young adults (about 64 percent of STDs occur in
people under twenty-five years old). They affect males and females
from all walks of life. Because people are becoming sexually active
earlier, there is a high instance of sexually transmitted disease in
teenagers. In addition, as a result of the increasing divorce rate and
other factors, having sex with multiple partners has become more
common, which also increases the risk of STDs.

Sexually transmitted diseases are dangerous for both genders but worse for females because they are often asymptomatic, which means the diagnosis is made later often after it has spread to internal organs such as the uterus and fallopian tubes. This can cause pelvic inflammatory disease, which in turn causes infertility and tubal pregnancies. STDs are also dangerous because some can cause cervical cancer as well as warts. They can also be transmitted to the fetus during pregnancy sometimes causing disabilities and even death. Most sexually transmitted diseases can be treated if diagnosed early. That's why it is very important that teenagers receive appropriate education about prevention, diagnosis, and treatment of sexually transmitted diseases.

Prevention of STDs is best accomplished by not having sex. If a teenager is sexually active it's preferabe if it is with one person who she knows does not have a sexually transmitted disease. Use of a male condom also decreases the transmission of STDs to a significant degree, although it should be noted that even the use of the male latex condom only reduces the risk and is not 100 percent effective. Many sexually transmitted diseases make the probability of others more likely, specifically HIV/AIDS. Thus, prevention and treatment of sexually transmitted diseases will hopefully cut down on the amount of HIV infections. Starting sex at a later age and having as few partners as possible decreases sexually transmitted diseases. Condoms lubricated with spermicides are not necessarily more effective than other condoms. Appropriate education about condom use is very important as incorrect use could lead to slippage and breakage and thus diminish the effectiveness of the use of the condom. Inconsistent use is an issue (see "Safe Sex" at the end of this chapter). Condoms are associated with a lowered risk of cervical cancer as well.

There are two ways in which STDs can be transmitted:

1. The "discharge diseases" are transmitted by infected semen or vaginal fluids that contact mucosal surfaces such as the urethra, the vagina, or cervix. These include the human immunodeficiency virus (HIV) as well as gonorrhea, chlamydia, and trichomoniasis.

2. The genital "ulcer diseases" are transmitted through contact with infected skin or mucosal surfaces and these include

genital herpes, syphilis, chancroid, and the human papilloma virus.

Sexually transmitted diseases are those diseases that you get by having sex: genital intercourse, or oral or anal intercourse with someone who already has an STD. Sexually transmitted diseases are caused by both bacteria and viruses. Bacterial STDs include chlamydia, gonorrhea, trichomoniasis, and syphilis. Viruses also cause sexually transmitted diseases and include HIV/AIDS, genital herpes, genital warts, and cytomegalovirus. While the bacterial ones can be cured with antibiotics the viral ones can only be prevented and treated, to some degree, but not cured.

In addition to using a condom and making sure a partner is not infected, getting regular checkups, especially if a teen has sex with more than one person, is important. A doctor might be able to see the signs of an STD before the teen knows he has the illness.

Signs and Symptoms of Various STDs

- **Gonorrhea:** This is a bacterial infection that affects the cervix, urethra, rectum, anus, and throat. Incubation period is up to two weeks. It is possible to have no symptoms. Males will notice symptoms before females. In females there is a change in vaginal discharge to a yellow or green color with a strong odor, pain, or burning sensation when passing urine, and irritation or discharge from the anus. In males there is a yellow or white discharge from the penis and irritation or discharge from the anus. Gonorrhea is passed on by sexual intercourse when the penis enters the vagina, mouth, or anus. Gonorrhea is diagnosed by a doctor examining the genital area and taking samples with a swab; in females by an internal pelvic exam and sometimes a sample of the urine. Treatment is easy and includes antibiotics. If untreated, females can get pelvic inflammatory disease and also pass it on to a baby; If untreated, males can get inflammation of the testicle and prostate gland and a narrowing of the urinary tract.

- **Chlamydia:** This is the most common of the treatable bacterial STDs. Some females have no symptoms of this disease.

Sometimes there is a slight increase in vaginal discharge or some increased urination. Sometimes menstruation is affected. With males there might be a mild discharge and some mild burning when urinating. Usually chlamydia causes no symptoms. Like gonorrhea, the genital area is examined and samples are taken. Treatment is with antibiotics. Like gonorrhea, this disease, if untreated, can cause pelvic inflammatory disease and infection of the fetus if a pregnancy is involved. There are fewer complications in males.

- **Syphilis:** Another bacterial infection that used to be much more common than it is now, although there seems to be an upsurge in certain areas of the country. It can also be passed to a child and congenital syphilis is not uncommon. There are three stages of syphilis. The first stage is the development of a chancre, or shallow ulcer, on the area where the person is infected: in females either around the vagina, the uterine cervix, or around the anus or mouth; in males often on the penis or anus and mouth. The chancre could appear after up to three weeks of being infected. Up to six weeks after becoming infected, the secondary stage can occur. Essentially this is a skin infection appearing on the whole body, a feeling of being ill, some mouth lesions, and even hair loss. If both the primary and secondary stages do not lead to diagnosis then latent syphilis or the third stage becomes a possibility. This affects the heart and possibly the essential nervous system; it can be fatal. The most accurate test for syphilis is a blood test. If there is a chancre sometimes a specimen can be taken from it. If diagnosed early, treatment is rather easy and often involves the injection of antibiotics.

- **Genital herpes:** This is a viral STD. It affects the genital area and the skin around the anus and fingers, and may affect the mouth. The virus called herpes simplex virus lives in nerves and occasionally, under certain circumstances such as being stressed, migrates down the nerve to form the typical herpes lesion. There used to be two types (Type One and Type Two),

but the differentiation between Type One—oral herpes—and
Type Two—genital and anal herpes—is less easy to make these
days. Symptoms of a herpes infection are usually an itchy,
burning, or tingling sensation in the area and then the erup-
tion of small fluid-filled vesicles or blisters that can be quite
painful. These can take weeks to heal. Sometimes the vesicles
all coalesce to become one large one. Other symptoms include
pain while urinating or having flulike symptoms. The disease is
transmitted through direct physical contact. Genital herpes is
not curable and seems to come in episodes. It is not possible to
know if you will have one or many episodes. Treatment is
mostly symptomatic, such as taking pain killers when you have
an outbreak. Avoiding excessive sun also is important during
an outbreak. If herpes is untreated during a pregnancy, it can
be passed on to a child causing serious neurological disease.

- **Genital warts:** These are caused by HPV, called the human
  papilloma virus. These are usually small bumps or even large
  cauliflower-shaped bumps in the genital area around the
  vagina, sometimes on the penis and scrotum, and on the anus.
  They are usually painless, sometimes they itch, and sometimes
  they can develop inside females and are not visible on the outside, such as when they occur in the vagina and on the cervix.
  Like herpes these are spread through physical contact. Usually the diagnosis is made by clinical examination. Sometimes
  warts are frozen, treated with lasers, or treated with podo-
  phyllin. Some types of genital warts may cause cervical cancer
  although that has not been proven.

- **Hepatitis:** There are three forms of hepatitis. Hepatitis A is
  caused by the oral ingestion of the hepatitis A virus (such as
  eating contaminated shellfish). Hepatitis B is contracted differently and includes being spread through sexual penetration.
  It may also be transmitted by transfusions of blood, either
  medically indicated or through the use of contaminated needles or non-sterilized equipment used for puncturing the body.
  It can also be transmitted from mother to fetus. Symptoms of

hepatitis include gastrointestinal disease including nausea, vomiting, and diarrhea; weight loss; turning jaundiced or yellow; or having itchy skin. Some people may develop chronic liver disease and even liver cancer. Blood tests usually make the diagnosis. Treatment is usually not required as the inflammation of the liver that occurs with hepatitis is usually not too severe. Today, many children get immunizations. Hepatitis C is also an inflammation of the liver that can spread the way hepatitis B does. It is similar to hepatitis B in many ways. People remain infected for many years and hepatitis C has increased as a cause and concern in the medical system in this country. People can be chronically ill with recurrences and exacerbations, and can develop hepatitic cirrhosis or liver cancer. There are various treatments with antiviral drugs and interferon as well.

- **Trichomoniasis:** This is a parasite disease. Two to three million Americans get this each year. It is mostly manifested in females who experience itching, burning, and redness in the genital area. Sometimes there is a vaginal discharge, painful urination, painful sex, and abdominal pain. Males sometimes have a discharge and painful urination or tingling inside the penis. Examining secretions from the penis or vagina can often make the diagnosis. It is treated with antibiotics, usually Metronidazole also called Flagyl.

- **HIV/AIDS:** AIDS is caused by a virus that affects the immune system and blocks the body's ability to fight infection. As a result, many people get life-threatening infections and even cancer. HIV is a sexually transmitted disease that is viral and spread during sexual activities as well as through blood and sharing of needles.

What to Do

- Any teenager who is sexually active should have regular checkups for STDs, even if there are no symptoms.

- Parents and teenagers should learn the symptoms of STDs.

- Tell teens that anal intercourse should be avoided, but the use of a male condom is important if it is practiced.

- Douching should be avoided. It may increase the risk of getting some STDs because it removes protective bacteria that live in the vagina.

- Treatment is necessary to reduce the risk of transmitting an STD to an infant.

- All sexual partners should be notified if your teen finds that he or she has a STD.

- All sexual activity should be avoided when being treated for an STD.

- Parents should make it clear that they are available to their teens for help and discussion about any aspect of STDs.

Safe Sex and How to Practice It

Safe sex actually means having sex so that you do not get ill as a result of contact with a partner's blood, semen, vaginal fluids, or breast milk. It also means protecting others from contact with these fluids in your body.

One should always use a condom and the best ones are lubricated latex condoms. Lambskin condoms do not stop contraction of HIV and STDs and polyurethane condoms break more frequently. Lubrication should always be water-based. (Oil breaks down latex.) Condoms have to be fresh and should be unrolled appropriately and as far as it goes. After using a condom, the male partner should always hold on to the bottom of the condom so it does not slip off. It should then be thrown away as quickly as possible and never reused. If sexual devices or "toys" are used, they should also have condoms on them, a new condom per different partner. If inserted into the anus, they should not be inserted into the vagina without having a new condom put on them. If oral sex is being performed on a penis it is advisable that the penis be sheathed with a condom. It is now advised that semen not go into the mouth, as it is known that

HIV can be transmitted in this way, especially if the receiver has any oral lesions or sore gums. Safe sex also may include getting vaccinations for hepatitis B and hepatitis A. Safe sex also requires washing hands with hot water and an antibacterial soap if the vagina or semen has been touched. This also is important if your teen touches a partner's anus. Antibacterial towelettes are also useful.

SEE ALSO:

Sexual Development

29. Sexual Abuse

"Mom, I don't want to visit Uncle Andy on Saturday, okay? I know he's been generous and stuff, but I just don't want to!"

THIRTEEN-YEAR-OLD Billy doesn't like his uncle's attentions. He's too affectionate, touchy-feely. He likes to "wrestle," and it's gotten out of hand. Though he can't bring himself to tell his mother this, Uncle Andy has been groping him in places he shouldn't. Uncle Andy has, in fact, been sexually abusing the boy.

Sexual abuse is usually committed by adults or older children known to the abuse victim. The abuser usually has power over the victim or is in a position of authority. This is true in 85 to 90 percent of cases. Often the abuser is someone the child trusts, loves, and respects, which includes parents, relatives, family friends, and even teachers, coaches, clergymen or –women, or baby-sitters. When abuse occurs in the family it is called incest.

Generally speaking there are two types of abusers: pedophiles, persons who are sexually excited by children and teenagers and tend to act out their desires with them; and incestuous offenders, who often commit the abuse under the influence of drugs or alcohol. Sexual abusers are often seductive, often exposing children to sexually stimulating ideas and pornography. They exhibit themselves, talk about sexual themes with children, and may become quite "protective," inducing isolation and secrecy in the potential victim.

Sexual abuse is defined as occurring when the child or teen is engaged in sexual activities that he or she cannot comprehend, for which he or she is not developmentally prepared, to which he or she cannot give consent, and which violate laws and social taboos. Sexual activities included under abuse may include all forms of oral genital, genital, or anal contact by or to the child, or non-touching abuses such as exhibitionism, exposing the child to pornography, or using the child in pornographic situations such as photographing or filming him or her. It can also include activities ranging from fondling to rape. Asymmetrical development among participants in sex play (an older child and a much younger child) is also considered sexual abuse. Children who vary significantly in age and indulge in sexual play can be considered to be engaging in sexual abuse. The perpetrators are usually dependent individuals who experienced disruption and often abuse during their childhoods. Although most offenders are men some are women as well.

Presenting symptoms of a teenager who has been abused may include sleep disturbance, abdominal pain, fears, wetting the bed, or more specific signs like rectal or genital bleeding, sexually transmitted diseases, inappropriate sexual behavior such as promiscuity, or complete avoidance of sexual behaviors. In some teenagers it is difficult to diagnose sexual abuse because they feel they are actually consenting partners when in fact they are being sexually abused by an older person. Some laws are also a bit hazy about the cutoff for statutory rape; for instance, some states allow boys over the age of eighteen to have sex with girls under eighteen. This makes it difficult to assess when sexual abuse legally occurs. Most teenagers are secretive about sexual abuse. They often feel guilt, shame, and are fearful, especially due to the threats made by the abuser/perpetrator. In addition, there are often conflicting loyalties and worries that a teenager might have about revealing that a family member or other important person has committed the sex abuse act. This all makes the disclosure of sexual abuse a difficult issue.

Sexual abuse has been correlated with such future conditions as drug and alcohol abuse, low self-esteem, divorce, and general distrust of other people. It is often shocking and shattering to people. People often feel extreme shame, anger, hurt, and disappointment. For boys who are sexually abused by a man, it usually raises worries about homosexuality. Feelings of humiliation may result in boys becoming bullies. Girls are more likely to take out their feelings against themselves; for example, by cutting, developing eating disorders, and so on. They may also become promiscuous, sometimes eventually turning to prostitution. Other symptoms of sexual abuse include agitated behavior, frightening dreams, repetitive play, cruelty to others, and running away from home.

Teenagers who are sexually abused may lose interest in sex or avoid things of a sexual nature, get depressed, have sleep problems, make statements that their bodies have been damaged, and become truant, delinquent, secretive, aggressive, depressed, and even suicidal. These signs should be a concern to parents. Sexual abuse also has been linked to the development of dissociative identity disorder, or what is known as multiple personality disorder, later in life. It also has been associated with borderline personality disorder, mood disorders, substance abuse issues, and post-traumatic stress disorder. Sadly, the problem of sexual abuse is common. It is estimated that one in four girls and one in six boys will be sexually assaulted before the age of eighteen. Although the median age is nine years old it certainly continues throughout adolescence.

Remember that every teenager is vulnerable to sexual abuse regardless of cultural background. Giving children knowledge about sex and sex abuse as well as skills to avoid it is most important for their safety. However, we should also remember that there are often no signs of sexual abuse; many cases go unreported. Also there is little evidence that teenagers make false allegations. More often teenagers will deny that the abuse ever happened. Incest and sexual abuse are a betrayal of trust, often making it hard for teens to trust anyone, sometimes far into adulthood. Other long-term effects are fear of intimacy and eating disorders. Post-traumatic stress disorder or post-sexual abuse trauma disorder often is experienced by teenagers who have been sexually abused.

What to Do

- Most important, if you feel your teenager has been sexually abused and has, in fact, disclosed this, the teenager should be listened to and understood. He or she should be reassured that even if he or she is close to the person he or she should not feel guilty. He or she did the right thing by disclosing. Children should not be blamed for being victims of sexual abuse even though we are anxious and often angry at the time of disclosure. Parents have to offer protection.

- Parents should report any suspicion of child abuse to Child Protective Services if it happens inside the family, or to the police or the district attorney's office if it occurs outside the family.

- The sexually abused teen should undergo a physical examination.

- The teen should be evaluated by a child and adolescent psychiatrist.

- Sexual abuse allegations by teenagers should be believed, although in very few situations such allegations tend to be untrue, especially when they are made during divorce custody litigations.

- Appropriate psychiatric treatment of any symptomatic disorder is necessary. In addition family, group, and individual therapy is helpful.

- Although he or she is usually ignored in the process as he or she becomes a focus of hatred by society at large, the perpetrator of sexual abuse also needs treatment.

SEE ALSO:

Stress and PTSD
Depression
Suicide
Borderline Personality Disorder
Self-Injurious Behaviors
Sexual Development
Homosexuality
STDs and Safe Sex
Anorexia, Bulimia, and Overeating
Drugs
Getting Help

30. Gender Identity Disorder

*"I don't know how else to put it, Mom and Dad. I
just got born in the wrong body. I've felt this way
my whole life . . ."*

TEENAGERS with gender identity disorder have a desire to be or even insist that they are the other sex. They experience a persistent discomfort about being the sex to which they've been assigned—a deep sense of inappropriateness in the gender role of the sex they're biologically "supposed" to be. In other words, boys want to be girls and feel uncomfortable being boys, and girls want to be boys and feel uncomfortable being girls. Males outnumber females with this disorder. The prevalence of this disorder is unknown but based on those seeking sex-reassignment surgeries, it appears to range from one in thirty thousand adult males to one in one hundred thousand adult females. This disorder is usually identified by the age of two to four years old.

Gender identity disorder usually dissipates in children but there are reports that about 70 percent of boys who have this disorder as children report being homosexual or bisexual when adults, although they no longer have gender identity disorder. In the teenage years there may be a solidification of cross-gender identification and actually the beginning of sex-reassignment surgery and preparation for it. Teenagers who persist in having gender identity disorder often develop gender confusion or dysphoria.

Some people develop this disorder in early adolescence and not as young children; in other words, later than the typical childhood time of onset. Some of them become transvestites. There is less homosexuality in that group although higher than in the non-gender identity disorder population; there is also less desire for sex reassignment. According to most studies, people who have gender identity disorder and become homosexual tend to have a lifelong history of gender identity disorder.

In younger children, gender identity disorder often manifests as the child's insistence that he or she is a different sex than he or she has been assigned. Boys tend to want to dress like girls, and girls want to wear only masculine clothing. Accordingly, boys usually wish to play with girls, participating in "girl" games (playing with dolls, dressing up, playing house, and so on), and girls to participate with boys in rough and tumble "boy" games. As the child matures into an adolescent, he or she usually states more overtly the desire to be the other sex, or that he or she feels trapped in the body of the wrong sex. By adolescence, the teen with gender identity disorder usually has learned to "pass"—through dress and mannerism—as the other sex. Many teenagers want to rid themselves of primary and secondary sexual characteristics, and it is common for teenagers to request special hormone therapy to change their bodies as well as surgery to change their anatomies. They subscribe to the real belief that this is being done in order to fulfill the fact that they were actually born the other sex.

The adolescent boy or girl with gender identity disorder usually is secretive; therefore, the diagnosis might be difficult to reach. Sometimes those young adolescents are teased, rejected, or bullied, withdrawing from social interaction, and this leads to a referral. Age-appropriate milestones of same-sex peers are not met and this often leads to distress and depression. Depression can be severe due to the despair engendered by this disorder; school may be missed and education interfered with; relationships become difficult; isolation from the family is often an issue; and often teenagers feel stigmatized.

The cause of gender identity disorder is not known although genes and possible hormone imbalances in the uterus may be contributing factors. Also, some studies show that birth order and physical appearance may have some contributory role. Sometimes parental desire for a child of the other sex also can have an impact.

Nothing has been proven but conflicts with parents, varying parental influences (overbearing mothers, under-involved fathers, and so on), and various other pathologies exhibited by parents may also have an impact.

It should be remembered that as part of their development toward normal sex roles, young children will often try to be the other sex as they learn the distinctions between masculinity and femininity. This means that some young boys act feminine, sometimes even wearing dresses, performing feminine types of play, using cosmetics, and even nursing infants. Many young girls will pretend to be their daddies or adopt other masculine behaviors. This is usually temporary and passes. "Sissy boys" and "tomboy girls" are *not* pathologically gender disordered. It is only when children become inflexible and persistently hold to the patterns of the other sex that the possibility of gender identity disorder is considered.

Psychological therapy can alter the course of gender identity disorder, especially when early intervention is made, and this can lead to less transsexual behavior later in life. However, some adults and even teenagers request sex-reassignment or sex-change surgery. Prior to this surgery there is usually some hormone therapy to suppress same-sex characteristics and accentuate cross-sex characteristics. Many gender-disordered people have psychological distress including anxiety, stigmatization, depression, and even suicidal thoughts. Supportive counseling, group counseling, support groups, and family education and therapy are necessary in order to ameliorate this distress.

What to Do

- If your teenager is diagnosed with gender identity disorder, it is extremely important that you be supportive, not punitive. Your child is probably having a hard enough time not being a "real teenage girl or boy" and thus he or she needs a lot of love and understanding at home. Don't try to talk your teenager out of the gender identity he or she feels.

- Professional help, including a medical examination, is necessary since there are some rare conditions that present with gender distortion such as Klienfelter's Syndrome.

- Some parents are made quite anxious and sometimes become overtly, even violently punitive because of not having a "real boy or real girl." It is extremely important that this subgroup of parents receive education and sensitivity training for what might be a lifelong difficulty, especially if this condition has been diagnosed late in the teen's life.

SEE ALSO:

Depression
Homosexuality

IV

The Body

31. Hypochondria and Body Dysmorphia

"Mom, I know something's wrong! I feel so achy.
It doesn't matter that I don't have a temperature.
It could still be the flu! And why is my face
always so red? Can't you see?"

AT SIXTEEN, Andrea's complaints to her mother about her health have increased in the past several months. At first, because she'd rarely complained about not feeling well before, her family was concerned that she might really be sick. But after thorough examinations by her doctor, no physical problem was found. Andrea's mother wonders why her daughter suddenly seems to "need" to believe that she's ill. Andrea has friends and has always done well in school. The possibility that she might be pretending to be sick to avoid something just doesn't seem to fit. But Andrea really believes she's sick—she's not putting on an act. What's the problem?

Hypochondriasis is an irrational preoccupation with or fear of having a serious illness or disease. While more common in adults, children sometimes and teens more often can be hypochondriacal. Physical complaints should never be taken lightly; Andrea's mother was wise to get her daughter to a doctor when she first complained of feeling sick. But Andrea's persistence in believing she is ill does indicate hypochondriasis, which (although Andrea's mother may not yet have found out the source of it in her daughter) in teenagers is virtually always a symptom of anxiety.

153

More specifically, hypochondriasis, diagnosed only when physical causes for symptoms have been ruled out, is considered akin to narcissistic disorders; that is, disorders having to do with a fear of loss of control over some aspect of oneself psychologically. Because teens experience heightened concern with appearance, self-image, and "being normal," hypochondriasis tends to be more common in adolescence than in early childhood. The good news is that such hypochondriasis is usually transient: as Andrea matures, it is likely that her fears and concerns about her physical health will pass.

The American Psychiatric Association's specific diagnostic criteria for hypochondriasis include: a) preoccupation with fears of having, or the idea that one has, a serious disease based on the misinterpretation of bodily symptoms; b) that the preoccupation persists despite reassurance after medical evaluation; c) that the belief is not of delusional intensity; that is, the teenager can entertain the idea that something might not be wrong with him physically, and is not restricted to a circumscribed concern about appearance, except in specific syndromes such as body dysmorphic disorder (see following); and d) the hypochondriac's worries cause difficulties and impairment in social or other important areas of functioning. Hypochondriacal disorder is only diagnosed when it is differentiated from generalized anxiety disorder, obsessive-compulsive disorder, major depression, separation anxiety, and sleeping disorders.

Body Dysmorphic Disorder

Because it begins in adolescence, and has characteristics similar to hypochondriasis, body dysmorphic disorder deserves attention here. Most teenagers are concerned about appearance to a heightened degree (compared to other times in their lives), but with body dysmorphic disorder, obsessive attention is paid to a particular part of the body that the teen feels is abnormal or "wrong." The teen obsesses over an imagined defect, or exaggerates an actual physical trait or abnormality that is minor, such as thinning hair, hair texture, wrinkles, acne, moles, and so on. A teen may decide that one side of the face is different from the other, that the nose is crooked, or that there is excessive hair on face or arms. Specific focus tends to be on areas around the head, such as eyes, ears, nose, throat, teeth, and lips. (Andrea's certainty that her face is "always so red" is an example.) However, any part of the body can be the focus of the teenager's obsessive concerns.

This is an intensely painful and disturbing disorder to the teen who has it. It is difficult for afflicted teenagers to control their distress, and they may spend hours if not days preoccupied with it. Because of their extreme self-consciousness, they avoid many activities that bring them in contact with other people, often spending hours in front of mirrors, taking inordinate amounts of time grooming themselves or examining, scratching at, or otherwise trying to make defects, such as of the skin disappear. Teenagers with body dysmorphic disorder typically need continuous reassurance about how they look. Elaborate camouflaging rituals are often engaged in, such as wearing a hat indoors and outdoors to hide hair considered defective, wearing baggy clothes to hide legs or arms, and sunglasses to hide "abnormal" eyes. Social withdrawal, dropping out of school, becoming a hermit, losing friends, and avoiding dating are all common outcomes for the distressed teenager. Severe instances of this disorder can lead to suicidal ideations and even, in rare cases, suicide.

Teenagers who manifest any of these symptoms need medical consultation to rule out other possible diagnoses such as anorexia nervosa, gender identity disorder, depression, avoidant personality, social anxiety disorder, OCD, and sometimes (although rarely) psychotic syndromes like schizophrenia, in which the child is unable to relate fully to reality.

What to Do

- Parents should realize that any child with physical complaints may be sick and take these complaints seriously. Seek medical attention to rule out any illness.

- If hypochondriasis or body dysmorphic disorder is diagnosed it is important that the parent set limits so that the teen's behavior doesn't rule the house and disrupt the family. Expressing sympathy is appropriate, but setting limits is also necessary. Children must go to school, do their chores, and not be pandered to. In this way, the child's disorder can stay relatively well encapsulated and the family won't be torn apart.

■ Most hypochondriasis and even some aspects of body dysmorphic disorder pass in time. If it lasts for longer than several weeks, professional help is indicated, the aim of which is to rule out other diagnoses.

■ Some medications are found to be useful for children with hypochondriacal and body dysmorphic disorder. These include some of the drugs used for obsessive-compulsive disorder, especially those within the antidepressant serotonin reuptake inhibitor class.

SEE ALSO:

Anxiety
Social Phobia and Shyness
Obsessive-Compulsive Disorder
Depression
Suicide
Schizophrenia
Gender Identity Disorder
Anorexia, Bulimia, and Overeating

32. Anorexia, Bulimia, and Overeating

"My thirteen-year-old Amy once ate everything in the kitchen. Now, in the past six months or so, she's become a health nut and just picks at her food. She's losing weight right when she should be gaining it. She jumps down my throat if there's even a suspicion I've put 'fat' into her meal: 'Mom? Did you put cream in that sauce? How could you! I never would have eaten it if I'd known there was cream in it!' What can I do?"

ANYONE who has a teenager, especially a teenage girl, knows that counting calories and determining the percentage of fat in food have become an obsessive national ritual. Talk to her and she may give you a very reasoned, even plausible defense of her eating habits. And with all the media attention anorexia and bulimia have received, she probably knows more about their symptoms (and how to hide them) than her parents.

Anorexia

Anorexia is a condition in which a youngster, usually a teenage girl, develops an intense, almost phobic fear of being fat and, as a result, restricts the intake of food. She will sometimes "purge" to lose weight; for example, by inducing vomiting or using laxatives or diuretics. Often, she also exercises obsessively. The typical teenager with anorexia misperceives her body as being too fat and will not relinquish this belief however much her parents try to convince her of her irrationality. Although any teenager can develop anorexia it seems to be more common in ballerinas, athletes, and others who are involved in rigorous physical training activities.

An anorexic's capacity for denial knows few bounds. And in a society where girls as young as nine, ten, and eleven worry obsessively over calories and gaining weight, there is considerable inducement to keep that denial alive. The big taboo for these girls (and boys, although a far smaller proportion—one out of nine—are male) is fat, which most will do anything in their power to avoid. (You may wish your child were as good at algebra as she is in calculating the calorie value and fat percentage of anything edible you put in front of her.) The good news is that the great majority of anorexic teenagers—97 percent—grow out of it on their own.

However, I wouldn't underestimate the probable pressures girls feel now that they've physically matured. Some young teenage girls are frightened of the physical changes they undergo and want to hold on to childhood a little longer. By limiting their intake of food, they may believe they won't grow breasts or otherwise assume the contours of a woman, changes they don't feel ready for emotionally. And although these girls don't seem to have a hard time "navigating" puberty, they may well have anxieties about growing up that they don't feel comfortable sharing.

If your teen persists in "eating like a bird"—and her weight falls to or below 85 percent of the optimal weight for her height and age—and especially if she stops menstruating—then you do have cause for greater concern and should seek outside help. There is plenty of help available; check with your doctor. But the best thing you can do right now is to encourage your teen to talk about her "health nut" theories without arguing them down or getting angry at her for having them. If you listen carefully to her concerns about her diet, you'll more than likely hear what her deeper concerns are, too. The freer she feels talking about her feelings, the less obsessed she's likely to become about what she eats.

The first fact about anorexia is that it's fairly rare in its severest forms. Don't assume your child is suffering from an intransigent case of anorexia—the great likelihood is that she will outgrow it soon. However, be alert to warning signs that don't go away, like the following:

- Loss of weight at or below 85 percent of her expected weight
- Mental obsession with weight, food, menus, recipes, and eating, along with a phobia of fatness
- An irrational estimation of body weight usually in the form of insisting she's fat when she is actually underweight
- Complaining of being fat in certain areas of the body and always examining these areas in the mirror, or constantly weighing herself
- A rigid style of behaving with an excessive need for control, a seeming lack of enjoyment in life, and a fear of eating in public
- Physical symptoms such as constipation, fatigue, and intolerance to cold
- Loss of menses, or menses never starting
- Depression
- Emergence of fine hair over the body

About one out of every 100 to 200 teenagers suffers from this disorder but many more live on the fringe of it, evincing many subtle symptoms. Most girls recover from one episode, which often begins at age seventeen, but a very few go on to develop a lifelong disorder and some even get seriously ill and require hospitalization.

Bulimia

Bulimia is another common eating disorder. It is characterized by episodes of binge eating. Binge eating is different from overeating because it takes place in a discrete period of time, usually two hours or so, during which the binger feels somewhat out of control, consuming a very large amount of high calorie, usually sweet, food typically in secret. The binger eats to the point of causing abdominal pain, as well as shame and self-disgust. These binges usually occur several times per week and are sometimes triggered by certain emotional events; they may also seemingly come out of the blue. Sometimes bulimic teenagers say that binging relieves depression at first, but the binges are often *followed* by depression as well. After a binge, the bulimic usually resorts to procedures that are meant to lose the weight thought to have been gained in the binge, such as self-induced vomiting, frantic exercise, laxatives, diuretics, and even enemas. These behaviors are like those of the anorexic; in fact, some teenagers have aspects of both disorders together.

Warning signs of bulimia:

- Witnessing binges or evidence that it has occurred (like finding quantities of food packaging secreted away)
- Missing food
- Finding vomited food in hidden areas
- The odor of vomit in the bathroom
- Frequent disappearances (to vomit in private)
- Depression, anxiety, or substance abuse (especially appetite-depressing stimulants like "speed" or diet pills)
- Theft of food and resultant trouble with the police
- Erosion of dental enamel from vomiting
- Telltale tooth marks on the hand used for inducing vomiting
- Addiction to laxatives

Like anorexia, the ratio of females to males with bulimia is on the order of nine to one. It is slightly more common than anorexia and is associated with normal or slightly above normal body weights. Unlike the rigid anorexic, the bulimic is often impulse-ridden in other areas, "addicted" to sex or romantic relationships, and addicted to drugs, alcohol, and other substances, among other erratic behaviors.

What to Do If Your Teen Is Anorexic or Bulimic

- Don't panic. Most teens who go through periods of unnecessary dieting grow out of them soon—usually by the time they hit their mid-teens. As always, do what you can to keep the lines of communication open with your teen. Encourage her to talk about feelings and assumptions about food and diet, no matter how irrational they may seem to you. The more you get your teen to talk in detail about these feelings, the clearer the underlying anxieties may be.

- Be alert to the examples you and other family members are setting. Is fat as big a no-no to you or your spouse as it has become to your child? Examine the messages you're sending out to your teenager about food; you may be surprised about some of them. Don't judge her opinions and emotions. Let her give full play to whatever she's thinking and feeling. Once again, the greatest likelihood is that the crisis will pass.

- If the warning signs listed above indicating either anorexia or bulimia persist, it is essential that you have your child examined by a physician. The doctor will be able to evaluate her and determine if there are any physical consequences that need to be dealt with urgently. The doctor may well tell you that your child is simply indulging in an exaggerated form of culturally sanctioned behavior—that she is not yet in any real danger—but that you should remain alert, patient, and observant.

- It's important to stress to your teen her positive and constructive traits, so that her self-esteem becomes more dependent on personal qualities and achievements and less attached to weight or physical appearance. Cultivation of a positive self-image is the key to avoiding the development of and overcoming these disorders.

- Treatment for eating disorders includes one or more of the following: nutritional counseling, family counseling, group therapy, support groups, individual psychotherapy, and hospitalization for severe cases.

Overeating

Often the teen who overeats to the point of obesity is afflicted by many of the same anxieties that best the anorexic or bulimic teen.

Despairing that he or she will ever fit in or "make the grade," the
obese teen frequently turns to eating as a means of assuaging anxiety.
The teen may feel soothed by eating more. Sometimes the teen outwardly rebels by sneaking food, with an outward defiance of "not
caring" about his appearance. The problem of overeating is com-
pounded by the vast availability of junk food, which can be found at
the mall, in movie theaters, and even in the school cafeteria. Eating
to allay anxiety is common among teens. Some studies also link obesity to depression. One puts the odds of an obese teen developing
depression as double those who do not.

Obesity is a major public health problem in the United States. In
some rare cases obesity is caused by a physical condition, but more
typically it's caused by simply eating too much. Obesity seems to run
in families. Family dysfunction tends to be implicated as well. In addition to self-soothing, a teen sometimes resorts to overeating to quell
feelings of anger, irritability, rage, and other forms of distress. Poverty
and lower socioeconomic status are linked to a greater likelihood of
becoming obese. Being obese leads to a host of secondary emotional
problems ranging from poor self-esteem to social isolation.

Obesity also foretells significant medical problems. More than
three hundred thousand deaths are linked to it each year, and among
the medical problems obesity causes are hypertension, cardiovascular
disease, some cancers, type 2 diabetes, osteoarthritis, and stroke.
While overweight teens may not initially be as at risk as older people
healthwise, their obesity does not bode well for future good health.
Although the causes are unknown, both obesity and depression are
increasing worldwide.

Helping the obese teen almost always involves family counseling, with an emphasis on making sure parents learn how to model
healthy eating habits. Emphasis must also be placed on developing an
eating program the teen will follow. Compassion and fair boundaries
are key.

What to Do If Your Teen Is Obese

- Educating your teenager about healthy eating is important,
  especially about portion size, calorie intake, and healthy food
  choices.

- Parents should provide good examples of healthy eating: a parent who overeats is more likely to have a teen who overeats. Showing by example is more powerful than lecturing, particularly if parents themselves are not abiding by the rules they want their teens to follow. Families should be sensitive to the role they may be playing in inducing the teen to resort to overeating. Counseling can help families address these concerns and help them make changes for the better.

- Avoid harsh criticism or putting down your teen for overeating. Understand that there are almost always emotional problems underlying the teen's urge to overeat. Open up the channels of communication to encourage your teen to talk about his anxiety.

- Consulting a good nutritionist or source of information on healthy nutrition and then working out a healthy eating plan with your teen is also important. Let your teen decide on food choices, and make an effort to find healthy foods the teen likes.

- Make it clear to your teen that many body types are acceptable and attractive. The aim in helping teens who overeat to eat more healthily is not to turn them into magazine models but rather to help them become happier with themselves.

- Parents should have a say in what's offered in school cafeterias. Many parents and students have successfully advocated for changing what's served in middle and high schools.

- If obesity is severe, it is advisable to schedule a diagnostic consultation with your teen's doctor.

SEE ALSO:

Anxiety
Obsessive-Compulsive Disorder
Depression
Hypochondria and Body Dysmorphia
Drugs
Getting Help

33. Psychosomatic Disorders

*"You know how I get when the weather changes,
Mom! I have a headache and my stomach hurts
and I feel achy all over. Can't the doctor help this
time? I'm not making this up!"*

GWEN TRULY doesn't feel she's "making this up," although her family
has gotten to the point where they don't take her seriously anymore.
At first her mother took her to the doctor when she got her "allergic" reactions, but test after test revealed no medical problem. Gwen
swears she's just "sensitive" to weather changes; when the humidity
goes up or down she's back to her bodily complaints. Her mother is
exasperated. She hates seeing her daughter in such physical distress,
but she's begun to lose patience. She's started to tell Gwen to "snap
out of it."

Often bodily symptoms express underlying emotional issues for
teenagers. Sometimes this results in what is called a psychosomatic
disorder. Officially, these are now called somatoform disorders of
which there are two major categories:

1. **Conversion symptoms** (like those that afflict Gwen): These
   are manifested by problems in a teenager's sensory or motor
   functions, and often seem to indicate a neurological or medical condition. These are triggered by psychological conflicts
   or stress. Typically teenagers with conversion disorders complain of weakness and sometimes even paralysis, or they
   may simply have "funny feelings" or numbness. Sometimes

they appear to be experiencing problems as serious as seizures. Pain may be experienced anywhere but especially in the abdominal area and in the head. Often these same teens complain about light headedness, faintness, generally feeling unwell, and nausea, and may vomit or experience intestinal distress.

2. **Somatization disorder:** This is the most common somato-form disorder of teenagers. In this disorder we see a pattern of many bodily complaints that last a long time; this contrasts with conversion disorders, which are usually short-lived episodes. Somatization disorder is persistent, tends to be recurrent, and involves many different symptoms. Officially, according to *The Diagnostic and Statistical Manual of Mental Disorders Fourth Edition* (DSM-IV), teenagers suffering from somatization disorder have at least four different pain symptoms (in the head, abdomen, back, legs/arms, joints, chest, rectum, and during menstruation, sexual intercourse, or urination); two gastrointestinal symptoms (nausea, vomiting, bloating, diarrhea, and food intolerance); at least one sexual symptom (sexual indifference, erectile or ejaculation disturbance, irregular menses, excessive menstrual bleeding, and vomiting throughout pregnancy); and one symptom that appears to be any part of a host of neurological conditions.

Both conversion disorder and somatization disorder are usually caused by stress. Females get this more than males; the ratio is about four to one. Social, academic/educational, and athletic stress; physical or sexual abuse; dysfunctional families; the death of a family member; and secret identification with parents who also have many bodily complaints constitute some of the stressors that can cause the onset of a somatoform disorder. Sometimes having a real physical injury can result in long-lasting psychosomatic symptoms; for example, the pain of a broken arm may continue to be felt even after the arm has healed, or a child who has had an actual upset stomach can end up having long-standing abdominal pain even after the physical source of the pain has disappeared. Of course, one of the keys to diagnosing somatoform disorder is first to rule out any medical condition through a complete medical examination.

Like many other symptoms in psychiatry, it is unclear why one child develops a somatoform disorder and another doesn't. We know that trauma and abuse tend to increase the likelihood of conversion disorders. We also know that somatoform disorders have a tendency to run in families, which might be evidence of a genetic predisposition. It might also be an expression of learned behavior. Some children simply have trouble expressing their emotions and learn to use their bodies unconsciously for the purpose instead. Somatoform disorders are not consciously willed: Gwen isn't "putting it on" when she complains of pain and physical distress.

What to Do

- It is extremely important that any teen with recurring physical complaints be completely examined and diagnosed by a physician.

- If your physician rules out physical illness, be sure not to minimize the enormous impact that emotions can have on your teen's bodily functions.

- If your teen has been diagnosed as having somatoform disorder, don't panic or express anxiety; this will result in your teen having more symptoms.

- Try to discuss with your teen what the triggers might be for upsurges in bodily complaints. Sometimes just the fact you and your teen are working together in this process can be helpful and healing, giving your teen a greater sense of control over what before seemed uncontrollable.

- Your child's doctor may refer you to a adolescent psychiatrist for a complete psychiatric evaluation, which may result in psychotherapy, family therapy, or another form of psychiatric intervention that can be helpful to your child.

- If you are a "body reactor," with feelings that quickly manifest in physical complaints, try to curb this behavior in front of your teenager.

- After your teen has been cleared medically, avoid any further non-indicated, expensive, recurring, and unnecessary medical tests; this will just reinforce your teen's belief that there's something wrong.

- Your psychiatrist may suggest medication for your teen, various forms of which, including antidepressants, antianxiety agents, and mood stabilizers, have been found effective. Psychoeducation will also be an important part of treatment, helping the teen to learn more about his body and how to interpret his feelings in the body more appropriately.

- Be compassionate. Do not minimize, belittle, intimidate, or make fun of your teen for expressing psychosomatic symptoms. They are real to your teen even if they may not be to you.

SEE ALSO:

Anxiety
Stress and PTSD
Depression
Hypochondria and Body Dysmorphia

34. Athletics, Weight Training, and Muscle Dysmorphia

"Hey, have you seen Brad lately? Yeah, I know
he's been workin' out like crazy. It's all he does.
But he's startin' to look like a freak. You think
he's takin' 'roids?"

CONCERN with body image is heightened for nearly all teens. Bombarded by various versions of "the perfect body" in the media, the notion of physical appearance, muscular strength, looking "hot" or "buff," and trying to conform to these standards of beauty and perfection often make teenagers tense, stressed out, and depressed. We know that the development of anorexia and bulimia have much to do with girls worrying excessively about how they look (girls greatly outnumber boys with these eating disorders). Less is known about another syndrome, more predominant in boys, known as muscle dysmorphia.

Self-consciousness about body image for teens is provoked by a variety of factors: pubertal changes, cultural acceptance issues, peer competitiveness, and athletics, all of which focus more and more on how one looks. Girls are generally more prey to developing negative body images than boys but boys do as well. Some feel that how a teenager feels about his or her body is often based on the influence of parental acceptance or rejection, although many other factors (particularly having to do with peer and cultural pressure) clearly have a strong impact. The repercussions of this body-image anxiety can be severe. Some children go on to develop anorexia, bulimia, or even body dysmorphia (discussed in a previous chapter).

Boys are greatly affected by cultural norms. Their intense preoccupation with body image may develop into muscle dysmorphia, which primarily has to do with feeling that his body is not muscular or lean enough. Like the anorexic girl worried about being fat, obsession with not being "buff" can preoccupy a teenage boy cripplingly, causing great anxiety, shame, and interfering in many aspects of life. Social opportunities (especially gym class or going to the beach) are often skipped for fear of exposing the body. Excessive working out at home or at a gym not only often causes teens to neglect other aspects of life but may even perpetuate injuries. Teens often turn to special high-protein or low-fat diets, consuming supplements such as protein powders, creatine, and amino acids. They may also take the dangerous turn toward drugs called anabolic steroids.

The teen suffering from muscular dysmorphia disorder frequently covers the body with loose clothing. Teenagers with this syndrome are constantly checking and measuring their bodies, and may spend hours in front of the mirror. Any activity in which their bodies may be even partially "on view," especially anything in the summer or during warm weather when people are more likely to wear less, is usually avoided. Often such teenage boys envy and are jealous of men who appear stronger than them. This syndrome is often known as "biggerexia nervosa" as well as "reverse anorexia" (the reverse of anorexic girls who feel they look too big, teen boys with muscle dysmorphia feel they look too small).

Since this is a psychological disorder, despite all the compulsive body building, weightlifting, and exercise to which they subject themselves, these boys don't find relief. Like other such disorders, causes are thought to be multiple, possibly including genetic factors and psychological influences such as the effects of growing up with family members who also share body image obsessions, in addition to the aforementioned tidal wave of "perfect body" messages in the media. Although some women get body dysmorphia, it mostly affects men. The teenage boy with muscle dysmorphia often is robbed of his friendships, either because of jealousy and envy or isolation and shame, and of romance as well. He often appears rigid and stilted, lacks spontaneity, and takes little enjoyment in any activity. Self-consciousness is a major issue, as is a general inability to relax.

Dangers with this disorder frequently involve the use of steroids. Steroids tend to increase muscle mass, strength, and stamina, but they also have severe physical side effects such as stunted growth, liver tumors, hypertension, mood swings, uncontrolled anger and aggression, and clinical depression, especially when the teenage boy stops using them. There are many national and local programs geared to helping teenagers avoid starting and, if they have started, to help them stop using steroids. ATLAS (Athletics Training and Learning to Avoid Steroids) is one of the more active programs.

Normal Weight Training

Despite the aforementioned issues, strength training is a common aspect of many programs for young people. It can constructively be used to enhance muscle size and definition and includes free weights, weight machines, and other weight-lifting accessories. Teenagers who get involved in weight training, also known as resistance training, often get stronger, prevent injuries, and enhance their long-term health—as long as it is done in moderation. However, no studies have shown that running speed or overall performance is particularly increased by working out. Teens must exercise care so that they don't cause weight-lifting injuries, such as muscle strain, lumbar back injuries, and injuries to the wrists and spine. Proper technique should be learned and supervised. The teen should also be evaluated by a doctor before embarking on a weight-lifting program. National pediatric associations counsel that competitive weight lifting, power lifting, and body building should not be done until the teen reaches full physical maturity.

What to Do

- Parents of teenagers should encourage their children to get involved in sports, athletics, weight training, and body building, but only to a degree that does not interfere with the rest of their social, academic, athletic, and family lives.

- Special diets—especially dietary supplements and steroids—should be assiduously avoided. If you notice that your teen is getting compulsive about weight training or obsessive about his body image, and/or seems in any other way to suffer from muscle dysmorphia, a psychiatric evaluation is usually necessary. This is a relatively severe disorder, one that needs professional intervention.

- Expect that the teen who is obsessively involved in weight training may resist attempts to get him help. Parents should take charge in this case. Not only will physical injury be avoided, but individual, family, and group therapy may well address underlying issues of low self-esteem, negative body image, and depression. This will help the teen in every aspect of his life.

- Teens with severe cases of muscle dysmorphia occasionally will be advised to take, and often benefit from, medication such as antidepressants and even antianxiety drugs, especially at the beginning of therapy.

SEE ALSO:

Obsessive-Compulsive Disorder
Hypochondria and Body Dysmorphia
Anorexia, Bulimia, and Overeating

35. Chronic Illness

"Oh, Mom, c'mon. I won't get sick. Let me go.
I never get to do anything!"

SIXTEEN-YEAR-OLD Dave has severe asthma. It's affected every moment of his life, every thought and plan he's ever had. He puts himself in real danger every time he goes outdoors, especially in the late spring when pollen is high. He feels humiliated by having to rely on medication. He hates all the big words his doctor uses—metered-dose inhaler, oral corticosteroids, beta2-agonists. What other kid did he know whose life was filled with such stuff? Most of his friends just cared about baseball and who they were going to take out on Friday night.

For a teenager, chronic illness is very stressful, for both the child and his family. It seems to crowd out everything else in the teen's life: few decisions are made that do not take it into account. Chronically ill teens typically feel great anxiety, anger, and guilt, and sometimes shame, panic, and blame. Like Dave, they feel constitutionally "different" from other teens, and terribly isolated. Often they can't do many of the things that other teenagers do. They often feel terrified about their powerlessness over bodily functions, a mastery that most teenagers increasingly gain and a mastery which, when the teen is not chronically ill, gives great pleasure and pride. Parents of chronically ill teenagers often feel guilty for not having done the right thing, even feeling that they may have caused the illness. As a result, they often become overprotective and try to shield their children, unwittingly increasing feelings of anxiety and isolation. Sometimes their often unacknowledged shame, anger, and anxiety lead to rejection of the sick teenager.

Unlike younger children, most teenagers understand a good deal about their diseases (Dave's ability to understand words like "corticosteroids" is an example of this). Fortunately, as they get older, most teens become adultlike in their abilities to care for themselves, and to understand their diagnoses, prognoses, and any of various interventions that may be necessary to manage their diseases. However, for some teenagers anxiety persists and can become displaced in obsessions about various medications and treatments. Others express and attempt to assuage anxiety by becoming almost encyclopedic in their understanding of the specifics of their illnesses and treatments. Others may deny that they have an illness. Some use their maladies as part of a typical teen oppositionalism and defiance, and don't take care of themselves. These teens recklessly rebel against being ill by not adhering to a particular diet, taking insulin or asthma medication, and so on.

The chronically ill teenager's self-image is often hindered. Some teenagers end up feeling innately flawed because, however unintended, the family's response and other aspects of the environment are not conducive to feeling any other way.

What to Do

- Be sure you don't confuse your child with the illness. He will always remain first and foremost, a person, a person who has an illness but who should not be completely identified with it. There are many aspects of the teenager that will remain healthy and constructive and these need to be continually, enthusiastically, and authentically acknowledged.

- Parents need to be protective of chronically ill teens but should try to avoid being overprotective. Try not to interfere too much in your teenager's life and don't invade his privacy. A teenager should be treated as normally as possible under the circumstances. Thus discipline, punishment, risk taking, and moving forward are as essential to and for the sick teen as for the healthy one.

- Make sure your teenager does not become too isolated. He will always feel "different" to some degree. But fostering continual social contact, joining support groups of teens with similar illnesses, and continual family involvement and support are essential for the sick teenager's overall development.

- Allow your child to give voice to all of his feelings regarding the illness, and remain calm while you listen. This can be an agonizing aspect of having a chronically ill child, but parents should learn to be strong enough to bear the emotional pain. The rewards for the teen of "letting it all out" are great and should be encouraged.

- Teenagers understand a lot and they should be treated with respect, fairness, and dignity. They should receive as full an explanation of the illness as they can take in. They shouldn't be lied to about the illness. Parents should be calm, direct, and reassuring without overstating positive prognoses or understating the degree of suffering.

- Your child should remain very active in all sorts of activities that he enjoys and can do safely.

- It's important to allow yourself to experience your own painful, completely normal feelings attendant with having a chronically ill child, such as regret, shame, anxiety, and anger. Dealing with them means admitting and accepting them, and then sharing them with people who are empathetic. If necessary, seek professional counseling to help you with this. Joining support groups for parents of ill teens can be very important.

- Allow the physicians involved in your child's care to explain to you all pertinent details, facts, and procedures, what to expect, and the prognosis for your child's illness. Knowing the truth, even if aspects of it may cause distress, will enable you to deal with the situation and concomitant feelings more compassionately and effectively. Knowing the facts will also help reduce blame. Dealing with your stress and grief in appropriate ways will enable you to set a good example for your child.

- Don't forget that teens look to their parents for reassurance when they are sick as much as when they are healthy. They look to parents to remain calm and not panic. They look to parents for guidance about tolerating various stresses and strains involved with recurrences and relapses.

- Teens with physical illnesses often occupy center stage in families and sometimes overshadow the needs of siblings and spouses. Just as you don't want your teen to be identified with his illness, you also don't want to be identified solely as the major caretaker of a physically ill child. It is important for parents to stay healthy both physically and mentally, to pay attention to the needs of others in the family, and to pay attention to their own needs.

SEE ALSO:

Anxiety
Depression
Anger
Getting Help

V

—————

Drugs

36. Substance Abuse Overview

"Yeah, so I smoked pot. So what? You said you got stoned in high school! Why should I be any different?"

MARIJUANA; cocaine; beer; booze; heroin; LSD; "club drugs" like ecstasy, "Special K," and crystal meth; the drug culture of those all-night parties called "raves"—all warrant serious parental concern. But how worried should parents be? How widespread is teen alcohol and drug abuse? What is normal experimentation and what are the signs of real trouble? How do you square what may have been your own teenage (or current) experience with alcohol and drugs with the possibility or likelihood that your teen may do the same thing? What control can or should parents exert over teens in this area?

These are big questions that require some context. We'll start by providing general statistics about teen drug and alcohol use and then elucidate some common risk factors. Next, in separate entries covering alcohol, marijuana, club drugs and rave parties, inhalants, hallucinogens, opiates, cocaine, and a variety of other drugs (from barbiturates to steroids) commonly abused by teens, we'll investigate the effects, dangers, and realities of these drugs. Also provided are the signs of drug use to look out for and a "What to Do" section with suggestions specific to each substance discussed. At the end of the book, in Additional Resources, is a list of drug and alcohol counseling and information sources (most with toll-free numbers) for further investigation.

One kind of help should be emphasized at the start: initiating and sustaining an ongoing dialogue with your teen. The aim isn't to lecture or chastise your child about drug and alcohol abuse, but to give both of you a chance to express your fears, questions, hopes, difficulties, and experience. Nowhere is communication with your teen more important than here.

Statistics

All teenagers will be exposed to drugs and alcohol at some point or other. Recent studies show that about 65 percent of teenagers try marijuana during high school, but for many children drug experimentation begins even earlier, in grade, middle, or junior high school. Substance abuse among teenagers is an alarming problem. It is implicated in the three most common causes of violent teenage deaths: homocide, suicide, and fatal accidents such as driving while intoxicated. Also associated with drug use are psychiatric difficulties, psychosocial problems such as teenage pregnancies, sexually transmitted diseases, and association with substance addiction later in life.

Of all substances, alcohol is most frequently abused in teenage years. While more boys than girls drink, the numbers for girls are rising. Binge drinking, defined as having five to six drinks in rapid succession, has been reported by as many as 30 percent of high school seniors. According to a study, 18 percent of the U.S. population over the age of twelve is expected to have engaged in binge drinking during the past thirty days. Binge drinking starts to increase significantly at age seventeen and over. Males are more likely to binge drink than females, and Hispanics more than blacks. A serious national problem, especially in high school and early college, binge drinking can cause death through alcohol poisoning and/or by depressing the central nervous system, which causes breathing to cease. Teenagers often get to emergency rooms too late to reverse this.

Tobacco ranks second as the most commonly abused drug. As many as 50 to 60 percent of all teenagers have used cigarettes, alcohol, or other drugs to some degree. (Marijuana is used by as many as 50 percent of all teenagers.) Third on the list of most commonly abused substances is amphetamines. While there has been a slight decrease in usage of inhalants (for example, paint thinner, gasoline, and glue) and cocaine, LSD usage appears to have increased slightly. Alarmingly, heroin usage is also on the rise—at its highest level in thirty years. This is attributed to the fact that it is relatively inexpensive and has become more accessible.

Risk Factors

For teenagers, these appear to be both external and inherent. Among external factors is the fact that alcohol and most other drugs are affordable and accessible enough for teens to obtain easily. In addition, the media (from beer ads to rock videos) bombard teenagers with the suggestion that use of substances can be fun, lead to social success, help them to live the "high life," and be sexy. The stresses teens feel as they experience bodily changes, unfamiliar social and peer pressures, the desire to separate from parents, and the urge to establish an independent identity make them vulnerable to the use of substances that promise to alleviate states of inner anxiety and despair. The grandiose illusions of invincibility that many adolescents have, and that they're too "smart" to get hooked, often make them more reckless as well. Many teens don't think about the cause and effect correlation of drugs and alcohol with the greater likelihood of becoming involved in criminal activity, suffering from suicidal depression, or facing other life-threatening dangers. Peer pressure is a major risk factor, especially for teens who are impressionable and easily influenced to begin with.

Fortunately, most teenagers who use drugs and alcohol will eventually grow out of it and stop using them, but others will become regular users and suffer from a variety of problems that will afflict them in later life. The earlier the onset of substance abuse, the more likely it is that a teen will have continuing problems and progress to serious addiction later on. Psychiatric disorders, poor self-esteem, a history of disruptive behavior, prior abuse, and suffering from learning disorders all are implicated in teen drinking and drug use.

Antisocial or "bad" behavior is often cited as a major risk. Children and adolescents known to be aggressive, oppositional, defiant, rebellious, and/or to act without thinking are more prone to substance abuse. According to the DSM-IV (the standard manual used for psychiatric diagnosis), conduct disorder is a major factor associated with teenage use of alcohol and drugs. According to one study, if a teen suffers from ADHD (attention deficit hyperactivity disorder) in addition to conduct disorder, he or she is at even more risk. (It should be noted that adolescents with serious emotional problems were about 400 percent more likely to become dependent on alcohol and other illicit drugs than teenagers without these problems.) Mood disorders such as anxiety and depressive disorders, as well as post-traumatic states as the result of sexual, emotional, and physical abuse and neglect, are also implicated in teenage substance abuse. There are also statistical correlations between drug and alcohol use and poor school performance, both academic and behavioral. Cutting, truancy, disruptive interactions with school personnel, and dropping out of school are all risk factors. Eating disorders such as anorexia or bulimia also make it more likely that a teen will abuse drugs and alcohol.

While there is no definitive proof of the role of genetic inheritance leading to substance abuse in teenagers, studies of twins who were separated at birth and adopted by different families indicate that there may be some genetic correlation. Apart from genetic considerations, families appear to have a strong influence. If the teen is raised among other family members who abuse alcohol and drugs, he is more likely to abuse them as well. A teenager who has experienced abuse or neglect in the family is far more likely to indulge in alcohol or drugs. Hypocrisy, rejection, unkept promises, harsh discipline, parents not setting appropriate limits, and poor parent role-modeling all make it more likely that the teen will have a problem.

Clearly, the causes of substance abuse are complex and appear to involve a combination of genetic, family, social, and external influences. While no one factor has been proven to be the definitive cause, concerned parents are well advised to view all of these factors and see which may apply. This will help parents gain a greater understanding of the particular issues their teens are facing. Most important is to establish parental communication with teens and improve negative family dynamics, or counteract unhealthy influences that may make it more likely for teens to turn to drugs and alcohol to relieve anxiety.

37. Alcohol

OF THE TWENTY-FIVE MILLION American adults who drink alcohol, 45 percent of them started drinking when they were teenagers. Alcohol is the most commonly used drug in the United States. It is widely advertised, easily bought, glamorized in the media, and many parents of teens drink themselves. Possibly for these reasons, parents seem to tolerate alcohol abuse in their teenagers far more than they would any other drug often with the idea, sometimes reinforced by their own youthful experiences, that occasionally drinking to excess constitutes a part of a teenager's "normal" experimentation.

Not every person who drinks alcohol becomes alcoholic. But teaching your teenager to drink responsibly means underscoring its possible dangers, the first and simplest of which is that it is illegal for a teenager to drink alcohol. Even parents who are moderate social drinkers need to teach their teens that alcohol can become addictive, affects the brain and body physically, and alters good judgment. Alcohol slows reflexes, impedes memory (sometimes to the point of blacking out, not remembering anything that happened while drunk), and disturbs vision. Alcohol can damage the liver, kidney, and other vital organs. It can cause a variety of diseases, from cirrhosis to alcoholic hepatitis and even cancer. Its effects on good judgment can be disastrous, disinhibiting teenagers so that they indulge in risk-taking activities that can threaten their lives. The possibility of contracting sexually transmitted diseases such as HIV escalates as a result of alcohol abuse, which often encourages sexual promiscuity. Close to 42 percent of all traffic deaths in the late teenage years are related to alcohol.

Possible signs of alcohol use in your teenager include:

- Slurred speech
- Uncoordinated movements
- Giddiness or other altered moods
- Fatigue
- Serious health problems
- Troublesome relationship with parents
- Poor grades at school
- Hanging out with "new kids"
- Feeling run-down
- Experiencing blackouts
- Getting in trouble with the law
- Rationalizing that alcohol is good and necessary for social life

More serious drinking problems are indicated by the following:

- Using alcohol to deal with all problems
- Needing to drink more alcohol to get "high" (increased tolerance)
- Obsessive thinking or talking about alcohol
- Drinking to self-medicate
- Drinking alone
- Chronic blackouts
- Binge drinking

What to Do

- Family communication is key. Make sure your teen is informed about alcohol's dangers, and encourage him or her to talk about pressures or anxieties that may contribute to the desire to drink. Parents are the most influential role models teenagers have. Demonstrating responsible drinking and good judgment regarding alcohol is worth a thousand lectures. If your teenager goes to a party and you are concerned about drinking, contact the parents in whose house the party is being held and ask that they monitor the partygoers' behavior and report to you any drinking your teen may do. Firm parental limits are necessary. The point is not to berate your teenager or to mete out harsh punishment but rather to make it clear that use of alcohol is not permitted and will not be tolerated.

- Depending on severity of use, family interventions may be necessary to awaken the teenager to the necessity of getting help. Interventions should never be carried out except under expert supervision. (Contact the National Council on Alcoholism and Drug Dependence at the toll-free number provided in the Additional Resources section.) If alcohol abuse becomes serious enough to warrant even the notion of an intervention, seek professional help. Depending on severity, treatment may be in- or outpatient. Twelve-step programs like Alateen have been enormously helpful to thousands of teenage drinkers who want to stop. Al-Anon, a 12-step program for loved ones of problem drinkers, is also a wonderful source of help, guidance, and information.

- If professional consultation indicates psychiatric problems such as ADD, depression, or anxiety disorder, these must be treated as soon as possible. But whatever the nature of your teen's possible drinking problem, let him know he has your unwavering, unconditional support for what may be a rocky road (possibly involving relapses) to recovery. The good news is that recovery is achievable.

38. Marijuana

MARIJUANA is the second most popular drug in the United States. Up to 63 percent of teenagers admit using it during high school, and some teens smoke it on a daily basis. Controversy exists over whether marijuana is a "gateway drug," one that leads to further and more serious abuse of other substances. While this debate has not been settled, it is known that a high percentage of people who use more serious drugs such as cocaine or heroin started by using marijuana. Marijuana leads to some degree of physical as well as psychological dependence. While its peak usage occurred in the seventies and declined in the eighties, its usage increased to approximately 60 percent "lifetime usage" by 2000. Its active ingredient is THC, tetrahydrocannabinol, which directly acts on the nervous system, altering the user's sense of time, impeding coordination, and inducing euphoria—all of which affect the teen's judgment and physical capacity. In addition, marijuana contains large amounts of cancer-causing tars that are present in cigarettes as well.

In some people, marijuana causes hallucinations and can precipitate severe anxiety to the point of paranoid mental states. Sometimes marijuana may provoke the emergence of underlying psychotic disorders that may require hospitalization. Its proponents' assertions that it is not dangerous and not addictive is clearly false.

Signs of marijuana use in your teenager include:

- Bloodshot eyes
- Short-term memory impairment
- Apathy or lack of motivation

186

- Acting silly or "drunk"
- Impaired body coordination
- Smell of sweet acrid smoke on hair or clothes

What to Do

- Because of marijuana's positive "rep," even with many adults, parents may be tempted to minimize its dangers. Educate yourself about this fallacy. Set the appropriate example for your teenager. Make it clear that marijuana use can impede functioning and possibly lead to more serious future consequences. Parents who experimented with marijuana in their own teenage years, and have shared this with their teens, and subsequently stopped use are encouraged to emphasize their reasons for stopping. The aim is sparing their children the same hard lessons they learned.

- Consult your family doctor, or a substance abuse counselor or other mental-health practitioner if you believe your child is smoking marijuana and cannot or will not stop.

- Investigate Narcotics Anonymous and various spin-off 12-step groups that deal specifically with recovery from marijuana use; some are geared to teens. (Consult one of the appropriate drug information agencies listed with the toll-free numbers at the end of this book.)

39. Club Drugs and Rave Parties

IF YOU'VE GOT a teenager in the house you've more than likely heard—and probably felt some trepidation—about "raves." A rave party is typically an all-night ear-splitting rock-band dance often held in places like warehouses, rental halls, barns, and open-air spaces where kids go crazy and, almost always, find drugs in great abundance. The drugs available at raves may not be familiar to you, but they ought to be. Their effects are alarming and potentially life threatening. Many teenagers expect their parents not to know about what goes on at raves or the kinds of drugs frequently passed around at them. This section will ensure you are not the uninformed parent they may hope you are. Being informed may help you save your teen's life.

The rave party phenomenon is approximately twenty years old. It started in the United Kingdom and quickly spread to the United States, especially taking root on the West Coast but soon after spreading across the rest of the country. Although the popularity of raves has diminished in the the early years of this century, the drugs associated with them are now taken at many other teenage dance clubs. The function of drugs at raves and clubs is primarily to keep kids energetic and dancing all night, which most of them do all too well. Few teenagers are aware of their dangers.

The dangers are legion. Most of the drugs we'll describe in this section are made illegally, come from unknown sources, and are made with various mixes of unknown chemicals. On their own or mixed with alcohol and other drugs, they can be catastrophically toxic and sometimes fatal. Adding to their danger is that not a lot is yet known about their toxicity or how to treat it. Because many are colorless, odorless, and tasteless they can be added to beverages without the recipient's knowledge. Since some of these drugs cause amnesia, unrecalled sexual assault is one frequent outcome. Teens who take these drugs frequently engage in risky sex that they may not even remember they had and this exponentially increases their risk of contracting diseases such as HIV and hepatitis C.

Club drugs include:

- **Ecstasy:** The most popular and well-known club drug is ecstasy, which is also known as E, X, Adam, and clarity, among other names. Its chemical appellation is methylenedioxymethamphetamine, the acronym for which is MDMA. This drug is similar to amphetamines and mescaline (a hallucinogen), which means it both stimulates and can have psychedelic or hallucinogenic effects. It is usually taken as a tablet or capsule, and its effects typically last from three to six hours. It increases heart rate and blood pressure, and because it enables its user to dance all night, often provokes dehydration (users are told to drink water to combat this). It can lead to heart and kidney disease, brain damage, and in rare cases can cause a marked muscle breakdown, high body temperature, heart attacks, strokes, and seizures. In other words, ecstasy is a highly dangerous drug.

- **GHB** (gamma hydroxybutyrate): It is also known as G, liquid ecstasy, and Georgia homeboy. This is a very common drug at rave parties and is often manufactured with mail-order ingredients. GHB is a sedative and a euphoriant. Because it is a central-nervous-system depressant, it causes its user to feel relaxed and sedated, but at higher doses it can slow breathing and heart rate to dangerous levels. Overdose on GHB can occur rapidly and be fatal; lower doses can cause extreme drowsiness, nausea, loss of consciousness, and impaired breathing. GHB is ingested as a clear liquid, powder, tablet, or capsule. It is most often used in combination with alcohol, which makes it even more dangerous.

- **Rohypnol:** Also known as roofies, rophies, or the forget-me-pill, it has gained special notoriety as a date-rape drug. Similar to and in the same family as Valium and Xanax, rohypnol is usually taken orally and can easily be sneaked into beverages, especially carbonated ones. It produces memory loss from the moment of taking it; hence its "forget-me-pill" tag. It lowers blood pressure and can cause dizziness and confusion as well as urine-retention.

- **Ketamine:** Also known as special K, K, vitamin K, new ecstasy, keltlar, and super K, it originally was used as an anesthetic for both humans and animals and is similar to the dangerous drug PCP (short for phencyclidine), also known as angel dust. Ketamine often causes psychotic reactions. It is sometimes snorted or smoked with marijuana or cigarettes. Some people inject it. At high doses ketamine can cause very serious neurological, blood pressure, and breathing problems.

- **Methamphetamine:** Also known as speed, meth, crystal, glass, Tina, and chalk, it is very common at rave parties. Serious health problems can ensue from methamphetamine, including memory loss, uncontrollable aggression and violence, psychosis, and body and nerve damage. It is an extremely disinhibiting drug and its users frequently engage in unsafe sex, thereby frequently contracting sexually transmitted diseases such as HIV and hepatitis C. It acts as a stimulant and for the most part is similar to amphetamines.

- **LSD** (lysergic acid diethylamide): Also known as acid, LSD is a hallucinogen and wreaks havoc with perceptions, thoughts, and feelings. Familiar for decades, LSD was once thought to have a therapeutic "mind-opening" value, a claim that has since been discredited in extensive testing. Swallowed as a pill, liquid, or on a saturated piece of blotter paper, LSD can cause severe psychotic reactions that may persist for extended periods, sometimes as flashbacks long afterward. Physically it dilates pupils, and raises body temperature, blood pressure, and heart rate. Some people who use LSD regularly suffer from neurological trembling and severe nausea.

Research has shown that club drugs have long-lasting effects on muscle tissue and on the brain, especially memory functions. Combined with alcohol, as they often are at rave parties, their effects become potentially fatal. Alerts have been issued nationwide by various national drug clearing organizations to communities about the dangers of these drugs. They cannot be taken safely.

Signs that your teen may be using club drugs include:

- Severe memory problems
- Pronounced lack of coordination
- Confusion
- Depression
- Chills and sweating
- Slurred speech
- Dizziness
- Nausea
- Bizarre speech or behavior
- Fainting

What to Do

- Most important is to let your teen know that you are informed about these drugs and let them know what the dangers are in detail.
- Make sure you have a way to contact your teen when she goes to a club, party, or rave. Have her call at regular intervals. Set a curfew. Know where she's going and who with.
- If your teen returns and appears to be under the influence of any drug, don't scold her but monitor symptoms closely; if they appear to be severe, seek medical help.
- If drug use continues seek therapeutic and/or drug counseling. (See list of resources at the end of this book.)

40. Inhalants

"INHALANTS," particularly a type called volatile solvents, as well as other sprays and gases, are among the first drugs that children, even very young children, encounter. Partly this is because they are found so readily around the home.

There are four basic types of inhalants:

1. **Volatile solvents:** liquids that form a vapor even at room temperature, such as paint thinner, gasoline, glues, felt-tip marker fluids and dry cleaning fluids

2. **Aerosols:** sprays that contain solvents, such as spray paint, fabric-protector spray, deodorants, and hair spray

3. **Gases:** those used in medical areas, especially nitrous oxide (known as laughing gas), the most abused of gases (frequently used in dentist offices), as well as chloroform, ether, halothane, and nitrous oxide (sometimes found in whipped cream dispensers)

4. **Nitrites:** amyl nitrites, known as poppers, snappers, and boodle nitrites, usually used as sexual enhancers

Inhalant abuse usually peaks during the freshman year of high school. Boys use inhalants more than girls. Like a number of other drugs, their use decreased approximately a decade ago but has recently increased.

Inhalants rapidly get into the bloodstream after they are breathed in through the nose and mouth. This leads to an immediate intoxication that has some of the effects of alcohol: slurred speech, feeling good, disinhibition, and an inability to completely control muscle movement. Some inhalants can produce hallucinations and psychotic delusions. Sniffed or snorted, or sprayed directly into the mouth with aerosol cans, inhalants may also be breathed in from bags or balloons, such as those filled with laughing gas. After the euphoria has passed, inhalants often have an anesthetic effect, leading to loss of sensation and sometimes of consciousness.

Inhalant abuse can lead to serious medical consequences such as suffocating and choking, as well as accidents caused by loss of control while under their influence. "Sudden sniffing death" thought to be the result of heart-rhythm defects and heart failure that can ensue after even one session of sniffing, can also occur. In addition, inhalants can damage the brain and the rest of the nervous system, as well as kidneys, liver, lungs, and heart. Even the more minor dangers of using inhalants are significant. They can impede daily functioning such as speech, and the ability to think or move the body. Sniffing glue may have certain irreversible damaging effects, such as hearing loss, peripheral nerve disease, arm and leg spasms, damage to the brain, bone-marrow damage, liver and kidney damage, and oxygen depletion in the blood.

Signs your teen may be using inhalants include:

- Slurred speech
- Unusual breath odor due to the chemical ingested
- A chemical smell on clothing
- Bloodshot eyes
- A coldlike runny nose
- Stains of the solvent or other inhalants on the face or body
- Appearing drunk

What to Do

- Because most of these inhalants are so accessible to children, ranging from nail polish to glue and propane gas, the most important action parents should take is preventive. Take measures to keep any possible inhalants under your scrutiny and (to the degree that this is possible) out of your teen's reach.

- If you have reason to believe your teen has been using inhalants, talk to him about their dangers, perhaps reading them verbatim out of this chapter.

- If symptoms are severe, and if your teen appears to be using inhalants with regularity, seek medical and therapeutic help. (Consult list of resources at the end of this book.)

41. Hallucinogens

ALSO KNOWN AS psychedelic drugs, hallucinogens radically alter perception, affecting all senses and often causing pseudoperceptions called hallucinations, such as seeing and hearing things that do not exist, or distortions of things that do exist. There are many types of hallucinogens. Some occur naturally in plants; others are created synthetically.

There are virtually no limits to the distortions hallucingens can induce in the mind. All aspects of reality are fair game: shapes morph alarmingly, visions appear, objects may look smaller or larger than they really are, sounds become louder or softer. Hallucinogens can cause synesthesia, a transposing of sensory modes; for example, the user may feel like she is touching something that isn't there but, under hallucinogenic influence, it seems completely real. Such visions can be very frightening and lead to uncontrollable panic or excitement. Sometimes the affected teen can seem to be fleeing from terror, a terror that exists only in her mind. These experiences are referred to as "bad trips." Bad trips can haunt a person for a lifetime, reappearing as flashbacks without warning or precipitating a lifelong state of mental illness or even psychosis. Those who do not become mentally impaired are thought to have a predisposition to mental illness. Several types of flashbacks can occur: a) emotional flashbacks, which may manifest in feelings of panic, fear, and isolation; b) somatic flashbacks, which can consist of altered bodily feelings such as weakness, nausea, and shaking—experienced during the original "trip"; c) perceptual flashbacks in which the user re-experiences some of the sensory distortions of the original trip.

Hallucinogens tend to intensify the mood state the teen is in during the onset of their effects. If the teen is experiencing depression or inner conflict at the moment she ingests a hallucinogenic drug, her feelings may escalate into anything from suicide attempts to out-of-control violence against people or things. Any neurotic or psychotic symptoms that may have been buried will erupt with horrifying force. Under the power of the delusion, the user may suddenly decide she can fly or perform some other superhuman feat. In the attempt to perform it, she can cause herself severe injury or death. Hallucinogens are also implicated in brain damage, impaired memory, decreased ability to concentrate, confusion, and other cognitive dysfunction.

Here are some of the more common hallucinogens to which your teen may have access:

- **LSD:** Already covered in the rave and club-drug chapter (see previous description), LSD can be found in ergot, a fungus that grows on rye and other grains. Other names for it include white lightning, blue heaven, and window pane.

- **PCP:** A dissociative anesthetic that has hallucinogenic characteristics. It is also known as angel dust, crystal, jet fuel, and cyclone. It is often laced into other drugs such as marijuana and can result in severe agitation, disorientation, and uncontrolled violence.

- **Ketamine:** Also called special K, it already has been described in the rave and club-drug chapter (see previous description). Sometimes it can cause terrifying out-of-body or near-death experiences.

- **Ecstasy:** See description in rave and club-drug section.

- **Psilocybin mushrooms:** Certain types of mushrooms contain hallucinogens; psilocybin is one. These can be eaten or brewed in tea. They cause nausea and distressing physical symptoms before their effects are felt.

- **Mescaline:** Mescaline comes from the piody cactus and is either swallowed or smoked. It causes similar delusional effects to LSD.

There are other hallucinogenic plants, such as morning glory seeds, and angel's trumpet or jimsonweed, the last of which is poisonous and can cause death. All hallucinogens are dangerous because of the severe, often psychotic reactions they induce in the user. Some teens become psychologically dependent on the escape hallucinogens can provide, making them prey to a host of difficulties that only intensify the more the drug is consumed. The psychosis that hallucinogens can temporarily produce sometimes becomes permanent. They comprise a very dangerous class of drug.

What to Do

- Information is power. Make sure your teen knows all of the potentially terrifying and deadly effects of hallucinogens. Reassure your teen that people do not have to hallucinate to find meaning or joy in life.

- If you encounter your teen while she is still under the influence of a hallucinogen, remain calm, and don't attempt to lecture, scold, or even attempt to speak rationally; make sure that your child is physically safe; and stay with her until the worst of the effects pass.

- There are many treatment plans and centers for hallucinogen dependency. Consult the Additional Resources section at the end of this book. Seek advice from local clinics and mental-health practitioners with an expertise in this area.

- If your teen repeatedly seeks the escape of hallucinogens, help her obtain professional treatment. In addition, view this as an opportunity to understand what she may be trying to escape from so desperately. Teens don't continually resort to drugs—hallucinogenic or otherwise—without reason. Your best and most effective tool is to keep open the channels of communication. Listen to your teen, and try to understand what is causing her distress.

42. Opiates

HEROIN is the best known of the opiate drugs. (Others are opium, morphine, Demerol, codeine, and synthetic opiates such as pethidine, and methadone.) All opiates are strong painkillers and are sometimes prescribed for pain by doctors and dentists.

Although the use of heroin had decreased somewhat up to about ten years ago, its use among teens has since increased. Heroin is used by teens in all socioeconomic classes, possibly because it has been glamorized in recent films and videos, but also because it has become cheaper and more widely accessible. It is highly addictive and has many dire health consequences, such as disinhibition, resulting in unprotected sex and contraction of STDs; increased violence and crime; the possibility of contracting tuberculosis; damage to the fetus in pregnant users; causing family dysfunction, and in general wreaking havoc in the life of teens who fall into its devastating grip.

Heroin is made from morphine, a naturally occurring substance that comes from the seed pods of poppy plants. Most heroin is combined with other drugs or, when bought on the street, such substances as milk, starch, or sugar. The fact that no one knows what is in the heroin they obtain increases its danger. Heroin can be injected, smoked, snorted, or sniffed. Intravenous injections induce the most rapid onset of effects, usually in ten or fifteen seconds. However, any route of administration leads to addiction.

Soon after taking heroin the user feels a rush or high. A warm flushing of the skin sometimes is followed by nausea and vomiting. This may be followed by drowsiness, with breathing and heart rate sometimes slowing to the point of death. Virtually every heroin user becomes addicted: over time, more of the drug is needed to produce a high, and ultimately addiction defines the entire life of the user. Once physical dependence is reached, withdrawal becomes dangerous and must be achieved under supervision. Withdrawing from heroin is a very painful state involving diarrhea, vomiting, severe agitation, and involuntary muscle spasms. It can last from one to a number of days after the last dose. Physical abnormalities can result, including disease of the blood vessels, liver, kidneys, and lungs. Because of needle use, infections are more likely to occur as well, including HIV, and hepatitis B and C. Pregnant users transfer addictions to unborn children.

Signs your teen may be using heroin include:

- Euphoria
- Impaired mental functioning
- Drowsiness
- Constricted pupils
- Slowed respiration

What to Do

- Treatment for heroin addiction includes the use of methadone, which is not intoxicating or sedating but suppresses narcotic withdrawal. Methadone also relieves the craving for heroin. LAAM is a synthetic opiate that is used to treat heroin addiction.

- Detoxification is necessary for many addicts. This is usually done in a residential center but sometimes in an outpatient facility.

- Behavioral therapy is often effective, involving contingency-management therapy and cognitive-behavioral therapy. As with other drugs, 12-step programs can help reinforce the decision to stop using heroin once the addict has navigated the difficult straits of withdrawal.

43. Cocaine

INTRODUCED in the mid-nineteenth century as a local anesthetic for conditions of the head, eyes, ears, nose, and throat, and championed by no less than Sigmund Freud for its stimulant properties, cocaine, made from the leaves of the cocoa bush, has since been mostly discredited as a medication. It certainly stimulates the central nervous system and increases alertness, inhibits appetite, causes insomnia, and produces intense feelings of pleasure and euphoria. It is also highly addictive.

There are two forms of cocaine: salt (the powdered form, which dissolves in water and can be taken intravenously or intranasally) and freebase (a crystalline form meant to be smoked). On the street cocaine is known as coke, snow, flake, or blow. Crack cocaine is another name for the freebase form, so-named because it makes a crackling sound when it is lit and inhaled. Crack can give a teen an intense high in less than ten seconds and is much less expensive than powdered cocaine. The use of crack in teenagers has increased over the last decade. Between 3 and 4 percent of teens reported using crack in 1998 alone.

Cocaine can be chewed and snorted as well as mainlined (injected) or smoked. Some people rub cocaine onto the insides of their mouths or other mucus membranes. Others mix it with heroin to make what is known as a speedball. Cocaine can be highly toxic, leading to brain and heart damage that can be fatal. Cocaine users develop an increased tolerance for the drug, requiring more and more over time to achieve the desired state of a "high." People who take cocaine usually feel very happy, hyper, talkative, overly alert, and oversensitive to external stimuli. Its effects include widening of the pupils, hypertension, and increased body temperature and heart rate. Psychologically, it can lead to violent, bizarre, and even psychotic behavior. Some users start shaking and twitching; others get paranoid. Sudden death, usually from heart failure, is not unheard of. Users often go on cocaine binges that last for days. Some people develop a psychosis similar to schizophrenia as a result of cocaine use.

Other medical consequences include damage to the nose and trouble swallowing. Some people drink alcohol when they use cocaine, which increases the danger. Those who inject it are at risk of developing needle-borne diseases (HIV, hepatitis C, and so on). The crack-baby epidemic of the past several decades is a testament to what happens to the unborn children of pregnant users. Crack babies are now known to have developmental disorders including learning disorders and difficulty concentrating, among other cognitive problems.

Signs your teen may be using cocaine include:

- An unnatural alertness or talkativeness
- Grinding the teeth
- A continually running nose
- Bizarre or paranoid behavior
- Disappearing for hours at a time, or going to the bathroom more frequently than is necessary
- Abrupt change in personality

What to Do

- Seek professional help. Treatment of cocaine addiction sometimes involves the administration of antidepressants to cut down the craving for the drug, and your health practitioner may suggest medications such as these for your teen.
- In addition to therapy and 12-step options, other medications are currently being tested to help cocaine addicts make the transition back to sobriety, among them selegeline (ask your doctor about this and other medication options).
- Out- or in-patient treatment may be indicated.
- Contingency management and cognitive-behavioral therapy also have been used successfully.

44. Other Drugs

IF YOU HAVE acquired one prevailing notion from riding the roller coaster of these chapters on teens and substance abuse, it may well be the idea that if there's a drug out there, it has been and will be abused by someone. Unfortunately, there is little in the realm of drugs and alcohol that hasn't been discovered and abused by teens. This is why education is of such paramount importance. The best thing you can do, in addition to keeping those lines of communication open and setting a good example yourself, is to learn as much as you can about even the more arcane "club drugs" and their effects. Forewarned is forearmed.

Other drugs teens commonly abuse are:

- **Painkillers:** Prescription drugs such as OxyContin, Darvon, Vicodin, Dilaudid, and Demerol (all opiates). It is very common for teens and others to become "hooked" even to medications legitimately prescribed by their doctors. If your teen is taking a prescribed pain medication, monitor his use of it carefully.

- **Downers:** Barbiturates, which are central-nervous-system depressants, are also frequently abused, even when they're legitimately prescribed. Tranquilizers often abused include Valium, Librium, Xanax, and Klonopin. In addition, sleeping medications such as Halcion and Prosom can tempt a teen user to overuse.

- **Stimulants:** Includes those used to treat ADHD in children, which are sometimes abused by teens. Stimulants also include Dexedrine and Dexedrine derivatives, such as Adderall, and all forms of methylphenidate including Ritalin and Concerta.

A new phenomenon among teenagers is snorting Ritalin, which produces a high but can also lead to seizures. Recent studies show that teens' use of painkillers and stimulants indicate that currently they are the two primary drugs of teenage abuse. Older teens seem to be abusing Percodan and Vicodin.

- **Steroids:** Steroid abuse, specifically of anabolic steroids, which are synthetic substances related to male sex hormones called androgens. They tend to increase muscle mass and bolster male secondary sexual characteristics, and are used medically to treat impotence and body wasting (in people suffering from severe disease). They are abused by literally millions of youths. They are taken as tablets, capsules, or injections; sometimes they are rubbed on the body as well. Steroids have numerous negative health consequences including aggression, depression, mood swings, increased chance of contracting blood-borne diseases (when it is injected), acne, liver and heart disease, premature decrease in growth, testicular shrinkage, impotence, and breast enlargement. It sometimes reduces sperm production as well.

One final important suggestion: Make it absolutely clear to your teen that if he or she indulges in drugs and alcohol, however much it may be against your wishes and rules, he or she should contact you as soon as possible. If your child is going to a party, club, or dance, make sure you have a way of contacting him or her. Have cell-phone numbers, addresses, and names of people he or she will be with. Let your child know that even though you do not approve of the use of alcohol or drugs, you will still be there to help. Parents must let their teens know that they're always the people to contact when and if they get into trouble.

VI

Family Issues

45. Teens of Alcoholics and Substance Abusers

"But I told you I was going out tonight, Dad! You said I could. Rick is picking me up in a half hour. I can't just flake out on him! Mom, help me out. You were here when Dad said I could go. Maybe if you hadn't had six drinks when you came home from work you'd remember stuff. What? No, I didn't say anything...."

MICHELLE'S FATHER is an alcoholic. She never knows when he'll blow up at her, change his mind, pass out, become over-affectionate and—maybe the worst—apologize, crying, for what he's done the morning after. Michelle's mother puts up with him much as Michelle does, attempting to placate and maneuver him so that chaos doesn't completely rule in the family. But so far it's a losing battle.

If you're reading this chapter, my strong hope is that if your teen has suffered because of you or your spouse's drinking or drug-taking, that your abuse of alcohol and drugs is now a thing of the past. If you do not use drugs or alcohol but your spouse still does, there is still much you can do to help your teen and your family. In fact, whatever the current state of alcohol and drug abuse in the family may be—past or present—this is still an important chapter to read. The effects of a drug- or alcohol-abusing parent are often felt long after a parent has stopped abusing substances. How Michelle has

learned to cope with her alcoholic father affects her self-esteem, how
she performs in school, interacts socially with other people, and her
assumptions about what's possible in her life now and in the future.

Living with an alcohol- or drug-abusing parent in the family
wreaks havoc for all. Not that each family member is affected in the
same way; indeed, alcoholic families may react to the stress caused by
the abuser in ways that range from denial (pretending that nothing's
wrong) to violent recriminations and severe withdrawal and isolation (Michelle is used to spending hours in her room alone when
she knows her dad's been drinking). Teens with an alcohol- or drug-
abusing parents score lower on measures of intellectual-cultural orientation, active-recreational orientation, and independence, and may be
hampered in their ability to grow in developmentally appropriate
ways. Teens often stay in their rooms for long periods and don't
relate to other people (even friends), often claiming that they have no
one to talk to. They may show depressive tendencies, be highly per-
fectionistic in their endeavors, hoard belongings, become excessively
self-conscious, and sometimes even develop phobias.

Potential problems don't end there. They suffer more injuries and
poisonings and use outpatient medical services more often than teens
whose parents aren't substance abusers. They have a greater likelihood of suffering from any of the following syndromes: attention
deficit disorder, learning disorders, and other behavioral disorders.
In short, these teens tend to feel helpless, perplexed, dependent, isolated, and "different," unable to cope with many of the day-to-day
challenges that face every teen. Children of addicts and alcoholics
often irrationally feel that they may have caused the problem.
Clearly, having a parent who is an addict or alcoholic takes a terrible toll.

It is estimated that seventy-six million Americans, or over 40 percent of the adult population in the United States, have been exposed
to alcoholism in the family, and almost one in five Americans lived
with an alcoholic parent while growing up. Alcoholic parents are
demonstrably lacking in basic parenting skills. Alcohol induces violence in families, abnormal mood swings, financial strain, and constant fighting, and tends to develop what are called co-morbid
psychiatric illnesses. Statistics about drug-abusing family members

are not as clear, but since so many abusers are "cross-addicted" (abusing both drugs and alcohol), clearly the problem is widespread. Indeed, there are now an estimated 26.8 million children of alcoholics in the United States. Recent research indicates that over eleven million are under the age of eighteen.

Alcoholism and drug addiction tend to run in families. Children of alcoholics are four times more likely to become alcoholic than children of non-alcoholics. Genetic factors may play a role in this, as does a range of family influence. The model the substance abusing parent sets clearly has a major impact on a teenager. Almost one-third of alcoholics have been found to have had at least one alcoholic parent, and children of alcoholics are more likely to marry into other alcoholic families. Teenage children of addicts also may turn to the escape of drugs and alcohol because of negative parental influence or negligence, learning to "get around" an alcoholic or drug-abusing parent in many ways. Children of alcoholics are more likely to be targets of physical abuse and to witness or be the victims of family violence. They also exhibit symptoms of depression and anxiety far more frequently than the children of parents who do not abuse drugs and alcohol. Difficulties in school are very common, even though this usually does not indicate any lack of intellectual ability. A lack of demonstrated cognitive skills, problem-solving ability, and healthy stimulation in the home is implicated in the teen's academic problems. They are more likely to drop out of school, repeat grades, be truant, or be referred for behavioral problems to school counselors or psychologists.

Fortunately, much can be done to help the teen whose parent drinks or does drugs. If only one parent abuses substances, the parent who does not can exert very helpful influence. That parent can encourage the teen to develop autonomy and independence, stronger social skills, and a close bond with him or her, and help the teen cope with emotionally difficult experiences. The parent also can help the teen learn to perceive their lives constructively—seeing family crises as opportunities to grow and become stronger as people. Self-help groups like Al-Anon and Alateen are tremendously helpful to teens of parents with addiction problems. Remember, even if you or your spouse have ceased drinking or drugging to excess and are getting help to stay sober, it's more than likely your teen still bears the scars of having lived with parents who were addicted. The following specific suggestions are thus geared both to the teen with an "active" addict as a parent and a parent or parents who are now recovering from former addictions.

What to Do

- The worst thing a teen can do is to run away from the problem. Investigate Alateen (a 12-step group specially geared to teens) and Al-Anon for support. Encourage your teen to talk to any trusted adult—a relative, friend, counselor, coach, clergyperson, and so on. Isolation is toxic to the child of an addict.

- Remind your teen that she is not being disloyal by sharing difficulties, past or present, with appropriate people. Keeping the "secret" of a parent's addiction is part of what will make the effects of parental addiction worse on the teen.

- If you are the non-addicted parent in the family, your role is crucial. Be as consistent and clear about your expectations as you can. Don't bad-mouth the addicted parent; understand that he or she is suffering from a disease for which help is needed. Attend Al-Anon meetings yourself, perhaps with your teen, to understand more about the impact of this disease on the entire family.

- Encourage your teen to help others. This may seem like odd advice, especially if your teen feels she is the one who needs help. But sometimes volunteering on a part-time basis to take care of preschoolers in nursery school, sitting with elderly people in a nursing home, visiting sick patients at a hospital, or tutoring younger children can provide a lift, and a sense of well-being and self-esteem that can be gained in no other way. Participating in activities such as these will develop feelings of competence, and that the teen is important and has something to offer.

- Develop day-to-day coping strategies that do not involve lying or manipulation. Be pragmatic: If an intoxicated parent is clearly in no condition to communicate with the teen, make sure the teen keeps his or her distance from that parent.

- Support any alcohol- or drug-prevention strategies in your community, schools, and religious institutions. If none are in place, taking measures to see that they are instituted will be of great benefit. Consult authorities familiar with the disease of addiction for guidance. They can be found at hospitals, clinics, and through referrals from your family doctor.

- If you are not a parent but a concerned observer, talk with the teen's teacher(s), clergyperson, or any other person whom you know the teen respects, and perhaps investigate the possible benefits of staging an intervention. Interventions must be carried out very carefully and only with the supervision of an expert who oversees such group encounters, whose aim is to awaken the alcoholic and drug addict to the havoc he or she is wreaking in the family, without scolding or excoriating the person. Clearly, if the teen appears to be suffering from acute abuse of any kind, immediate intervention by the police or medical caretakers must be sought.

- If you or your spouse is an active alcoholic or drug addict, please consider getting help now. The potential rewards can be literally life-saving—for you and your teen.

SEE ALSO:

Anxiety
Stress and PTSD
Depression
Drugs
School Problems
Getting Help

46. Internet Use, Abuse, and Addiction

Sherry's Kute: well, it does sound like we have a lot in common

ManABOUTtown: Oh, honey, we got more in common than you know. We should really meet...

"SHERRY'S KUTE" and "ManABOUTtown" met in a chat room on the Internet. "Sherry," whose real name is Suzanne, has conveniently not told "ManABOUTtown" that she's only sixteen. "ManABOUTtown" has, however, revealed his age (thirty-six) but not the fact that he is married and an experienced Internet sexual predator. He's found it a great way to meet women for "on-the-side" trysts.

If this sounds like a parental nightmare come true, there may be good reason for thinking of it as such. Teens plus the Internet can be a volatile mix. Recent news stories about abductions and rapes of teens who began relationships with people in chat rooms on the Internet make the point all too forcefully. Parents need to be on the alert when their teens log on.

Not that they need to be paranoid. Cyberspace is a wonderful place. Surfing the Web through the Internet has become commonplace for well over a one hundred million people in our country and many more across the globe. Teenagers have access to vast resources on the Internet including news sources, libraries, and encyclopedias, among infinite others. The amount of information that is one click away is overwhelming, as are the distances that can be traveled right in your teenager's room. We are clearly in the age of cyberspace, and there's

212

much here to encourage your teen to take advantage of. A teen who is not Internet-savvy will be left behind as far as accumulation of knowledge goes.

This is not to say that the Internet is a substitute for education, only that it is a modern and increasingly necessary tool. Exclusive use of the Internet for doing homework and other school research often decreases a student's ability to utilize libraries, read, and write well. Thus, purely from an educational standpoint, parents should encourage teens to strike a balance between seeking information on the Internet and developing abilities to use their own brains, eyes, and hands to acquire and process knowledge, and to learn how to communicate effectively.

As "Sherry's Kute" knows, the Web and Internet are also used to chat with others through instant message services. Even apart from the danger of a "ManABOUTtown," and from the undeniable plusses of being able to communicate instantly with anyone anywhere at any time, this has a downside in the sense that it fosters less personal and more mechanized social interaction. There is still an important place for the human voice, presence, and the carefully composed "snail mail" letter or note. Teens should be encouraged to balance the use of a computer to communicate and the older tried-and-true methods of picking up the phone, writing a letter, or seeing a friend face-to-face.

Parents need to remember that teens often feel invulnerable, as if getting hurt driving a car, having sex, or surfing the Internet, is something that always happens to someone else. But it is a fact that teens do court real danger even if they think they don't; and teenagers get in trouble on the Internet more than any other group. First, there is very little supervision or control over the use of the Internet. Internet service providers try to exercise some control but most Internet activities are freely accessed by anyone who wants to use them. Mentioning this is not intended to promote paranoia. The majority of teenagers who are online every day do it safely and appropriately, so there is no reason for a parent to automatically panic if the teen goes online. But what are the full range of dangers, and how can parents reasonably protect teens from them?

One obvious effect of the Internet is its tidal wave of advertisements and the endless links flooding teens with too much stimuli and information. Excessive time is often spent wading through this huge morass of data and come-ons and can interfere with developing other interests and more profitable ways of spending time. For some teenagers the Internet causes anxiety and discomfort. So much of the material offered up is violent or sexual, or both. A curious teenager will often click inappropriate or "on-the-edge" Web sites that can reveal very upsetting pictures and stories. There is also the obvious danger—faced by "Sherry's Kute"—in which the teen may reveal personal information about him- or herself (address, phone number, and so on) or make in-person contact with someone only met in cyberspace. Teens may also run up very high credit card bills surfing pay sites often offering pornography. Harassment can take place over the Internet as well: the ease with which people can meet strangers sometimes ends up in meeting very unbalanced people. Obscenity is prevalent on countless Web sites and resorted to by many unsavory Internet users in e-mail. Some Web sites spout racist, demeaning, or explicitly violent manifestos. Chat rooms on the Internet allow people to engage in conversations in real time, and chatting is considered the most dangerous aspect of Internet use for teenagers. Many chats are private conversations, and many so-called buddies or friends are not buddies or friends at all. They may be pedophiles, pornographers, violent people, or others who pose a real threat to teens. Spammers that send out invitations to log on to pornographic Web sites catering to very specific fetish or "kink" interests are also common. People use phony names that are not always obviously phony. E-mail news groups, also called bulletin boards, can also be dangerous. Teens may be tempted to reveal too much about themselves when they post opinions about a subject on the bulletin board. There also is the danger of computer viruses. No one should respond to e-mails or download attachments from unknown senders.

Internet Addiction

For some teens, the sheer bulk and allure of what the Internet provides, from Web sites to ways to meet people, can crowd out every other interest and activity. This leads to what is known as Internet addiction: the ever-present craving some teens feel to be in front of the computer screen. Social isolation, withdrawing into the self, or obsessing over one particular aspect of the Internet, which can range from an obsession with cars to rock bands and pornography, such that the teen seems to have no aim in life other than logging on all indicate real trouble. Teens who spend too much time in front of the computer screen are shortchanging themselves in many often quite destructive ways.

Some people don't believe that there is such a thing as Internet addiction disorder, but we do know that excessive use of the Internet occurs, especially with teenagers, and can have consequences that are very like those of other addictions. Some observers have gone as far as developing criteria for Internet addiction disorder. One symptom is that the "addict" needs to spend an increasing amount of time on the Internet to feel good just as, over time, an alcoholic needs to drink more to get high. Withdrawal symptoms after Internet ceasing use include anxiety, and obsessing, dreaming, and fantasizing about the Internet, among others.

Other symptoms of addictive use are that many aspects of life are given up. Internet "addicts" actually feel distress and sickness if they are not allowed to use the Internet. As with other addictions, Internet addiction is often concealed by lying. Some people relate Internet addiction disorder to pathological gambling since, as with gambling, no drug is involved. However, whether or not Internet addiction is a bona fide addiction is really not important. What is important is that if you see your teenager overwhelmingly consumed with using his computer and the Internet for any reason that interferes with his education, and social, athletic, or physical well-being, then you should step in and put a stop to it. Remember that your teen's overuse of the Internet may be stimulated by his wish to avoid major areas of life that are anxiety-provoking or feel threatening. As always, finding compassionate ways to get your teen to face these fears more directly is the best approach to take.

What to Do

- In general, staying safe means staying private both on the Internet, in news groups, in chat rooms and even in e-mails.

Children are taught not to talk to strangers, let unknown people in the house, or give out information indiscriminately, and these same rules should apply to your teen's use of the Internet as well. Meeting people should never be done unless both parents and teen are sure who the person is, the arrangement has received parental approval, and the meetings take place in a public place, usually with another party present that the parents know.

- Parents should limit the amount of time that the teenager spends online. Chatting and browsing can become highly addictive and distract teens from their everyday activities such as homework, chores, and bedtime. How much time your teen spends on the computer needs to be controlled and monitored. Don't be fooled that teens are just doing their homework online.

- Parents should go over privacy issues with their teens, especially in the appropriateness of giving out names, addresses, telephone numbers, and credit card numbers. Some Internet services provide parental control features with which a parent should become familiar. These features allow parents to limit access to certain kinds of information and may allow them to personalize settings so that teens cannot get into certain objectionable Web sites or chat rooms. However, remember no screening program is perfect, and there are some sites that appear to be okay but aren't. Help your teen understand why his use of the Internet must be monitored. Tell him that the Internet is not like TV or other media since there are no controlling networks or censors.

- Set family rules about the computer. Keep the computer in a central location in the house. Sit down with your teen and work out reasonable boundaries and schedules. You might think of setting rules similar to those about phone usage: when and how long they can use it, whom they can call, and what they should reveal in conversations.

- Teach your teen about computer viruses and what they can do to prevent them, specifically never opening a downloaded attachment from anyone they don't know.

- Keep the lines of communication open about the use of the Internet, and encourage your teen to discuss any aspect of it that makes him uncomfortable. Most of all, don't let your teen become the only cyber-savvy person in the house. You should learn about the use and misuse of computers so that you have a hands-on sense of what to look out for—as well as what to profitably pursue.

SEE ALSO:

The Media

47. The Media

"Yeah, I heard you, Mom. I'll be down in a minute. What? Yeah, I know I said that a half hour ago, but I'm doing something! Yeah, it's important! All right, all right, I'm coming down already!"

ACTUALLY, ZACK would wait another twenty minutes before he came down and faced his irate mother. Finally he was going to wash the car and mow the lawn as he'd been promising to do for the past three days. He was watching his favorite movie video for the zillionth time. He loved the raw thump of its heavy metal sound and the cool guys in black leather throwing their biker girlfriends around. Damn, he wished his life could be like that. Zack isn't only glued to this particular music video, however. He has about a dozen cable TV programs he "can't miss," and spends hours on the Internet surfing "edgy" biker Web sites of which he knows his parents would disapprove. There was just so much cool stuff to watch and do on TV and the 'net! It sure beat washing cars and mowing lawns. And pretty much anything else he could think of.

The media's influence on teens has never been more intrusive or powerful. In addition to the tens of thousands of hours that most teenagers will have spent in front of the television by the time they are seventeen, teens like Zack are bombarded by an unprecedented deluge of movies, music videos, Internet content, and radio. The prevalence of violence (80 percent of television programs are violent) and sex are understandably troubling to parents of teens. However, sex and violence aren't the only worries. The media tend to err on the side of reducing complicated issues to simplistic judgments and stereotypes. There's reason to worry about teenagers becoming passive audiences for this deluge of media stimuli. Unfortunately, since TV has baby-sat so many of them throughout their childhoods, they've been conditioned to become this kind of glazed-over audience. Being glued to a TV or computer screen is a very difficult habit to break.

Unlike the past when news was disseminated by a newspaper or two and a couple of television networks, now it pours out of hundreds of cable TV channels and countless Web sites on the Internet on a twenty-four-hour basis. Children are thus exposed to an enormous amount of gore, disaster, and sexually charged and other possibly trauma-inducing topics and themes. Bombing, shooting, murder, sex crimes, kidnapping, rape, and explicit medical procedures are offered up on the air continuously. Music videos depict graphic sex and violence as if it were completely normal and desirable. Many radio shows seem obsessed with different forms of violence and cult followings, and give explicit sexual advice. The Internet offers its own media assault (see previous chapter). All of this has a confusing and deeply disturbing impact on teens.

Although some have questioned whether the media have in fact had the destructive impact on children attributed to it, we know now from various studies that they do. We now know that violence in the media affects teenagers both immediately and sometimes later on as a kind of delayed reaction. Teens who watch violent movies have been found, on the strength of their influence, to resort to violence themselves. For other teenagers, violent movies induce fear, numbness, or insensitivity, and similarly serve as a model for their own acting out. Because sexuality is ubiquitous in the media, it can serve as a false reassurance to teens, increasing a dangerous and unwarranted sense of invulnerability and convincing them they don't need to be careful sexually. It can induce superficial sexualizing of relationships at an immature age. The glamorization of drugs in the media can also lead teenagers, especially vulnerable ones, to see drugs as a thrill, solution, and/or escape.

With all the influence the media have on teenagers, it's important that parents become vigilant about limiting their teens' exposure to the more provocative, destructive, and disturbing aspects of it. While we don't want to diminish a teen's constructive use of the media, we want to limit the harm caused.

What to Do

- Parents should find out what media engage their teenagers. This means knowing how often your teenager watches television, listens to the radio, and surfs the Internet, as well as knowing what music and music videos he listens to and watches. This task of educating yourself about your teen's media exposure is extremely important. It may involve watching television shows you know your teen habitually watches (with or without your teen); and listening to music, radio shows, and so on that personally you may not find palatable but your teen does. You can't understand the impact of media on your teen if you don't know what in it attracts and absorbs your teen.

- Set rules in your home about the media. Reasonable limits should be set and adhered to.

- Encourage your teen to get involved in athletics, the arts, or other activities. Teenagers should not be allowed to become passive recipients of an overload of media.

- Talk with your teen about what he is watching and listening to. Try to get a sense of why it absorbs him. This is especially important in the areas of sex and violence. Let your teen know that these are important issues and that they shouldn't be dealt with superficially.

- Parents should find out what is constructive in the media and encourage teens to take part in it. There are many programs, talk shows, and even musical experiences that can be quite thrilling, uplifiting, fun, and educational. Much worthwhile culture can be gleaned and enjoyed through the media.

- Stay around your teen when he watches TV or videos or surfs the Internet. The simple presence of a parent is often enough to remind the teen of limits you have agreed to about what and how much media to consume.

- Help the school system your teenager attends develop educational programs about media exposure.

- Become as familiar as possible with cultural and sub-cultural trends to which the media exposes your teen. This is not meant to imply that you should pretend to be as "cool" as your teen, but simply be knowledgeable about what's going on. Again, you can't help your teen deal with media influence if you don't know what that influence is. (This also applies to learning how a computer works, knowing what instant messaging is, and so on. Again, consult the Internet chapter for more information.)

SEE ALSO:

Internet Use, Abuse, and Addiction

48. Divorce and Stepfamilies

"First off, Mom, that man you married is not my father and his kid is not my sister. So quit trying to make me act like this is The Brady Bunch!"

IN ONE FELL SWOOP, fifteen-year-old Jenny expresses the anxiety and pain typical of teens whose parents divorce and remarry. Despite the fact that divorce has become commonplace (50 percent of marriages end in it) dealing with its harsh impact on the family is not much easier than when divorce was less common and carried more of a stigma. Fortunately, because teens generally have a greater capacity to understand the conflicts that lead to divorce than younger children, they often enjoy better prospects of adjusting to it. But it's still a bombshell, and helping your teen deal with the abrupt changes in her life that divorce almost always brings about will be the focus of this chapter. The issue of stepfamilies is a related one, of course, and will be dealt with later in this chapter.

The impact of divorce on teens can be profound. Children of divorced parents often have difficulty forging intimate relationships later in life. Their self-esteem and feelings of security and safety are sometimes badly damaged. Pain, grief, and feelings of abandonment and hopelessness are part of the common emotional menu for a teen. Because few divorces aren't preceded by years of growing conflict between the teen's parents, the teen's shaky feelings of well-being often have a long history, sometimes going far back into early childhood. It's typical for young children to believe they are the cause of their parents' enmity toward each other, and while teens are better able to understand that this is not the case, a childhood spent believing they were to blame has tenacious negative effects on teens, even if they know these feelings are irrational.

As a result of these strains, by the time a child reaches the teen years, she often experiences behavioral problems and difficulties at school. Nearly all teens of divorced parents show signs of sadness, sometimes even depression. The period prior to divorce is particularly difficult for teens who have long had emotional problems due to their parents' bickering and evident dislike of each other. Added to this is the fact that divorcing parents' own self-absorption in their problems often keeps them from being fully "present" to their teens. After the divorce, changes in economic stability, having to move and change schools, and adjusting to their parents' new relationships can be traumatic to teens.

Fortunately, there is much parents can do to ease their teens' passage through this difficult period. Being available to listen, not trying to overcompensate by being both mother and father, making sure the teen is not used as a scapegoat or a go-between, minimizing the changes a teen must undergo during and after a divorce, helping the teen understand that feelings of anxiety and anger are completely normal, helping her uphold relationships in her life that are steady and nurturing, and, above all, making sure that the teen doesn't bottle up her feelings about the divorce all constitute the kind of informed and compassionate approach that divorcing and divorced parents are strongly advised to adopt. The following suggestions are based on this approach and offer more specific help.

What to Do

- Explain to your teen why you are getting divorced without confiding inappropriate information (such as sex or fidelity issues). Underscore that sometimes people find they cannot live together in harmony. One parent may have changed in some ways and sometimes the other cannot adapt; sometimes people simply drift apart over time. Emphasize that none of this is the teen's fault and that there's nothing the teen can do to heal the rift. It is simply what sometimes happens in relationships. Assure your teen that both you and your ex-spouse still love him and that you will both take every measure to make sure that his life is not unduly disrupted and that your teen can have access to both parents.

- Plan to attend special events—recitals, sports activities, or graduations—that involve your teen with your divorced spouse. Invite the teen to suggest compromises with regard to attending events important to him. ("I'd like Dad to come to my football games, Mom, but when my teacher wants to talk to somebody, would you do it?")

- Encourage teens to live their lives—to stay as fully and actively involved in school, athletics, and social activities as possible.

- Parents should be sure to take care of themselves emotionally, seeking the counsel of a friend, trusted authority, or therapist to work out their feelings. This will help parents be clear with their teens and refrain from bad-mouthing their spouses or in other ways putting the teen in the middle.

- Concentrate on the positive aspects of the family's post-divorce future. Many teens find they are happier once their parents have become happier apart. Gently suggest this to your teen. Remember that staying together "for the kids" is almost always a recipe for disaster.

- If you and your spouse have decided to divorce but are still living together, do everything you can not to argue or fight in front of your teen. Keep family life as normal as possible under the circumstances.

- After the divorce, remember that going back and forth between the father's and mother's homes can be very tough for the teen. Don't impose some arbitrary schedule; involve teens in these plans and ask them their preferences.

- Counseling and psychotherapy can help both you and your teen. Seek out individual or family therapy, support groups, and so on to help all of you get through this difficult time.

Stepfamilies

Not every parent who divorces remarries, but many do, and the impact of bringing teens into a whole new family and living situation, dropping them into a milieu of strangers whom they are often encouraged to call "Mom" or "Dad" or "brother" or "sister," can cause enormous confusion, anger, and anxiety. Sometimes it is difficult for a man and woman who bring great love and optimism to remarriage to understand that this good feeling is not automatically shared by children. Teens tend to feel competitive with a new spouse or new siblings. Even after the remarriage, they may secretly hope that somehow their "real" parents will reunite.

Here are some suggestions that can make the jolt of remarriage and a new stepfamily more manageable for your teen.

What to Do

- Remember that it will take time for your teen to adjust to the new relationship and family that remarriage entails. Don't attempt to coerce intimacy or insist that the teen "must" call the new spouse "Mom" or "Dad." Give the new family time to sort itself out.

- If you are a divorced parent and have begun a new relationship that you believe is moving toward marriage, discuss this gently and honestly with your teen, and allow your teen to vent whatever feelings this may bring up without dismissing or attempting to persuade him to feel otherwise.

- Remember that the older a teen is, the harder it will be for her to adjust to a new family. Don't insist that she do so. Let your teen know that her wishes for autonomy and independence will be respected.

- Prepare yourself for a long period of "testing" after the new household has been set up. Conflicts are probably inevitable, and it may take many patient conversations with your teen to help the family deal with them. Custodial parents should be in continual communication with non-custodial parents to make sure they do not appear to be embattled or in opposing camps. Patience is key.

- If you are the stepparent, do not expect to be accepted as an authority figure immediately. This position must be earned over time; remember, for many teens, the relationship with a stepparent can never be more than cordial. If your teenage stepchild presents discipline problems, discuss them with your spouse; and allow your spouse to have the final say about how to handle them.

SEE ALSO:

Stress and PTSD
Getting Help

49. Teens with Depressed Parents

"Hey, George, um, I don't think you better come over tonight. Yeah, it's my mom. She's . . . sick again, I guess. Got a headache or something. She says I can't have anyone over. Yeah, I know, same ol' same ol' . . ."

SIXTEEN-YEAR-OLD Doug's phone call to his best friend George doesn't sound too strange on the face of it. Mothers do get headaches, and sometimes they just don't want the noise of two teenage boys in the next room bothering them. But Doug's mother has a headache every night. Doug's mother rarely comes out of her room. Doug can't remember the last time they had a normal day like he imagined other families did: mom getting up, making breakfast, asking him if he'd done his homework, happy to see him when he came home from school. He can't remember his mom ever doing that. His father isn't much help either. He seems to stay away as much as he can, working late, going on business trips. Doug isn't surprised. His dad probably just wanted to get away from the whole dreary family . . .

Doug's mother suffers from depression, and her influence on Doug has been devastating, especially because Doug couldn't remember a time, even back in early childhood, when his mother wasn't "sick" or "exhausted" or otherwise unavailable to him. He'd gotten so little warmth and love and attention from her, he had a hard time recognizing, accepting, or trusting positive attention from anybody now. Teens with depressed parents adapt to some very harsh family realities. Many learn to tread very lightly—"walk on eggshells"—so that they don't make the depressed parent get even more "down," or lash out in anger. They tend to become withdrawn and depressed and isolated themselves. They rarely can have friends over and often lie about what's really wrong at home, almost like teens with alcoholic or drug-addicted parents. Such teens are likelier to develop a range of psychiatric problems, not only depressive episodes but various kinds of behavior disorders and hyperactivity, by the time they hit their teen years. Cognitive ability, school performance, and reaching appropriate developmental milestones all tend to be adversely affected by depressed parents. Depressed parents are unable to set limits for teens and are so mired in their own self-absorption and problems that they often barely notice their teens. If a teen has had to adapt to a depressed parent or parents (it's often plural because one depressed parent tends to have married another) since early childhood, it's likely he feels somehow to blame for the parent's distress. The anger frequently masked by depression can sometimes blow with great ferocity: family discord can reach unbearable levels. To escape, teens of depressed parents may run away, become suicidal, or turn to drugs and alcohol.

As with alcoholic and drug-addicted parents, the urgent hope is that the afflicted parent will seek help for this disease. If one parent is not affected by depression, it is up to him or her to bring warmth and guidance and love to the teen, to normalize the teen's life, and be as consistently available to the teen as possible.

What to Do

- If you or your spouse is depressed, get help as soon as possible. Psychotherapy sometimes combined with antidepressant medication has proven to be extremely effective. If you have children, it is imperative that you seek professional help.

- If you have been treated for depression and are recovering, you must still be alert to signs of your past influence in your teen, especially lethargy, listlessness, anger, poor school performance, low self-esteem, hyperactivity, and any self-destructive behavior. Explain to your teen that depression, like alcoholism, is a disease and that you know it will take both of you time to work through the pain of past disappointment and neglect. Without being inappropriately confidential about every last symptom or problem you have had, enlist your teen as an ally in getting better. Anything to bolster a sense of security, warmth, and consistency in the family will help the teen—and you.

- If you continue to suffer periodic episodes of depression, or if you don't but your spouse does, you can still do much to help your teen by enlisting the aid of friends and other family members to be there for the teen—to go to sports events, concerts, and other activities that have meaning to her, and to pay attention to her triumphs and disappointments.

- It is not only the shutdown of depression that harms your teen, but the hostility underlying it. This can sometimes explode with horrifying force and has a more damaging and lasting effect on your teen than you may know. Do all you can to manage anger in the family reasonably and compassionately.

- If your teen becomes intransigently depressed or manifests any other abnormal behavior, she may need psychotherapeutic help. See that help is received.

SEE ALSO:

Depression
Suicide
Anger
Self-Injurious Behavior
Behavior Disorders
Drugs
School Problems
Getting Help

50. Teenagers Whose Parents Are Ill

"No, Dad, really, it's okay you can't come to the game. It's not that important. I know you're on that new medicine. Really, Dad, it's all right. Yeah, I know you'll be with me in spirit. Thanks, Dad. Hope you feel better, Dad. . . ."

LOUIE is on his high school's junior varsity basketball team, and tonight was a pretty important semifinal game. Though he'd never tell anybody about it, sometimes Louie dreamed his dad was healthy and in the stands like his friends' dads were, shouting about how their son was the greatest. But he knew that wouldn't ever really happen. His dad was just too sick; he didn't have the stamina to last through a TV sitcom, much less a whole basketball game. He knew his dad loved him. But it would be nice, just once, to have a dad who could shoot some hoops with a guy. Or come to a game. Or didn't make him feel he had to walk on eggshells every time he walked into his own house. (Or make him feel that there was no one in the family who could take care of him if he got sick.)

When parents are seriously or chronically ill, many "normal" family scenarios are reversed. Often the child is placed in a caretaker capacity. So much daily life is lived in deference to the ill parent that sons and daughters often feel there is no one in the house they can turn to for comfort or guidance. Their problems may seem insignificant compared to those faced by their sick mother or father. Such teens, especially if they have lived with a chronically ill parent since early childhood, may also harbor feelings that they somehow caused the illness. Illness may seem to be the main way to get attention in the family, with the result that some teens become hyper-concerned about their own health. Sometimes this reaches the point of manifesting psychosomatic symptoms, often those that mimic those of the ill parent. Such teens are prone to isolation and depression. They may appear to be able to tolerate knowing about the parent's illness in great detail, but in fact the negative impact of this often goes much deeper than anyone knows. Nightmares, fears of abandonment, and poor school performance may also afflict the teen of an ill parent. They are prone to anxiety, sleep disturbances, frightening or upsetting thoughts, loss of appetite, angry outbursts, increased fighting, and overall social withdrawal.

Of course, the teen's underlying personality is important in determining how he will handle a parent's illness. Teens with pre-existing psychiatric problems are obviously more likely to be worse off than teens with a strong, healthy sense of self. Gender also apparently plays a role. A teenage girl is more likely to respond traumatically to her mother's illness, a boy more likely to be upset at his father being sick. Teens are also adversely affected if parents must be hospitalized or "sent away" because of their treatment. The healthy spouse's reaction to the illness provides an important model to the teen. If the healthy parent is stoic, in denial, falsely optimistic, or constantly upset or depressed, the teen can be expected to follow suit or simply withdraw from the family unit altogether.

Parents—healthy or sick—must realize that there is no greater blow to a child's sense of security and safety than a mother or father becoming seriously ill. Even though teens are generally more able to understand, accept, and adhere to the adaptations the family must make to the ill parent than younger children, they need to be reassured that they are loved and that there are still many normal activities in which the family can participate.

What to Do

- Parents should explain as clearly and simply as possible the nature of the sick parent's illness without being unduly optimistic but also not dwelling overly on the negative. Discussions about how to adapt to the parent's illness should be held by the entire family, with teens invited to contribute and suggest solutions and compromises. Who does what chores, when lights must be turned out, keeping noise down, and other practical considerations should all be worked out calmly. Reassure teens about what won't change in the family and that there will always be someone for the teen to talk to.

- Focus on positive family activities that can be shared by everyone. Perhaps have a "family night" where the family watches a video, plays a game, or has a special indoor "picnic" or "barbecue." Again, invite teens to come up with their own ideas about how the whole family might have a good time together.

- Parents should be aware of their own reactions to the illness and realize that they are providing models to their teens about how they should react. Panic and despair will encourage teens to panic and feel despair. But neither should problems be whitewashed. Be honest about what the ill parent is going through, and invite teens to vent their distress and anxiety openly. Correct any distorted view of the parent's prognosis or condition.

- Consider getting help with cooking, cleaning, and other household chores to cut down on family stress. Make sure the teen has someone (a close family friend if not a family member) who can go to athletic events, academic conferences, concerts, and other activities important to the teen.

- If you are the ill parent, gently prepare the teen for any changes that may happen to you and reassure your teen that such changes are normal in the progress of your illness. Stress the positive, not the negative.

- Keep an eye out for any signs of psychiatric, academic, or social problems in your teen. It may be wise to inform the school of a parent's illness so they can be on the lookout for problems that may need to be treated.

SEE ALSO:

Anxiety
Stress and PTSD
Depression
Psychosomatic Disorders
School Problems
Getting Help

VII

School Issues

51. School Problems

*"What use is algebra ever gonna be
to me anyway?"*

SCHOOLING AND EDUCATION are a major focus of adolescence and are one of the most frequent reasons that parents call me for psychiatric consultation for their children. Teenagers spend most of their time during the day at school and thus it is easy to understand why problems at school are a major focus of a parent's—not to mention the teen's—anxiety. It is also easy to understand that problems in school are often an indicator of problems elsewhere, and it is important that parents be able to differentiate the two. As with athletics in some families, school performance becomes a major focus of parents' anxieties, ambitions, and vicarious living. In addition, they may project problems in their own lives onto their children's performance.

It is normal for teenagers to experience some problems at school that are not particularly serious, especially during what are called the transition years, moving from middle school to junior high school or from junior high school to high school. It's unusual to find teenagers who don't experience some degree of stress at these times. But when school problems persist long past these transitions and become more deeply entrenched, there is a problem.

Underachievement

What are some of the common indicators and risk factors for particular teenage school problems? What should a parent look for?

Some problems may have been present during the teen's childhood; for example, if your teenager had problems paying attention in school when she was younger or behaved disruptively, the teenager is more likely to have the same problem during high school. If poor grades, being left back, or other signs of academic failure occurred during primary schooling, this is an indicator or risk factor for failure. Behavioral problems in primary school and as a teenager also increase the risk for possible school failure, as does being absent more than a week or so per year. Teenagers who have pre-existing or current psychiatric problems are also set up for a higher level of school failure.

Underachievement in school has many sources, and it is up to parents to compassionately investigate the reasons teenagers may be having difficulties. Problems such as learning disorders, attention deficit disorder with or without hyperactivity (ADD and ADHD respectively), as well as behavior disorders are all indicators or risk factors associated with underachievement, as are emotional problems, especially depression and/or school phobia (see page 242). A chaotic or disorganized family life, fighting to the point of domestic violence, and the effects of a "bad" or ill-handled divorce can also set the stage for school problems. Single parent and stepparent families have to take extra care to ensure that school achievement is not undermined, although it is not known why these situations are high risk factors. Teens have to be in good physical health to do well in school. It is important that parents know their children hear and see well, and they don't have serious illnesses that can interfere with school problems such as undiagnosed seizure disorders or untreated or under-treated diabetes, asthma, or migraine headache symptoms.

Heightened or unrealistic expectations and blaming teens for not doing well cause stress and interfere with school functioning as well as sometimes provoking rebellion. Sometimes there is simply a poor match between the child and her teacher and/or school setting that may need to be tended to. Along these lines it should be noted that our culture tends to put such an emphasis on grades and productivity that the most important part of education—taking joy in learning—is often left out. A parent who compliments the grade and not the process of the achievement undermines the child's developing self-esteem, confidence, and further school success. We have to be careful that while on one hand we support success at school, on the other we support building confidence and appreciating one's assets and weaknesses compassionately. We should also remember that laziness is probably a misnomer and what appears to be a lack of motivation is a manifestation of other problems. No teen is inherently lazy but under the influence of stress, psychological problems, learning disabilities, and sexual anxieties, and as a result of wanting to rebel and defy parents who are putting unusual pressures on them, teens might appear "lazy."

Learning Disorders

Learning disorders can have a serious impact on a teen's performance. For most teenagers, learning problems have probably been diagnosed earlier on or there have been some strong previous hints of difficulty. Learning disabilities or disorders are better called information-processing disorders because that is, in fact, what the teenager is actually struggling with. What does this mean?

Learning well depends on mastering the processes of input, integration, and output. Input is how information gets to the brain; thus any problems in the visual or auditory areas can cause problems. Problems in the central nervous system can cause children to read backward or rotate letters or numbers and not be able to focus on specific letters or words when reading or working. Problems with auditory perception interfere with hearing; some words sound similar and are confused with each other, making processing words impossible. This creates the impression that the child does not hear as fast as people might be speaking.

Integration involves the ability to call up the relevant information or sequential processes the teen has learned. Visual ability thus not only affects input but it also affects integration, how the brain processes all the data that it is sent. A teenager with an integration problem may not be able to remember that one adds a column of three digit numbers from right to left. He may have similar trouble integrating information received from areas of vision, touch, and balance, which means gross and fine motor skills may be affected.

Putting words, letters, and numbers in the right order may be affected
due to sequencing learning problems having to do with integration, as
may difficulties with abstraction, memory, and organization.

Output involves the expression of language or appropriate use of
the body to convey what a child knows. Problems with output can
create difficulties in the way children talk, thus leading to a language
disability diagnosis, or in the way they write, which may result in a
motor disability diagnosis.

All of these processing problems lead to difficulties in the three
R's: reading, writing, and arithmetic, or what is now known as the
three D's, dyslexia, dysgraphia, and dyscalculia. Children usually
have problems in more than one area; that is, they most commonly
experience overlapping difficulties in input, integration, and output.
Problems can show up in one or many areas of school learning.
Nearly all children with learning disabilities have normal intelligence.
It is the difference between their achievement and what can be
expected from their IQ—those who don't do as well in achievement
tests as in their intelligence testing—that tips us off to the diagnosis.

Learning disorders cause much misery and depression in children
because of the frustration they cause. Often a child with an undiagnosed learning disability develops despair, low self-esteem, rebelliousness, defiance, and complex acting out if untreated. This acting
out can lead to suspensions, antisocial behavior, truancy, and eventually even dropping out of school. It is imperative to make the
appropriate diagnosis of a child who has learning disorders. It is also
important that the parent understands that teens who have problems
learning do not necessarily have a learning disorder but might be
depressed (for example) instead. Differentiating the depressed teen
from the teen with a learning disorder and knowing which came first
is very important. In other words, appropriate treatment of the
depressed teenager can lead to the abolition of apparent learning
problems.

The specific cause of learning disorders is not known. They tend
to run in families, which suggests that they might be inherited. Some
people feel that the "wiring" in the brain is different for the learning
disordered teenager than the normal one, but nothing definitive

about this has been demonstrated. There are some known risk factors, such as the teen's mother's use of drugs and/or alcohol during pregnancy, difficult deliveries, and low birthrate. Learning disorders are often coupled with attention deficit hyperactivity disorder (discussed in a separate chapter). A moderately large percentage of children with ADHD also present with one or more learning disorders. Parents should be alert not only to learning problems but the symptoms of ADHD, including a short attention span, distractibility, hyperactivity, and impulsivity. These symptoms are usually present earlier in childhood as well.

Homework

Along with poor academic performance and behavior disorders (discussed in a separate chapter), other problems confront teenagers and their families regarding school. The issue of homework is an important one. Doing homework in an organized and timely fashion not only helps with performance in school but leads to a good set of values and the understanding of discipline, time planning, organization, and perseverance. It increases your teen's confidence and self-esteem. It is important that parents provide adequate light and space and lack of distraction for teenagers. Although many teenagers state they like to lie down while they do homework, play loud music, or keep the TV on in the background, it is known that a lack of distraction, sitting up, setting aside time, and keeping a schedule book all help in developing good work habits. While parents should assist in homework when asked, parents doing homework is a no-no. Questioning, helping a child expand his knowledge, making suggestions, and stimulating thinking are all advisable parental outputs, as are withholding various rewards and disciplining appropriately if the teen does not carry out his homework obligations.

Cheating

With pressures such as anxiety about getting into college, a teen's personal belief that he is unintelligent, or feeling hampered by a learning disorder, cheating becomes more common in high school, as it was in early kindergarten or first grade. Teenagers who cheat eventually lose confidence in their own abilities. Parents who find out their children are cheating often react with horror, rage, and severe anxiety. It is important for parents not to give into these feelings but rather try to understand the source of the cheating.

Of course, cheating can be part of a larger behavior disorder such as a conduct disorder or antisocial behavior; in that case it is only a small piece of a larger picture. However, usually cheating is not associated with a complex behavioral disturbance but is an indicator of a child struggling either with external demands, fears of future functioning and college admission, psychological difficulties, or learning disorders that had not been diagnosed. It is important to be firm yet compassionate about this situation. Often at this time, if a child has been caught in school cheating, meetings with the school personnel are held. Parents are advised to support the school's handling of the cheating but at the same time try to bring to the school personnel a compassionate personal understanding of the unique and specific issues that motivated their teenagers to cheat.

Attendance, Truancy, and School Phobia

School attendance—and non-attendance—constitute another big issue with teenagers. Some teens may cut particular classes or stay out of school entirely. Again, if truancy is part of a larger behavioral disorder then this has to be addressed appropriately. If it is not, the specific stressors, social issues, or other reasons for cutting school have to be explored in a firm yet compassionate way; for example, transient problems with bullies may be the source of the problem. Avoiding shame and humiliation about athletic performance or social rejection can lead to transient cutting or truancy. Problems with a particular teacher might lead to avoiding a particular class or a learning disability in a particular area might lead eventually to a child cutting to avoid the humiliation of continued failure. If truancy continues then school authorities as well as local governmental authorities will eventually get involved. It is rare that things go that far in most cases, unless the truancy is part of a larger antisocial behavioral pattern.

School attendance is also affected by the well-known syndrome of school phobia. School phobia is usually found in children who earlier in adolescence have shown anxiety about separation from parents, overall timidity, and a tendency to want to stay at home. Although it frequently occurs in middle or elementary school years it tends to increase as adolescence approaches. Often children won't get out of bed in the morning because they are so frightened to go to school; they won't leave the house no matter how severely parents threaten them with punishment. For a school-phobic teenager this is the only way they know to decrease their anxiety. They feel they really can't go to school; it is not planned defiance or rebellion, as many parents feel. Often the onset of school phobia happens when the teenager moves, switches schools, has an illness, or develops a learning disorder that becomes obvious. Although these are common precipitants they are usually also evident earlier in a child's life. Acute stress sometimes leads to acute school phobia, such as that caused by sexual and other abuse. Stress in the home can cause school phobia as can stress at school or social rejection. The school-phobic teenager feigns illness, especially stomachaches, feeling "feverish," or having headaches.

School phobia is often misinterpreted by parents and can lead to fights between them and their teens. Since parents are often insensitive to the high degree of anxiety in the school-phobic child, teens tend to get more depressed, hostile, and panicky, and may even threaten or try to commit suicide. Some may run away if forced to go to school. Generally, school phobia is worse on Mondays and earlier in the day when anxiety is highest. School-phobic adolescents often develop secondary shame and humiliation about not being like other teenagers and become increasingly isolated. They often end up staying home all day in their withdrawn state. They often become quite depressed. Normally these children who feel anxious and timid and shy become more dependent on their parents, but this dependence is inextricably interwoven with mutual hostility as well.

Parents should keep in mind that the earlier the child with school phobia gets back to school the better. It is common for some parents to back off from their school-phobic teens, not wanting to upset them. They may join with the teenager (not always consciously), blaming the school, teachers, or other classmates for what is really an irrational fear in their son or daughter. However, to get school-phobic teens back to school involves giving them a sense of control over their lives, such as determining when they will return and how many hours they will spend there. Parents are advised to encourage whatever choice-making is appropriate to ease re-entry into school and to discuss the advantages of attending school without being over-bearing. When possible, parents should stay home in the morning in order to encourage their teens to leave for school, making them feel more secure that "somebody's there." However, it is extremely important that the teenager understands his parents are on the side of going to school, not staying home.

Often children with school phobia need individual and family therapy, as well as behavior modification interventions. Sometimes a change of school to a special-education high school for phobic teenagers is necessary, or even the temporary use of medication such as antidepressants or mild tranquilizers. It is rare, but some teens with school phobia become so entrenched in their syndrome that placing them out of the house and in a special treatment center or even a psychiatric hospital is necessary for a short period of time. Special schools designed to help school-phobic teens may also be appropriate.

Dropping Out

Dropping out of school seems to be a common course taken by teens afflicted with disorders. Teenagers who have experienced chronic school failure, have serious social problems, get pregnant, run with a crowd or come from families that do not value education, have been abused or subject to severe stress, have been cutting school exces-sively, or have undiagnosed learning disorders often drop out of school. There are many programs aimed at decreasing dropouts. They provide counseling and opportunities for students to learn about vocations and appropriate behavior. Some states facilitate stu-dent involvement in extracurricular activities, which also decreases dropouts.

Although dropout rates are declining, about 300,000 to 350,000 students still drop out each year. Often they leave before the tenth grade; one-fifth of students drop out by the eighth grade and four percent do not finish the fourth grade. Generally speaking, dropout rates are highest in some ethnic divisions. Hispanic students are slightly more likely than African Americans to drop out of school, while Asian American and white students are less likely than both groups. The dropout rate is higher in urban than in suburban or rural areas. Dropping out cuts earning capacity considerably. The economic gap between kids who drop out of school and more educated ones widens as time passes.

Many teenagers who drop out say they did not like school, were failing, or didn't get along with teachers. Many of them had disciplinary problems, were frequently suspended, and often did not feel like they fit in. Dropouts often got married quickly after leaving school, became pregnant, hung out with others who dropped out, had a substance-abuse problem, or had to get a menial job. Moving also increases the dropout rate. Often there were truancy, tardiness, and disciplinary problems, problems with the police, and a history of having lived in a group home or a group shelter. Some teens who drop out of school go on to get a GED certificate. Many end up in low-paying or dead-end jobs.

Fortunately, a great deal of institutional effort is now exerted to decrease the dropout rate in many school districts, with programs to enable teens to make up work when they are behind and receive psychological help. These programs also define a more appropriate specialized educational setting for teens who are at high risk for dropping out.

Special Remediation

There are many ways to help a child outside of the home. The field of special remediation has grown enormously. Usually after a child receives the appropriate psychological tests, generally including an intelligence test and a battery of achievement tests, specialists in remediation can be of great help. Remediation can occur in the area of language skills, speech, and learning problems in specific areas such as reading, spelling, writing, arithmetic, and sensory motor integration among others. This remediation also can be received at home by hiring specialists in remediation to work with the teen. Academic tutoring, organizational tutoring, and joining after-school remediation classes can also be beneficial.

Some mental-health professionals have combined degrees and not only work on underlying issues such as anxiety, depression, and family problems but also offer specialized remediation in which they integrate work on psychological issues with the effects on learning. There are also many resources at school. These are usually more affordable than hiring outside help and are actually mandated by the federal government to be provided to children who need help. Sometimes procuring this help takes a lot of advocating on the parents' part, but with enough effort any parent can get their teens the help they need.

Home Schooling

There is an increasing trend across the country of parents choosing to "home school" their children, even if they are able to attend school. It is estimated that two percent of children in this country are now receiving home education. This is a nationwide movement. Interestingly, and for unknown reasons, children who are home educated seem to score better on certain standardized tests. Home education is also often used for the phobic child.

What to Do

There are many different types of parenting styles and a teenager's parent should know what his style tends to be, and if necessary, alter or adapt it to suit the teen's needs, especially with regard to school. Some parents tend to be permissive, others authoritarian. The former often neglect to set limits and to supervise; the latter tend to emphasize limits and supervision. It's best to aim for a rational authoritative style, which offers a combination of the two kinds of parenting:

supervision with some latitude. Such parents are loving, kind, and warm but also are able to set standards for their children and communicate with them when issues arise. Establishing appropriate expectations rather than demands, and engaging in appropriate discussion of consequences if teens are not living up to those expectations, are profitable. Here are some ways parents can stay on the "rational authoritative" track:

- Parents should attempt to understand the teen's fears and concerns about school as well as set appropriate boundaries.

- Extracurricular activities should certainly be encouraged but they shouldn't interfere with school functioning. Helping a teen balance his life with regard to school, social, athletic, and other extracurricular activities is important.

- Parents should maintain contact with teachers and guidance counselors as well as attend school meetings and activities concerning their teens' education. They should take an active interest in their teens' schooling and show that they value education.

- Parents should regularly review teenagers' school work.

- Settling any ongoing family problems is important in creating a non-stressful atmosphere in which a teen's educational activities can flourish.

- Know who teens are hanging out with because peer pressure is never more pertinent than during the teenage years. We cannot expect teenagers to function well in school if their friends are cutting, "hanging out," and valuing other activities more than education.

- Parents should know if their teens are using drugs. School functioning is often subtly affected by drug use, and sometimes poor school performance is the first indicator of drug use.

- As with so many other areas of teenage functioning, parents' connectedness with their teenagers remains the best preventative and therapeutic factor for school performance issues.

SEE ALSO:

Stress and PTSD
Depression
Bullying
Attention Deficit Disorder
Behavior Disorders
Discipline
Sexual Development
Psychosomatic Disorders
Drugs
Divorce and Stepfamilies
Getting Help

52. The College Process

*"I don't want to go to that college; it's not
even in the top twenty-five schools! It's
only twenty-eighth."*

BRIAN, AGE SEVENTEEN, is referring to college rankings, an assessment
made by such sources as the *U.S. News & World Report* which,
whatever their merits of indicating college quality may be, have over
the past couple of decades fed on the anxiety of college-bound teens
everywhere. The notion of reducing a college to a "number," of
regarding the whole aim of going to college as having more to do
with prestige than with education, is symbolic of a wider troubling
anxiety that afflicts more teens every year. SAT scores, grade point
averages, and class standings trouble many teenagers to a degree that
can negatively affect their feelings of competency and self-worth.

Amazingly, the anxiety that hits so many college-bound teens
often begins even before preschool. Many parents of toddlers worry
over nursery school admission as much as parents of teens worry over
their sons or daughters getting into Ivy League colleges. Recent pub-
licity about nursery school admission and the large payoffs, bribes,
and other tactics used to gain entry have made the societal pressures
even more apparent. This anxiety, in other words, isn't limited to
teens, and it's often shared by, even contributed to, by parents of
teenagers. Living in a competitive, individual-centered and aggressive
society, it is not surprising so many parents and teens focus on college
admissions starting at such a young age. Unfortunately for all, but

especially high school students, this pressure leads to great stress and often to anxiety, depression, cheating to "succeed" at the college admissions game, and feelings of rejection and disappointment when the "perfect school" doesn't accept the teenager.

Parents should recognize that admission to a particular school does not guarantee fulfilling a child's potential or predict future success. Rejection from any one college will not cause long-lasting damage. The truth is that the overwhelming majority of students who go to college have a future not particularly dictated by what school they get into but rather by what type of people they are, how hard they work, and the values that were inculcated in them by parents long before applying to college. Competition to get into prestigious schools is great these days, but there are many wonderful and successful college programs that can match your particular teen's interests and strengths. One of the most important messages that can be relayed to your teenage son or daughter is that focusing on the teen's particular strengths, interests, aptitudes, and desires is far more important than trying to force the teen into a school solely because it has a high ranking or prestige value.

Unfortunately, high school for many teenagers in this country is basically a preparation for the PSATs and SATs, standardized admissions tests that hover over a teenager's life, often inducing intense anxiety that can lead to an overall withdrawal from many life-enhancing and enjoyable activities that have nothing to do with "making the grade." While there are many SAT and PSAT preparation courses, they often cost a lot of money, take up a lot of time, and don't necessarily raise scores all that much. But trying to convince many parents today that SAT preparation courses aren't an absolute necessity can be all but impossible.

Each year about two million students go to college. Certainly attending college has real benefits: a typical college graduate earns from a half million to one million dollars more in their lives than students who don't go to college. Despite the enormous expense of college, parents often see it as the most important investment they are going to make in their children's lives. It is an important investment, but its success doesn't depend on the prestige of the institution. A teen can be just as successful going to a state university as an Ivy League school.

Other anxieties attend the prospect of the teen going off to college. Even if it is a local school that the teen attends while living at home, it still represents a major, if not final, separation children make from their parents. Parents who were actively involved in their children's lives often worry about the void they may experience when teens leave, which is often referred to as the "empty nest syndrome." They will no longer play the roles of primary caretakers or be the major figures in their child's lives. Parents who live through their children vicariously may suddenly worry that they will become unimportant as their children prepare to go to college. Many parents who have focused most of their lives on their teenagers have avoided attending to their marital relationships, often worrying that they will face an empty and barren marriage after the children leave.

This crisis can turn into an opportunity for parents to reconnect with one another, sometimes precipitating a return to former interests, pursuit of new hobbies and activities, or even career changes. As couples, this can help parents grow in new and unique ways. Parents who worry that they will suddenly be made "unimportant" because their children are leaving for college should be reassured that this is far from the case. This is not only because of the financial support most parents offer their college-going teens, but because of the help they will continue to give their sons and daughters through any number of social, academic, and personal challenges and crises.

During the admissions process, parents should be active participants in the their teens' investigation of college possibilities, showing an interest and helping to define limits for their children, and discussing objective and subjective factors about school choices (having to do with size, location, programs, and social atmosphere). Often parents take their children to visit various campuses and engage with them on the spot about the school's evident pluses and minuses. For many parents these trips are remembered nostalgically.

Parents must be careful not to confuse their own ambitions or past disappointments with those of their children. It is important to encourage teens to have reasonable expectations and to be prepared for possible rejection. Choosing a range of schools, from "easy" to "hard" in terms of admissions prospects, is also important, but even the "easy" schools should be colleges at which the teen feels she has a good chance of being happy. Preparations should be made for the stressful day the "envelopes arrive." It's crucial that if the teen is rejected by a favorite school, parents offer support, advice, and consolation. Teens also need to know that even if they have been rejected by their first choices, their second, third, and fourth choices have real merits, and they can be just as successful where they end up as where they most wanted to go.

In helping teens to be realistic about getting into colleges, parents can make sure teens are aware of what test scores, extracurricular involvements, grades, teacher recommendations, and essays each school encourages applicants to have. Guidance counselors can help here, as can any literature provided by the college. After finding out what criteria schools seek, it is important that teenagers try to evaluate their own suitability. They should always ask themselves if they will be comfortable at the school if they are admitted. The size of the school is particularly important: some teens prefer the closer-knit atmosphere of a small school to the impersonal quality of a large university. Particular attention should be paid to programs in which the student is most interested. Sometimes programs at "easier" schools may be better than programs at higher ranking colleges: the actual education the school provides should be the determining factor. Finally, staying organized is important: a lot of information must be sifted through and compared, and parents can help their children to stay on top of various admission deadlines and requirements.

Many teens feel great anxiety when going off to college, even if they hide it. They have to give up the friends, familiarity, and family comforts at home, and try to fit into a whole new social situation. For many students, striking a balance among academic, social, athletic, and extracurricular activities at college is perplexing. Often there are worries about drug and alcohol use and the possibilities of exploring sexuality more freely. It is important for parents to educate their children as much as possible about these issues but allow teens to make their own final choices. Parents can only hope that the values they have instilled and the education they have given them will lead to good judgment. Most teens deal with these challenges well and make it through college just fine.

Not all students benefit from going to college right after high school. There are many reasons for this. Some teenagers are simply not mature enough to leave home at the age of eighteen. Sometimes they realize this, and/or their parents do, but this is nothing to be ashamed of. I have never seen any negative consequences of a teen postponing college for a year or even two. As a matter of fact, I have been impressed by the degree of maturity that particular teenagers have gained when they finally do go to college at nineteen, twenty, or twenty-one years old. Some teens don't want to go too far from home for various social and psychological reasons. This is not necessarily a bad choice. Some eighteen year olds need a more gradual separation from the comforts of home. Other teens have let me and their parents know that they only want to go to college to "party" and have sex. This is another indication that they are too immature to leave home and may profit by waiting a year or two before making the college plunge.

College anxieties don't end with worrying about getting in. The first year of college is often very stressful for teenagers; sometimes they are depressed and don't want to return to school when they come home for Thanksgiving or Christmas. This reluctance to return can be cloaked under the disguise of having "mono" (mononucleosis, known as "the kissing disease") or other feigned illnesses. Many students want to drop out of school and may come home for extended periods of time, which often upsets parents. In most cases, this is not severe enough to necessitate actually dropping out of school, but it certainly indicates that counseling at school and/or at home over vacation breaks may be very helpful. For a small minority of students college can represent a stressor that may precipitate modest or even major psychiatric problems. If your teenager comes home within the first year or later with evidence of severe anxiety, depression, drug abuse, or reckless and destructive acting out, this might be a sign that he or she should be home for a while to receive appropriate treatment while maturity is gained.

What to Do

- Be careful not to feed your teen's anxiety about getting into the "right" college with your own anxieties about prestige. Many different schools can be good choices for your teen. Encourage her to make reasonable decisions about where to apply.

- Remember that PSATs and SATs are not the be-all and end-all determinants of your teen's college success. Too many teens feel branded by their scores. Make sure your teen knows that many other more important factors go into ensuring success both in college and in life.

- Remind your teen that college is about education, not only partying or status.

- Help your teen throughout the college process by encouraging him to stay organized and select a variety of "hard" to "easy" schools in terms of admission, and by accompanying your teen to college campuses when feasible.

- Encourage teens to talk to other people they know who are already going to the colleges they are interested in attending. If you visit college campuses, try to arrange to meet some of the students who are attending; the admissions office should be able to facilitate this.

- College is not for everyone. Some students are better off at specialty schools, such as in the arts or manual vocations, than at college. Some students benefit from working a year or two before attending college. There isn't any specific right time or age to go to college. Keep in mind that your teen's temperament and maturity may make it better for her to wait a year or two before attending.

- If stress before getting into college or after attending is severe, encourage your child to receive counseling to get over the worst of it.

- If you, as parents, fear the "empty nest syndrome," remember that separation from your child does not mean you have lost importance in your child's life and that the time you are afforded can be seen as an opportunity to enrich other areas of your life and your marriage.

SEE ALSO:

Anxiety
Stress and PTSD
Depression
Risk Taking
Psychosomatic Disorders
Drugs
School Problems

VIII

Getting Help

53. When You Can't Do It on Your Own

"You know, honey, I hate to say it, but I think Robert's really depressed. I mean, it's not just a passing mood; I can hardly get him to go to school in the morning. And now two of his teachers have called me about it. We can't just keep giving him pep talks or getting angry with him. He doesn't seem to be able to help how he is. I think we should get him some help."

THROUGHOUT THIS BOOK it has been repeatedly emphasized that for nearly any disorder, stress, or issue that your teenager faces, the first line of intervention should be made by parents at home. Compassion and understanding comprise the most beneficial approach you can take to helping your teen. However, sometimes mustering up compassion and understanding is difficult because teenagers' issues can reverberate in us and cause great anxiety, anguish, and anger. Parents who are usually well-tempered adults can lose their tempers quite easily when dealing with adolescent moods, behaviors, and provocative discussions. Reflecting before blowing up—understanding that there are always reasons for your teens' misbehavior that may not readily be apparent—is sometimes difficult but is always the most rewarding tactic you can employ in helping your teenager.

Parental help is not always enough. Robert's mother's suggestion to her husband that maybe they seek this help for their son comes from her intuition that Robert's problems need a kind of care they just aren't equipped to give. But what help is available? This section will outline the variety of therapies and therapists available to you when you realize that help for your teen is necessary.

54. Mental-Health Professionals

AS YOU'VE READ in many chapters, at some point professional help may be advisable for your teenager. Where to turn for help is often a parent's first question. Consulting your teenager's doctor, teachers, school counselors, or your religious counselors, local mental-health association, hospital, or outpatient services are reliable ways to find a trained mental-health professional appropriate to your teen's problem. While many school-related learning/academic difficulties can be handled by the school system, for most other mental-health issues, turning to a mental-health professional is usually indicated. But parents are generally the best diagnosticians of their own teenagers and often the best therapeutic agents. Parents know their teens better in some important ways than any outside therapist or counselor could. With this in mind, I've offered various tips on understanding your teenager and what to do for him or her yourself in most of the previous chapters of this book.

The first step in getting help for your teenager usually involves a mental-health evaluation. Mental-health evaluations can be carried out by nearly all mental-health professionals. These include adolescent psychiatrists who specialize in the problems of teenagers, psychologists, social workers, and nurses. Adolescent psychiatrists are the most broadly trained of mental-health professionals; they have gone to medical school and pursued advanced training in adult and child/adolescent psychiatry during residency programs. The adolescent psychiatrist can also prescribe medication and do psychotherapy. The psychologist has received an advanced doctoral degree in

261

psychology and often has done an internship as well, prior to getting a license. Psychologists are trained not only in doing therapy but also in doing various types of testing, which helps in the evaluation of many aspects of a teen's life. Social workers who are licensed have also attended graduate school to receive their masters degrees in social work. Like psychologists and psychiatrists, they are also psychotherapists but generally have more training in dealing with family issues, cultural issues, and systems theory. Psychiatric nurses, especially those with masters degrees in psychiatry, are often trained similarly to a psychiatrist but not as extensively. The nurse will often have a strong background in medical sciences but also an expertise in psychiatric diagnosis, like the psychiatrist. Psychiatric nurses also do psychotherapy.

As you can see, nearly all four of the major professions provide psychotherapy, while psychiatrists and occasionally specially trained psychiatric nurses can also prescribe psychotropic medication. Any of the aforementioned mental-health professionals can and sometimes do go on for advanced psychotherapy and/or psychoanalytic training. This advanced training is extremely important because it is during this training that any mental-health professional gains a deeper understanding of underlying psychological issues that result in all of the various symptomatic states that have been mentioned in this book. Without such training, many therapies get bogged down in more superficial approaches that don't take into consideration unconscious psychological issues, family influences, and a host of inner conflicts that cause anxiety and symptoms in our teenagers. It should also be emphasized that work with teenagers requires training in the area of adolescent problems specifically, and while many in the field of mental health are adequately trained it is mostly in work with adults. Make sure that the mental-health professional to whom you turn has had specific training and experience in working with teenagers.

55. Clinical Evaluations

ALTHOUGH MANY SEEK the help of a mental-health practitioner only for a professional opinion, a one-time visit, or for reassurance, most often a full evaluation is needed. This can take several sessions if done correctly. Depending on the age of the teenager, sometimes the first interview is held with the teen alone. If the teenager refuses to come for an evaluation, is disabled in some way that would preclude obtaining an adequate history, or is simply too young to offer a complete history himself, then an interview is generally held with one or both parents first.

Gathering history and assessing the teenager are the two basic aspects of an evaluation. The mental-health professional will want to know what the primary complaint or problem is. Is it related to school, home, the use of drugs, behavior, social isolation, bizarre preoccupations, or eating? Is it a physical pain or other physical symptom that won't go away? Once understanding of the initial symptom has been reached, the evaluation will center on further history from both the teenager and the parents. Many teenagers will resist giving details; that's when work with parents becomes important. Although school teachers, administrators, or counselors sometimes want to offer their version of the teen's story, it is always best that the parent be the first person to provide information. Sometimes school reports and testing will be read by the initial evaluator but most important is getting a view from the teenager and his parents.

After hearing what the initial complaint is, further exploration of that complaint will be pursued. When did it start? How did it develop? Has it gotten worse? Has it gotten better? What have the parents or the teenager done to ameliorate the symptoms? Were vacations tried? Were curfews changed? Was discipline used? Was punishment used? Did the household move? Was schools changed? These and other similar questions will be asked. Additionally, the evaluator will ask whether this is the first episode of the particular problem or if it has occurred before. For most teenagers, the evaluator will try to get an understanding of the child's early development starting with the mother's pregnancy, characteristics of the birth, birth weight, early health problems, and any issues that occurred during preteen years, including school adjustment problems, behavior disorders, and/or learning disorders.

Also important are the characteristics of the family. What kind of household did this child emerge from? Was it a single parent home? Were the parents always fighting? Was it a placid, stable, and calm household? Have other family members had the same or similar issues? Here we are looking for role modeling as well as the possibility of genetic influence. Questions will also be asked about substance abuse. The teenager will be asked about this; parents will be asked if they have any evidence their teens have been using drugs or alcohol. Friendship patterns will be explored, as will relations with other family members outside the nuclear family. The evaluator will also want to know the history of the early developmental milestones of the teenager, such as when he walked, talked and was toilet trained and the character of his early social relations. These all give the evaluator valuable knowledge of the teen's former years.

The evaluating mental-health professional will also focus on the mental state of the teenager, noting such evidence as grooming, dress patterns, and overall behavior. The evaluator will note the teen's level of activity, his ability to establish rapport with the interviewer, evidence of any mood disorders such as depression, anxiety, bizarre thoughts, pseudo-perceptions (hallucinations), suicidal thinking, possible intoxication or disorientation, and the teen's attention span, distractibility, and tolerance for frustration, and ability to interact socially and use language and speech. The evaluator will determine the level of insight the teen has about his problem, degree of rebelliousness, ability to make good judgments, and will decide what type of therapy may prove most effective.

After the evaluation is complete, a psychiatric diagnosis usually can be made and treatment plan proposed. The psychiatric diagnosis will take into consideration the particular thinking, feelings, or behavior that led the teenager to be evaluated in the first place, as well as other personality traits, medical conditions that might be present, and stresses in the environment that might be causing or precipitating the outbreak of the symptoms; this will lead to a score of the teen's level of functioning. The evaluation will include recommendations for intervention, which can range from brief counseling to one of various different psychotherapies. Testing, further medical or physical examination, and/or the use of psychotropic medications may be suggested. The evaluation may conclude that treatment outside of the home, such as in a hospital or a residential treatment center, is necessary.

From this description it is apparent that the initial mental-health evaluation is broad and wide-ranging, focusing not only on the teenager but on the relationships between the teenager and his friends and family. It also entails an assessment of the teen's physical health, based on getting the teen an appropriate physical examination. This will include various blood tests: a complete blood count, a broad blood chemistry screening, and blood levels that show the degree of thyroid functioning. Other tests include an electrocardiogram, as some psychotropic medications affect the functioning of the heart. Hearing and vision tests are indicated for most teens, which are routine aspects of physical examinations.

56. Special Tests

OFTEN TEENAGERS will be referred for special testing to evaluate their functioning. These are sometimes called psychological tests, developmental tests, and achievement tests. It should be remembered that testing without a clinical interview does not give a whole picture of a teenager. Just as a doctor wouldn't rely solely on a blood test to make a diagnosis, a mental-health evaluator will not rely purely on the results of any one type of testing to diagnose what a teen has and determine what treatment is indicated.

Types of Tests

- **Intelligence tests:** These usually result in an IQ score, which is a measure of your teenager's intelligence, or ability to learn. A number is given for the full scale in intelligence, as well as broken down into verbal and non-verbal intelligence, among other categories. Not only is the ability to learn measured by these tests but also to think and act appropriately. Strengths and weaknesses of your teenager can be specified by these scores. The most common intelligence tests are the Wechsler Intelligence Scale for Children and for older teenagers the Wechsler Adult Intelligence Scale.

- **Achievement tests:** These are often given at the same time as intelligence tests because they provide a comparison between a teen's intelligence and what she has been able to achieve, which helps in the diagnosis of information-processing or learning disorders. There may not be a discrepancy; a low intelligence score generally results in low achievement score tests. Commonly used achievement tests are the Woodcock Johnson Psychoeducational Battery, the Wide Range Achievement Test, the Kaufman Test of Educational Achievement, and the Wechsler Individual Achievement Test. Essentially these measure achievement in the areas of reading, mathematics, and spelling.

■ **Adaptive behavior testing:** The Vineland Adaptive Behavior Scale helps the evaluator measure a child's day-to-day living skills and ability to socialize with peers, as well as motor and communication skills. Although more commonly given to younger children, some teenagers also receive this test.

■ **Personality/projective tests:** These describe personality issues of teenagers. They can help in leading to a psychiatric diagnosis and sometimes can help in assessing the suicidal propensities of the teenager as well as other areas of difficulty. Projective tests often delve into the underlying psychological issues in a particular teenager. They are usually given along with intelligence tests and other tests as part of a complete battery of psychological testing. The most common ones are the Rorschach (ink blot) Test and the Thematic Apperception Test. Sometimes drawing tests such as the Draw-a-Person Test and the Kinetic Family Drawing tests are also used.

■ **Neuropsychological testing:** These test perceptual motor problems, memory depth learning, and cognitive disabilities and often are used to indicate where there is a problem in the brain's functioning due to neurological deficits or damage. In other words, these tests indicate specific brain dysfunctions. Common are the Bender Visual Motor Gestalt Test, the Luria-Nebraska Neuropsychological Battery, the Beery-Buktenica Developmental Test of Visual Motor Integration, the Benton Visual Retention Test, and the Halstead-Reitan Neuropsychological Battery.

■ **Tests for attention deficit disorder:** Some tests specifically helpful in the diagnosis of attention deficit disorder include the continuous performance tests, the attention profile test, and the test of variable attention.

- **Speech and language assessment:** Before speech and language therapy can be given, a formal speech and language evaluation is necessary. The Peabody Picture Vocabulary Test, tests of language comprehension, the Clark-Madison Test of Oral Language, and the test of language competence are usually given by professionals who specialize in the speech and language area.

- **Forms or questionnaires:** Often parents are given forms or questionnaires to help in the diagnostic process. Sometimes simply the act of filling out the form by both parents, family members, and the teenager can be therapeutic and diagnostic as well. These include tests that measure depression, anxiety, and behavior. They are often given to the evaluator at the time of the mental-health evaluation and are sometimes done as an adjunct for the psychological tester as well.

In summary, it is important to remember that there are a host of adjunctive psychological tests and questionnaires that aid in the diagnosis of your teenager. It should always be kept in mind that these alone do not make a diagnosis but only help in the overall process.

57. Choosing a Therapist

CHOOSING A PROFESSIONAL for evaluation and or therapy is not always easy, as there are so many types of mental-health professionals and individuals within the mental-health field. Three basic criteria should be kept in mind:

- **Professional credentials:** Be certain that their training has involved work with teenagers. This means that a psychiatrist should have received training in adolescent psychiatry during a specific residency in that area. Those with psychology degrees should also have worked with teenagers. Social workers or nurses should also be able to demonstrate that they have had specific experience working with this age group. Once again, advanced training in psychotherapy and psychoanalysis is very valuable. Many people ask whether it is important to go to one particular type of professional over the other. In general, I would advise that for initial psychiatric diagnosis one try to see an adolescent psychiatrist, since he or she is likely to have received the broadest training and will also have medical expertise. If an adolescent psychiatrist is not available in your area, consultation with a psychiatric nurse with a masters degree in psychiatry and special training in teenage issues is advisable. Psychologists and social workers also do evaluations, but it is important that a medical doctor also be consulted to rule out medical conditions that might cause psychiatric symptoms.

- **Personal references:** These are extremely important. Personal recommendations from other professionals or school personnel are often valuable. Recommendations from other patients or their parents may be even be more important.

- **Gut reaction:** Assuming the professional's credentials are in order and there have been some personal references made, you and your teen's feeling about the person after the meeting is probably the most important factor. Although some initial anxiety can be expected, feeling persistently uncomfortable in a therapist's presence is a bad sign. When emotional help is sought, a good feeling about a therapist is crucial. Questions should be asked about scheduling, fees, how missed sessions are handled, and so on before deciding whether you are comfortable with the therapist's business arrangements. Don't feel bad if you don't like the person who friends describe as "the greatest therapist on earth." Once again, it is your own gut reaction to the therapist that counts most, and not all therapists can help all people. Be careful that you don't resent the therapist because your teenager gets along with him, a common feeling among parents, who sometimes feel left out of the therapist/teen relationship. It is difficult for parents of teenagers to tolerate the confidentiality between the therapist and the teenager that is necessary in successful psychotherapy. On the other hand, some teenagers have been upset with the fact that in certain emergency situations therapists have to contact parents. With self-destructive acting out, illegal activity, and other life-threatening issues, parents do have to be told. Indeed, the adolescent mental-health professional often has to walk a tight rope in handling areas of emergency notification and confidentiality. It is important to ask the mental-health professional what school of thought he uses and have him explain this to you. You should be comfortable with the therapist's assumptions, which affect the ways he provides therapy. Also, one should ask what the therapist's expectations are, what the prognosis is, and when some progress should be expected. You might be surprised to hear that progress may take a long time or even, in some cases, that a teenager might get worse before he gets better. Knowing this in advance will help.

In summary, credentials, references, and your gut feelings will help you choose the best therapist for your teen. Before starting formal psychotherapy, the following should be determined: the schedule of sessions, who will be present, fees, cancellation policies, and confidentiality/notification issues. There should be no surprises in these arrangements. Scheduling has to be convenient for all parties involved.

One last point. Sometimes the adolescent mental-health professional won't want to see the parents for a while. He is interested in forming a good, solid, trusting bond with the teenager first. This aggravates parents occasionally, but it shouldn't be seen as inappropriate. In fact, it is often the best way for the therapist to proceed with the teen.

58. Types of Therapy

IF ONE PAYS ATTENTION to the media, it seems like a new type of therapy is invented almost every day. However, there is a range of well-recognized and -regarded therapies that have proven helpful to teenagers over the years. They include the following:

- **Individual insight-oriented psychotherapy:** This is the classic talking cure therapy, also called psychodynamic or psycho-analytic therapy, where an individual goes for a session that lasts anywhere between thirty to sixty minutes. The frequency of this therapy can be anywhere from one to three times a week. The focus of this therapy is to explore the underlying factors that lead to particular symptoms, with an emphasis on having a teenager grow and get back on track toward normal development.

- **Group therapy:** There are various and many types of group therapy. Many group therapies focus on groups of individuals who have similar problems such as depression, addiction, or shared parental problems (such as children of alcoholics or children of mentally ill parents). For some teenagers, group therapy is indicated because of a lack of social skills, which a group can help to foster. Group therapy is often helpful, especially in conjunction with individual therapy. In this case, it is often done by the same therapist who gets a view not only of the individual teenager but how he interacts with others.

- **Family therapy:** Family therapy is also quite helpful because it gives the family a wider perspective on the teen's problems.

Countless times over the years I have seen that a "misbehaving teenager" represents only a small tip of the iceberg. Family therapy treats the family as a system. Often the misbehaving teenager is scapegoated by the family and is acting out the conflicts of the family as a whole. Family therapy sessions usually last longer than individual therapy sessions, since there are more participants.

- **Work with parents:** Sometimes a teenager doesn't even have to come for therapy. Extensive counseling, education, and supportive therapy of parents is sometimes enough to help a teenager indirectly. A subset of this is called parent work, which means that in addition to a child receiving individual therapy a parent gets help also, either from the same therapist or a different one. Work with teenagers has shown that work with a different therapist may be better so that the teenager won't worry about confidentiality being compromised.

- **Detoxification and rehabilitation:** Detoxification and rehabilitation are often used for teenagers who are involved in substance abuse. This can take place either in an outpatient or inpatient setting. It is very important for an addicted teenager to receive individual, group, or family therapy, but only after the teenager stops using drugs. This is why detoxification and/or rehabilitation often come first.

- **Cognitive-behavioral therapy:** Cognitive-behavioral therapy is another popular form of therapy, and has proven helpful in dealing with nearly all forms of psychiatric problems. It combines cognitive therapy, which focuses on negative thinking patterns, and behavior therapy which helps through various exercises to weaken the pathological reactions that people have to various situations. Less explorative than individual psychodynamic therapy, cognitive-behavioral therapy sticks to a plan, part of which is home work done by the patient. It often focuses on one particular symptom, not the overall life picture. Interestingly, it is the most studied of all therapies, probably because it is limited in time and is often the type of therapy referred to in comparisons between drug- and non-drug therapy. (Thus when one reads a study of whether drugs or psychotherapy is more effective, cognitive-behavioral therapy usually is the type of psychotherapy referred to.) Cognitive-behavioral therapy has been found to be specifically helpful for behavior disorders and attention deficit disorder. It has also been proven effective with mentally retarded teenagers, some bed wetters who are still wetting in the teenage years, and for some anxiety, depression, and phobias.

- **Dialectical behavior therapy (DBT):** A special type of behavioral therapy called dialectical behavior therapy (DBT) specifically addresses borderline personality disorders, especially teens with suicidal behaviors. Dialectical therapy draws from Eastern thinking, combining it with Western psychology. As its name implies it has to do with bringing together conflicting trends in a personality. Patients are accepted and validated in the present as they are also supported to change. It is done both in a group and individual settings. Various types of skills that might be helpful are worked on with disturbed teenagers, including how to interact socially, relate one's feelings, and tolerate distress.

- **EMDR:** EMDR, otherwise known as eye movement desensitization reprocessing, has become quite popular although its effectiveness is somewhat in question. It has recently been recommended for a host of disorders but mostly for those suffering from post-traumatic stress disorder and other forms of anxiety. Although the psychological and neurological basis for this therapy is debated, the advocates of this approach, which essentially has the patient move her eyes back and forth from right to left, say that difficult emotions are revealed and dealt with during this rapid eye movement.

- **Hypnosis and biofeedback:** Hypnosis has been proven effective in changing habits and has helped teenagers who have stress-related syndromes and headaches, and who overeat. Hypnosis is a form of focusing attention to a high degree, which leads to a type of relaxation and openness to suggestion. Biofeedback is a type of therapy that helps teenagers who suffer from chronic pain. It helps teenagers learn how to regulate the physical aspects of their being, in particular muscles, blood pressure, and pain, by noting information about what their bodies are doing.

- **Remediation:** Mentioned in the chapter on school problems, remediation should be seen as different from tutoring. Remediation is administered by professionals who have been trained especially in the area of learning disorders to provide therapies that are appropriate to a teenager's specific information-processing problem.

- **Hospitalization:** Sometimes teenagers need to be hospitalized to protect themselves and others, or property, from damage. Teenagers need to be hospitalized when they are suicidal, violent/homicidal, or have become psychotic to the point of disorganization and/or being unable to function appropriately in society. Hospitalization can either be voluntary or involuntary. Although hospitals are helpful to teens who are acutely disturbed, the experience of being hospitalized is often traumatic both to the child and to the parents. In a psychiatric hospital there is usually an immediate full evaluation by many different professionals and then the child usually receives a combination of psychotherapies, medication, family therapy, milieu therapy (therapy provided by the staff on the hospital board), and even recreational and/or occupational therapy. These days most psychiatric hospitalizations are short—sometimes too short. The old days of long-term psychiatric institutionalization seem to be waning.

- **Day and residential treatment:** Short of psychiatric hospitalization is day hospitalization, where the teenager receives treatment in a hospital setting as an outpatient and receives schooling there as well. Individual group therapy and medication, and occupational therapy are also given at the day hospital. Teenagers who require supervision but not confinement in a psychiatric hospital are referred for day hospitalization. Residential treatment is for those teenagers who have been unable to attain an appropriate level of safety in their home environments or are unable to utilize the various therapies that have been offered to them in an outpatient setting. Many chronically misbehaving teenagers, such as those who have violated probation, been chronically truant, and been antisocial to some degree, end up in residential treatment. These are not psychiatric hospitals but centers where children live, receive treatment, and get schooling. They are usually there, under supervision, for an extended period of time. Their supervisors are usually professionals who work at the residential treatment center and provide different types of therapeutic input.

59. Psychotropic Medications

PSYCHOTROPIC DRUGS affect the way we think, feel, and behave. The use of psychotropic drugs in the general population is increasing rapidly. Studies have indicated that the use of psychotropic medications in children and teenagers has been growing especially fast recently. These drugs treat target symptoms that are manifestations of psychiatric disorders. The increasing use of medication in this country is due to a general shift in thinking from the psychologic to the biologic in the field of psychiatry. In addition, the field of psychiatry, and child and adolescent psychiatry in general, have become more medically oriented. Many theories abound about the cause of mental illness, none of which have been proven beyond a doubt, including the famous and well-known chemical-imbalance theory. This theory implies that mental illness and target symptomatology has a lot to do with receptor sites on neurons, alterations in neurotransmitters between neuron endings, and other neurophysiological mechanisms. Despite the fact that much money has been spent and much biological research has been done, there is yet no known cause for mental illness. And to the surprise of many, the mechanism of action of many psychotropic medications is also unknown. There are theories about the way that medications work, but none have been proven definitively. When one hears about the serotonin hypotheses, the catecholamine hypotheses, and other neurochemical mechanisms that account for mental illness, one should keep in mind that the facts are not in and proof has not been established. Despite this we do know that psychotropic medications work in a significant percentage of people who take them. Usually psychotropic medications work better than placebo medications but often not to a very great extent. However, psychotropic medications save lives, prevent school suspensions, prevent child abuse, and prevent progression to psychoses. That's why the use of medication is an essential part of adolescent psychiatry. Although there is debate about the use of medication within the mental-health field itself, it is now a well-established fact that medication for some teenagers forms an essential part of treatment. Psychotropic medication should never be given without ongoing therapeutic intervention at the same time. The use of psychotropic medication to chemically control behavior, moods, or thinking is bad medicine.

The safety of psychotropic medication in young people is an important issue. Teenagers' neurological systems are still somewhat in development and this makes the effects of psychotropic medication on the maturing nervous system a cause for concern. In addition, there aren't many studies about the side effects of medication in young people. Nearly all psychotropic medications are approved for adults, while only a few are approved for children and teenagers. This means that most psychotropic medications in teenagers are prescribed "off label." Although the drugs have been approved for adults the FDA has not approved their use in children. On the medication's labels and in the physician's desk reference this is usually stated. Presently, many of these medications are undergoing studies in children and teenagers. This is not meant to say that off-label usage is either malpractice or dangerous. As a matter of fact, many medications have been used with great efficacy prior to approval. We know that psychotropic medications, approved or not for teenagers, do help as they do in adults.

Despite the fact that the chemical-imbalance theory has never been proven, that receptors have never been proven, and thus the causes of psychiatric illness are still unknown, we do know that psychotropic medications help. You should not fear the use of psychotropic medications. However, you should discuss any of your concerns and anxieties with the prescribing adolescent psychiatrist. Remember, one does not necessarily have to know the specific cause of illness to treat it appropriately and one does not have to know the specific mechanism of a drug action to also get good results.

After a mental-health evaluation, or sometimes during the course of a psychotherapy that is being conducted without your child receiving medication, a decision to start psychotropic medication might be made. Usually an evaluation by an adolescent psychiatrist will be made at that time leading to this decision. Feel free to ask any or all of the following questions prior to and during the course of administration and prescription of psychotropic medication.

- Find out the name of the drug, which is usually the brand name, and even the chemical or generic name if necessary.

- Discuss the reason why the psychiatrist has picked a particular drug for your teenager. (As above, please bear in mind that nearly all the drugs prescribed for your teenager have not been approved for use in teenagers. Also keep in mind that such off-label usage is common.) Ask the psychiatrist what experience he has had with the use of this drug in the teenage population, and also ask what studies have reported.

- Ask about the dosage and how it should be taken; for example, should it be taken on a full stomach or an empty one? Can it be taken with any foods? What if a dose is missed?

- Ask about side effects. Most side effects are mild such as dry mouth, changes in appetite, or minor changes in weight, but some could be more serious and you should know what to look for with the particular drug your child is taking. Although it is extremely rare with psychotropic drugs, also ask about the addictive potential of the medication.

- Ask about adverse reactions that might occur when taking the drug with other drugs. Ask for a list of any dangerous drug interactions.

- Ask how long your child is expected to take this medication, what is the specific expectation, and how the drug will be monitored by the psychiatrist. How long will it take to work? When will use be discontinued?

- Complete medical clearance is necessary before taking medication and a teenage physical examination, routine blood tests, and a cardiogram are necessary. Also, some blood tests might be required during treatment with certain drugs.

■ You can ask the psychiatrist about the cost of the medication, but it is probable that he is not familiar with the exact dollar figure associated with various drugs. Your pharmacist might be better able to supply that information.

Psychotropic medication has been found to be effective in conjunction with other therapies for a host of teenage psychiatric disorders. These include but are not limited to anxiety and depression, psychosis, aggressive behavior, violent behavior, attention deficit disorder with or without hyperactivity, obsessive-compulsive disorder, some aspects of eating disorders, and sleep problems as well. That is, nearly all categories of psychiatric disturbance in teenagers can be affected by one or more drugs. It should also be noted that it is common these days to prescribe multiple and simultaneous drugs for a condition and thus teenagers like many adults in this country may often be on more than one drug—sometimes three or four. This trend toward "polypharmacy" is growing in this country. However, you should not necessarily be alarmed if your adolescent psychiatrist suggests multiple medications. Also keep in mind that drugs are usually started at the lowest dose to be sure that there are no allergic reactions or other reactions to the drugs. It is then that the drugs are increased in dosage. Do not be alarmed by this.

What follows is a list of the brand names of drugs of different classes. The brand names are the most common names. Please note that each brand name has an associated or generic name; ask your pharmacist about these. When going to the pharmacy for prescriptions you can, after consultation with your psychiatrist, ask whether the generic name is available and whether it is cheaper. Remember, some brand names do not have generic prescription equivalents on the market yet.

Classes of Commonly Prescribed Psychotropic Drugs for Teenagers

Stimulants. The stimulant medications are commonly used in adolescent psychiatry. Stimulant medications are best known for treating attention deficit hyperactivity disorder but are also found to be useful in other behavior disorders in the teenage years, including oppositional defiant disorder and other behavior disorders. Stimulant medications are essentially of three varieties. There are the methylphenidate derivatives, the amphetamine category, and a new drug called Strattera (a drug that has been considered more desirable than the former ones due to its lesser potential for abuse).

Stimulants are chemicals that activate our central nervous systems and thus it might be surprising that we use them for syndromes including hyperactivity, impulsivity, inattention, and behavioral acting out. Paradoxically in these syndromes, the stimulant medication lessens these problems. Actually, if given to children who have been incorrectly diagnosed, such as those with only anxiety-induced misbehavior, we will often see an induction of hyperactivity and restlessness and not the calming effect found in teenagers with ADD and ADHD.

Over the years many parents have expressed concern about giving their children stimulants since some people become addicted to them. Some states have classified these drugs as controlled substances due to unscrupulous prescribing by some doctors and street use, combined with the potential for abuse. While it is true that stimulants can be abused, and can lead to tolerance and withdrawal (addiction, in those prone to this problem), and have recently even been associated with an increase in street use as inhalants, when given under appropriate medical supervision they are remarkably safe and well tested. In fact, there have been reports that proper use of these drugs in children actually leads to less substance abuse in teenagers because many of their behavioral problems will have been dealt with. This makes them less prone to antisocial acting out including substance abuse. So many authors have downright scared parents into taking the position of withholding these drugs, often comparing them to illicit cocaine abuse, that I have had to spend much time explaining to these frightened parents the many studies of efficacy and safety in this class of drugs and the fact that when properly used in conjunction with other interventions they can help enormously.

Stimulant medication has also been found to be effective in narcolepsy, which is an unusual syndrome in the teenage years. The most common side effects of stimulant medications are decreased appetite, abdominal distress, headaches, and sleeplessness. Some of them might cause tics as well, especially if there is a history of tics in a particular teenager or a strong family history.

Following is a table of the most common approved drugs used for ADD and ADHD with their brand and generic names along with durations of activity. Dosage amount and method of using should be left to your teen's psychiatrist. Please note that the introduction of sustained release stimulants has made prescribing much easier for your teenager, as once-a-day dosing is now possible.

ADD AND ADHD MEDICATIONS

METHYLPHENIDATE CLASS

Brand Name	Generic Name	Action Duration
Ritalin	methylphenidate	3–4 hours
Ritalin SR	methylphenidate	3–8 hours
Ritalin LA	methylphenidate	8 hours
Concerta	methylphenidate	12 hours
Metadate CD	methylphenidate	8 hours
Metadate ER	methylphenidate	4–8 hours
Focalin	dexmethylphenidate	4 hours
Methylin	methylphenidate	4 hours

AMPHETAMINE CLASS

Brand Name	Generic Name	Action Duration
Dexedrine	amphetamine	5 hours
Adderall	amphetamine mixture	4–6 hours
Adderall XR	amphetamine mixture	8 hours
Dexedrine sustained release	amphetamine	8 hours

OTHER

Brand Name	Generic Name	Action Duration
Strattera	atomoxetine	5–6 hours

Antidepressants. Although these drugs are called antidepressants they are used for more than depression. They are prescribed for generalized anxiety disorder, panic attacks, and phobias, and also have some use in bed-wetting, obsessive-compulsive disorder, post-traumatic stress disorder and even in attention deficit disorder. Some are used to treat teenagers with anorexia or bulimia.

There are basically two large classes of antidepressant medications. The original ones were called tricyclic antidepressants, named for their chemical configurations, which have become somewhat less popular because of their common troublesome side effects, especially dry mouth and tendency to cause constipation, blurry vision, heart effects, and toxicity in overdose. They have been replaced to a great extent by the selective serotonin reuptake inhibitors (SSRIs), named for what we think they do in the nervous system. There are other antidepressants that fall somewhere between the tricyclic antidepressants and the serotonin reuptake inhibitors with regard to their proposed mechanisms of action (see other antidepressants below).

Although no one is sure of the minute details, all antidepressants are said to work by altering the concentration of neurotransmitters (chemicals secreted by neurons in the central nervous system into spaces between neurons called synapses). After the body secretes the neurotransmitter it is absorbed by a neuron across the way or reabsorbed by the neuron that secreted it in the first place. It is proposed that in some way the antidepressant attaches to a receptor on a neuron that was meant for the body's neurotransmitter; for example, the SSRIs are thought to attach to a neuron that is involved with reabsorbing serotonin that has been secreted into a synapse. It is felt that depressed people don't make enough of the neurotransmitter serotonin to get across the space from one neuron to another, and if the drug can block the natural reuptake that goes on in all of us then the amount available in the space will increase. It is postulated that with this increase depression will be diminished. The same goes for other antidepressants, which inhibit reuptake of another neurotransmitter called noradrenalin. Some antidepressants inhibit reuptake of both types of neurotransmitters. Some people prematurely conclude that since so much research is being done with these chemicals and into the chemistry of our nervous systems, depression must be due to an imbalance of chemicals. Unfortunately, we don't know enough yet to determine exactly how these chemicals work and we certainly cannot conclude that our teenagers' problems with depression are caused by chemical imbalances (possibly depression causes the imbalance). But putting that argument aside, we do know that these drugs work better than placebos and are useful for treating symptoms of depression, preferably along with talk therapy.

The antidepressants take time to work, averaging from three to six weeks and sometimes more depending on how rapidly the psychiatrist raises the dose and whether side effects slow the pace or result. The selective serotonin reuptake inhibitors often cause upset stomach, can cause insomnia if taken late in the day, and also can cause tiredness, headaches, and even sexual dysfunction in adolescents; the older tricyclics are known to cause sedation, headache, dry mouth, constipation, low blood pressure when getting up quickly, and sometimes even cardiogram changes and difficulty initiating urination. While those are the most common side effects, there are more serious ones which, while rare, should be discussed with the prescribing psychiatrist. Most side effects are mild and often pass or become tolerated with time.

Following is a list of the most common antidepressants by generic and chemical name.

Dosage amount and method of prescribing should be discussed with your psychiatrist.

ANTIDEPRESSANTS

SELECTIVE SEROTONIN REUPTAKE INHIBITORS

Brand name	Chemical Name
Prozac	fluoxetine
Paxil*	paroxetine*
Zoloft	sertraline
Luvox	fluvoxamine
Celexa	citalopram
Lexapro	escitalopram

*Recent studies have led the FDA to warn against prescription of this drug to young people due to the possibility of increased suicidal ideation.

COMMON CYCLIC ANTIDEPRESSANTS

Brand name	Chemical Name
Elavil	amitriptyline
Tofranil	imipramine
Asendin	amoxapine
Anafranil	clomipramine
Norpramin	desipramine
Adapin/Sinequan	doxepin
Aventyl/Pamelor	nortriptyline
Vivactil	protriptyline
Surmontil	trimipramine

OTHER ANTIDEPRESSANTS

Brand name	Chemical Name
Wellbutrin (and SR)	bupropion
Effexor (and XR)	venlafaxine
Serzone	nefazodone
Remeron	mirtazapine

Antipsychotic medications. As the name implies, antipsychotic medications were originally developed to treat more serious forms of psychiatric illness called the psychoses, which often include hallucinations and delusions and syndromes such as schizophrenia, psychotic bipolar illness, and other psychotic disorders. Their use has been extended to include many other syndromes in young people including tics, serious behavior disorders, severe anxiety, and even teenage behavioral aspects of autism. The first antipsychotic medications caused many neurological side effects and were thus called neuroleptic drugs because they mimicked neurological illnesses. These original neuroleptic drugs included Thorazine, Mellaril, Prolixin, Haldol, Navane, and Stelazine. Because of the side effects, much research has been done in the development of the newer antipsychotic drugs, which are called atypical antipsychotics because they usually do not cause the neurological side effects of the earlier generation of drugs. It is this group of drugs that increasingly is used in psychiatry for indications including psychosis but also for the other conditions mentioned. Like other medications, there are a number of rather common and less serious side effects including fatigue, nausea, headache, and memory impairment. Some also cause abnormal blood sugar, electrical heart irregularities, and weight gain. Dosage amount as well as method of prescribing should be left to your teen's psychiatrist. He can also explain the more rare and serious side effects.

COMMON ANTIPSYCHOTIC MEDICATIONS

Brand name	Chemical Name
Risperdal	risperidone
Seroquel	quetiapine
Abilify	aripiprazole
Zyprexa	olanzapine
Geodon	ziprasidone
Clozaril	clozapine

Mood-stabilizing medications. Mood-stabilizing drugs were originally used for the treatment and prevention of the mood swings associated with bipolar disorder. Lithium is the most well known and still one of the most effective drugs in this class. In time, other mood stabilizers, especially drugs used in neurology for the control of seizures, were added to the list of mood-stabilizing drugs. These mood stabilizers are not only helpful in treating bipolar disorder but any mood-swing disorder, impulsive behavior, explosive disorder, and aggressive-behavior disorder. Mood stabilizers often cause intestinal upset, weight gain, slight shaking, fatigue, and sometimes dizziness. Some of the drugs cause increased urination and increased thirst, as well as trouble with thyroid functioning. Depakote, in particular, has been known to cause polycystic ovary problems in teenage girls, who should be monitored for this.

COMMON MOOD-STABILIZING DRUGS

Brand name	Chemical Name
Tegretol	carbamazepine
Topamax	topiramate
Neurontin	gabapentin
Depakote	divalproex sodium
Lamictal	lamotrigine

Antianxiety medications. Antianxiety drugs have been around for many years. They are helpful in the treatment of severe anxiety. They are also useful in the short-term treatment of insomnia. The most common and well-known ones are the benzodiazepines but drugs from the class of antihistamines also are used for the short-term treatment of anxiety. In addition, the atypical antipsychotics and previously mentioned antidepressants help with anxiety. There is some concern over the addictive potential of benzodiazepines. This is rarely seen when given at the correct dosage and for limited amounts of time. But because of the issue of addiction and withdrawal, including seizures, teenagers who take these should be monitored closely by their prescribing psychiatrists.

COMMON ANTIANXIETY MEDICATIONS

BENZODIAZEPINES

Brand name	Chemical Name
Xanax	alprazolam
Valium	diazepam
Klonopin	clonazepam
Ativan	lorazepam

ANTIHISTAMINES

Benadryl	diphenhydramine
Vistaril/Atarax	hydroxyzine

OTHER

BuSpar	buspirone

Sleep medications. Sleep medications are those used to induce sleep in teenagers who have insomnia. These should be used with great caution in teenagers, and only short term, keeping in mind that most insomnia problems are linked to and are often part of other psychiatric syndromes that can be treated with the appropriate medication and psychotherapy. Common sleep medications include the benzodiazepine antianxiety medications and the antihistamines. It should also be mentioned that some of the side effects for other psychotropic medications include sleepiness and thus some are given at night not only to treat the target symptomatology of the particular psychiatric syndrome but also to induce sleep. A common example is in a disruptive and aggressive teenager who also has insomnia and is treated with one of the newer atypical antipsychotics such as Risperdal. Often taking the Risperdal at night will induce sleep as well as decrease the disruptive behavior. Another example would be the use of Trazodone, an antidepressant, with particularly strong sleep-induction side effects. Benadryl is also commonly used.

COMMON INSOMNIA MEDICATIONS

Brand name	Chemical Name
Ambien	zolpidem tartrate
Sonata	zaleplon

Other Medications Helpful for Teenage Psychiatric Problems

There are other medications used to treat teenagers. Catapres and Tenex are used for behavior disorders and even sometimes for flashbacks in teenagers with post-traumatic stress disorder. Inderal is used for anxiety disorders and the prevention of migraine headaches. Enuresis or bed-wetting is often treated with DDAVP, which affects the pituitary gland and often results in a decrease in the problem. This is often available in pill and nasal-spray form.

Several things to keep in mind are that psychotropic medications should not be given alone and as the only form of therapy. Most are quite safe, although untested and unapproved for use in teenagers, and side effects are usually easily controlled by an immediate decrease in dosage. Multiple medications are often given. Lastly, comfort with your teenager's psychiatrist and his ability to explain what is going on are the most important considerations in choosing who will medicate your teenager.

IX

Frequently Asked Questions

Is my teenager okay?

This question, in one form or another, is the most frequent one I am asked. That's because parents are worried. Nothing is more upsetting than the thought that one of our children is sick and cannot be helped. Parents will do almost anything to help. There is no good answer until I have examined the teenager, her family, and environment. After an assessment I can usually come up with a pretty good estimate of how impaired a particular teen is and what might be the prognosis. Most parents are excessively worried, especially when it comes to mental problems. These problems usually have no physically measurable signs and appear strange and enigmatic. Most teenagers undergoing a period of psychiatric problems recover; few end up with lifelong illnesses. The chance of full recovery is heightened with appropriate professional intervention and especially with family changes that might be necessary to relieve stress. That last part is the hardest because often parents have no idea they might be part of the problem and may be resistant to changing their ways. But it can be done.

Are mental-health problems inherited?

Maybe. The answer to this question is not entirely straightforward. There have been many studies about the inheritability of mental problems. There is some evidence that our genes exert an influence on our mental functioning. But this is far from uniform, and there are a lot of questions still lingering when we try to compare the relative influences of our genes (nature) versus the way we were brought up (nurture). Recently there has been a shift to favoring nature, but I think this has more to do with the increased use of medication and rationalizing this trend than with reality. Parents, role models, and cultural and subcultural influences still hold plenty of weight both for the better and for the worse. At this point we can't do much for our genes but we can certainly do a lot for the way we nurture.

Do you think my teenager will be a criminal psychopath?
He seems so angry and seems to make his own rules?

Probably not. The overwhelming majority of teenagers who commit antisocial acts don't become criminals. Over 85 percent of teenagers commit antisocial acts at some point but less than 1 percent ever become criminals. Unless a teenager meets the criteria for a severe behavior problem like conduct disorder there is little to worry about as far as future prison time is concerned. Angry feelings are very common and are often indicators that your teenager is experiencing some degree of anxiety or helplessness induced by the normal stressors of adolescence like social or educational demands. Unless this anger presents as a danger to himself or others the best approach is to try to understand what is troubling him and give some aid, if possible. When anxiety decreases, anger goes away. No scars are left. And your help will have increased your bond.

Is depression a normal part of adolescence?

No! The teenage years can be very tumultuous ones. As a result, adolescents have variable moods ranging from giddy euphoria to the depth of despair. Unrequited love, rejection by a clique, college worries, academic stress, athletic competition, and the anxiety of moving away from parents emotionally and distancing themselves from the dependent comfort of home and the like, all feed into this mood variability. Usually these moods pass quickly, and many parents are actually more amazed and befuddled by the rapidity of change than the quality of these moods. All of this is quite different from depression, which is a clinical syndrome characterized by alterations in feelings, behavior, and thinking that usually don't go away. Deep despair, withdrawal leading to isolation, persistent sadness, thoughts of death, suicidal contemplation, dressing in black, and academic failure are different from the stressful but normal mood swings of the teenage years. Depression needs treatment; mood swings need patience.

When a teenager goes on medication is it for life?

Usually not. Most psychiatric disorders are treated for a circumscribed amount of time after which both therapy and medication is stopped. There are uncommon situations, such as with the more severe syndromes like schizophrenia or severe bipolar disorder, when medication might be needed for extended periods of time. Also when children take ADD and ADHD medications, this often is done for years but is stopped after a final successful adjustment is made.

I heard that all teenagers undergo an identity crisis. Is that true, and what should I expect when it happens?

It is not true that most teenagers have an identity crisis. Although adolescence can be a tumultuous time for both the teenager and the family, there is rarely a crisis of identity in which a teenager loses his ability to adapt to most circumstances. Identity crisis is an old term, popular a generation ago, that described a moderate to severe psychiatric syndrome such as an anxiety state, a depressive episode, and even a psychotic breakdown. While some psychiatrists called this "normal," we now know that it is a serious situation and needs professional intervention. Sometimes an "identity crisis" is the beginning of the expression of a borderline personality disorder.

I thought bipolar illness was only found in adults but my son's psychiatrist just told me he had it?

Bipolar illness, formerly known as manic-depressive illness, used to be diagnosed in adults only. It usually is characterized by periods of depression alternating with periods of being manic (high) or just about manic, called hypomanic. These periods of mood swing are often separated in time, but sometimes they occur together or separated by very little time. Sometimes the so-called manic periods are characterized by irritability as well as the other common symptoms of mania, which include a degree of euphoria, racing thoughts, hyperactivity, increased energy, rapid speech, and a decreased need for sleep. Recently it has been found that many youngsters suffer from bipolar illness but often are confused with those with attention deficit hyperactivity disorder (inattention, hyperactivity, and impulsivity) or those with just a behavior disorder. The key to diagnosis in young people is to remember that the periods of depression and mania are often not separated in time into discreet mood swings and that often the presenting sign of the manic shift is solely irritability and angry acting out behaviors. The good news: there are many more effective treatments for teenagers, so the suffering from this syndrome has been diminished considerably.

I have found out that my teenage daughter's friend is involved in using drugs and cutting school. Should I let her parents know? She's such a nice girl, but I worry that my daughter will be angry with me for interfering and that her friend might get in big trouble.

This issue is thorny and one which many parents face each day. There is no single satisfactory answer since there are many factors that will influence your decision. One is how you found out about the friend's problems. If your daughter told you then you might have an easy path because it is obvious that she wanted you to know and probably wants you to take action (although she might express great ambivalence when asked). On the other hand, if you found out in other ways you not only have to overcome your worries about her friend's problems and reactions but also about your own child's reaction and even her own involvement in such behaviors. I think the best route in these cases is to discuss what you know with your daughter first. After that you will have to decide together how to approach her friend so that she might get the help she needs, since that is what we are after in such cases. In cases of emergency, there is little doubt that the parents have to be notified one way or the other. It is the more common gray-area cases that give us most of the trouble. I would err on the side of notification, taking into consideration that there might be a period of time during which you and your daughter are on the outs. In the long run, most teenagers are thankful when parents step in and help their friends. Lastly, there may be a price to pay regarding the reactions of the parents who are being notified. Many feel insulted, invaded, and ashamed. Again, we have to keep our eye on the bigger picture—the help that might finally be received.

Is it true that teenagers are more violent than ever?

Believe it or not, this is not true, although you would not know that if you watch the news. With the recent explosion of twenty-four-hour news coverage we see and hear a lot more about violent teens. We are exposed to many gory details of teen violence. We also see the teens' homes, their parents in grief, and the victims either being carried out of schools in body bags or telling reporters of the ordeals they have endured. Despite this increased in-your-face coverage, there is no evidence of increased violence among today's teenagers. In fact, it seems to have decreased. What has changed is that the methods used are more lethal than in the past, when school-yard fights settled the score, and the detailed coverage has terrified parents.

Should I worry about what my teenager watches on TV and at the movies?

While you should not necessarily worry, you should be involved enough to know the details of your teenager's exposure to media influences, including on the Internet. Until recently, there was little evidence of the negative effects of media exposure to sexual and violent themes on children, but we now know the whole story isn't in yet. Current studies imply a far more deleterious effect on young people who watch strongly sexual and aggressive programs and movies. It is a parent's responsibility to know what is influencing her teen, to be available to discuss what has been seen, and to answer questions. Although a parent might be called old-fashioned or some such description, you can be sure teens fare far better with parental involvement in their lives than not. So get involved, tolerate the name calling, and have a positive influence.

Neither my daughter nor son has ever asked a sexual question of me or my husband. Should we be doing something in this area?

Yes. Most teenagers learn most about sex from their peers and this education starts way before the teenage years. The subject is a difficult one for the teenager and even more so for many parents. There is a common myth that if it is not discussed it isn't going on—or if discussed it will go on. In reality, most teenagers are very interested in sex and more are having it at younger ages than a generation ago. Guidance is needed to avoid premature and anxiety-provoking sexual involvement and/or the results of unsafe sex, including teenage pregnancy or a sexually transmitted and sometimes fatal illness. Let your children know you are available for a discussion. Be patient. Teenagers will come to parents if they know they aren't going to be judgmental. If you can't do it, ask your spouse, another family member, or even a friend. You also can ask your teen's doctor, school personnel, or a counselor for help. There are a host of books for teenagers on the subject. Remember, your teenager has questions and is probably worried about asking. Open the door, be available, and try to be accepting. Don't lecture and don't give advice before you know where your particular child is at with regard to the whole issue. Also, you don't have to share your sexual experiences; your child probably doesn't want to know about that. She or he just wants information, acceptance, and help if there has been some trouble in the area. Lastly, try to get the correct information about sexuality before you answer a question that is unfamiliar to you. This topic is still one that creates anxiety in parents despite the "sexual revolution," and much of the information we carry around is emotionally charged and sometimes wrong.

My son's therapist says information discussed during sessions is confidential, but as a parent and one who is paying I feel I should be informed about his treatment. Am I right?

You might be right about wanting to know what is going on in your son's therapy, but it would be highly unusual for a therapist to share such information with a parent of a teenager. Confidentiality is of paramount importance for a therapeutic relationship to develop. This is especially true with teenagers, who are in the final phase of emotionally separating from parents. The usual rule is that all information remains confidential between therapist and teenager while any information that comes from a parent is shared with the patient. The only exception is when a therapist diagnoses an emergency situation. In those cases a parent is notified.

Over the years my son has increasingly been drawn to other kids who I think are not great for him. They seem to have no goals, they hang out a lot, and I worry about antisocial behavior. What should I do?

This is a tough question and one which demands great control on your part. Friendships are of great importance during the teenage years and parents have less control over this area of a child's life as time goes on. The friends that your son has chosen in some way reflect some aspects of himself. It is your job to try to find out why he is attracted to this group. It might be that he is trying to distance himself from you and the rest of the family and has associated with a group of boys whose values and goals are different from those of your family. Or it might suggest that he is under some pressure to succeed that he considers stressful and is acting out this message. There are other psychological possibilities as well. It would be a mistake to forbid him to associate with his buddies. In fact, we all know that the forbidden fruit often seems even more attractive. Strict statements about not hanging out with certain individuals will often backfire, increase the behaviors you are seeking to diminish, and increase family tension. It is better to act therapeutically and explore what he likes about these other kids. You might learn a lot about him through such indirect questioning. If your son seems to be drifting to ganglike activities with group involvement in violence, substance abuse, and/or other antisocial behaviors, then a more direct approach is needed.

My whole family seems to have had trouble with alcoholism. Is it inherited? What should I do about my teenager's problem?

The jury is still out on the question of the inheritability of alcoholism. While there was some evidence from studies over the last twenty years, more recent inquiries have failed to substantiate the genetic link among family members. Regardless of biology, there are things you can do to prevent your teenager from abusing alcohol. First, be aware of her use. This is not always easy but being on guard for drinking behaviors, drunkenness, the odor of alcohol, the habits of her friends, hangover syndromes, increase in uninhibited behaviors, and severe moodiness are all pointers. Secondly, remember that the best deterrent is setting a good example. If you or your spouse have a drinking problem, get some help. You can bet that a child or teenager who sees her parents solve their problems by drinking is at increased risk herself. Thirdly, if you come to the realization that your child has an alcohol problem don't wait, don't listen to promises, and don't believe the rationalizations and denial mechanisms that you are told. Call your doctor, local substance-abuse organization, a center or professional specializing in this problem, or the school guidance counselor. And just in case you start to feel wishy-washy, remember that alcohol is involved in 40 percent of all non-natural deaths that occur in this country.

Are there other problems that girls with anorexia have besides the obvious nutritional ones?

Yes. Teenage girls with anorexia often have accompanying hormonal imbalances that often throw off or obliterate the capacity to menstruate normally. Some anorexics stop menstruating completely. The decrease in estrogen caused by low weight also affects the bones which often leads to osteopenia or even osteoporosis. These silent diseases only make themselves known when it is too late and fractures have occurred. In addition to any psychological or psychopharmacological treatment of anorexia, it is also very important to seek medical advice. Your anorexic teenager should have an endocrinologist (hormone specialist) examine her. A bone density study, often overlooked, is also very important. If bone thinning is diagnosed, treatment with safe amounts of female hormones can help.

Some professionals I see on television say it's good for kids to express anger; others say it's not. What's the story?

Anger is a perfectly normal human emotion. It is usually a response to a feeling of some degree of helplessness and signals that some assistance is needed to stabilize it. It is as natural as any other feeling. Anger is a great communicator of distress and can be a sign that a parent should step in and help. In fact, it is well known that if anger is ignored, denied, or reacted against in a harsh fashion, children will learn that this normal feeling is a bad one and they will try to repress it. If anger is repressed (pushed out of awareness), it can often contribute to a host of other psychiatric problems. Unfortunately, many parents are scared of angry teenagers who are often loud, bellicose, and volatile. Many parents learned the wrong message about this normal feeling from their own parents and are ill-suited to understand the communicative value of healthy anger. Instead of searching for the underlying reasons for the feeling of helplessness, they punish, lecture, and get rigid, thereby reinforcing the idea that anger is a bad feeling. Treating anger this way leads to even more anger, and the cycle just repeats itself. Only when your teenager's anger seems persistent and incomprehensible, despite your best efforts at understanding it, or if the anger seems a danger to others, the environment, or your teenager should professional help be sought.

My fourteen-year-old daughter has had weight problems for several years and is getting even heavier. Do you think it's a problem with her glands?

Probably not. Only about .5 percent of obese people have a physical problem such as a hormone imbalance or a medication-induced weight gain. Obesity (being greater than 10 percent of your normal weight) is a growing problem in the United States, including in the teenage years. Not only does it lead to many medical problems but it affects self-esteem and peer acceptance. The reasons for obesity are quite simple to understand, although much more difficult to change quickly. Simply put, overeating and lack of exercise are the root causes. There may be emotional reasons at the core like depression, stress, peer problems, and the like, as well as a household in which overeating is a cure for everything. The only way to treat this issue is to cut calories, increase exercise, and attend to the underlying emotional and family issues that stimulate the obese lifestyle. Pills, wonder diets, and other quick cures don't work. Changing eating habits is a major life change and takes time, effort, and support. Weight Watchers helps too!

My son came out to us about his homosexuality last year. I thought this would ease his worries, but he still seems depressed and uptight. I thought coming out was the beginning of the end of issues with being gay.

While it is a good sign that your son was courageous and comfortable enough to inform you about his being gay, unfortunately it is not the end of stressful times. Being gay is still somewhat stigmatized and frightening to those who lack knowledge and are prejudiced. Many gay teenagers feel bullied, harassed, rejected, different, vulnerable, and downright depressed about being gay in such a society. The suicide rate among gay teens is higher than in the non-gay teen population.

They often feel they lack the support they need. It is important that you continue to listen to his worries, support him, and also help him contact local or national teen gay support organizations.

We don't have guns in our house, but our son's friend's house is full of them. The friend's parents are gun enthusiasts. I worry when he goes there because he comes home talking about what he has seen. What should I do?

You are right to be worried. With about ninety to one hundred million people owning guns, we live in dangerous times. Accidents can and do happen and they are often fatal. Not only do they occur in teenagers' own homes but in friends' homes as well. About one-third of fatal accidents with firearms occur inside the homes of friends. The basic rule of safety is that there should be no guns around. But that is unlikely in our country. So we can only hope that all safety rules are adhered to, such as locking away guns, unloading them, and keeping ammunition locked elsewhere and never leaving them unattended. The problem comes when other parents own guns. How do we tell them about the rules? With courage and diplomacy. Since children's lives are at stake, try to err on the side of safety even if your teen is angry. Speak to the other parents, and be sure that all safety rules are being adhered to. You should not be hearing about your teen's fascination with his friend's family's guns unless you are sure that appropriate supervision is being offered at all times. It's a rough one but could be lifesaving!

Recently my daughter has gotten into weird music. She locks herself in her room and blasts "psycho stuff" having to do with sex, drugs, and mean-sounding music. What should we do?

Teenagers listen to music for many different and usually healthy reasons. By listening to music they fit in socially, try on different roles in their imaginations, and usually cause no harm to themselves or others. It might be difficult for parents to hear songs about drugs, nirvana, suicide, gangs, racism, sexism, and sex, but the music usually is just a phase. As with many other trends, it will pass without any lasting damage. Music only becomes a concern when your teenager is manifesting other emotional difficulties and is using music-listening to get away from problems, to substitute for real-life activities, and to accompany her in depressive withdrawal. In these cases the music is giving you a message about depression, severe social problems, drug use, and even suicide plans and parents must intervene. Parents shouldn't turn off the music but listen and learn about their teenagers' problems and get the required help. Don't panic about music per se but do worry if there are other signs of disturbance and take action.

Is sexual abuse an issue for teenagers or does this only happen to younger kids? How do I know if it is happening?

Sexual abuse happens to teenagers just as it does to younger children. Sexual abuse is a most serious and dangerous invasion of the boundaries of your teenager. Unfortunately, it is often kept secret for a host of reasons having to do with shame, guilt, fear, and in some cases family loyalties, so we don't find out about it for some time. Teenagers who are sexually abused are vulnerable to depression, confusion, feeling worthless, losing trust in all human relationships, becoming substance abusers, becoming prostitutes, and in general losing touch with the true meaning of sexual relations in loving relationships. There are no specific signs of sexual abuse other than a child disclosing it. But there are more general signs that might indicate something is wrong, especially if they occur rather suddenly. These include seductive sexual behaviors; increased sexual acting out; acute depression, secretiveness, and withdrawal; school refusal and/or failure; sleeping and eating changes; and heightened moodiness, anger, and even suicidal ideas or attempts. These signs can indicate other emotional problems and a professional will need to help diagnose sexual abuse.

Do learning disabilities affect teenagers?

Yes. Learning disabilities are considered neurological conditions that affect a person's ability to process information. While many such disabilities are diagnosed in childhood many are not. As a result teenagers still present with them when they enter junior high or high school. The lack of an earlier diagnosis complicates the picture since repeated failure often lowers self-esteem and increases feelings of failure, which in turn often lead to behavioral problems and being turned off to all aspects of school. But it's not too late. Adequate psychological testing and a thorough educational evaluation can still come up with the diagnosis and there are now many treatments specifically geared to remediating the problems. For some teenagers hope will have to be restored and for some psychotherapy will be advised to help them see that there maladaptive techniques, which evolved to cope with the undiagnosed disability, are no longer needed and in fact are detracting from their lives.

I've heard that talking about suicide might put the idea in a teenager's head. Is that true?

No. Teenagers commit suicide. Often there are signs before the act. Mostly it is depressed or psychotic teenagers who commit suicide. If you notice that your teenager is depressed (there are many signs including sleeping and eating changes, withdrawal, sadness, having the blues, anger, violence, loss of interest and pleasure in things, school failure, substance use, neglect of appearance, physical complaints, and boredom, to mention some) or acting bizarrely, hearing voices, and talking about unusual and incomprehensible ideas then there will probably be concern about suicide. This will become heightened even more if your teenager talks about feeling hopeless, useless, worthless; gives away important objects, a sign that he is putting his "affairs in order"; and talks of the afterlife, death, morbidity, and the like. Discussing your observations and asking about suicide can be lifesaving and not in any way the wrong thing to do. Not only will it open the way to getting immediate help, but it will also give the message that you are there, concerned, and attentive, and this will go a long way on the road to cure.

My sixteen-year-old daughter has been hiding what appear to be many cuts that she has inflicted on her forearms. She usually wears long sleeves, even in the summer, but I saw these when we went shopping last week. She had to change in the dressing room and called me for help. I almost fainted. Is she suicidal?

Odds are that your daughter is not suicidal, since teenagers who cut themselves (and there are many) are usually not out to kill themselves but on the other hand to soothe themselves from painful emotions such as anxiety, perplexity, and sometimes just vague feelings of being overwhelmed by emotion or despair. The cutting, and in fact any self-injurious behavior, seems to bring a temporary feeling of relief, a feeling of being alive, and even elicits a degree of post-cutting self-care that the teenager feels she is not getting elsewhere. While most cutters are not acutely suicidal they are disturbed and need help. It might be difficult since the cutting is often a source of shame and is hidden from parents and most friends. Although the reason that a youngster will cut or harm her body differs in each case, there can be some certainty that this behavior has been resorted to because of a feeling that there is faulty communication or emotional distance in the family setting. Your daughter and possibly the whole family will probably have to re-examine the usual modes of communication and restore a more natural interpersonal atmosphere.

I realize that most kids really start caring about how they look in the teenage years, but my fifteen-year-old son spends hours in front of the mirror checking out minor skin blemishes before he leaves the house. His skin looks normal to us. Is he going crazy?

No, he's not. While the teenage years bring increased self-consciousness and a focus on looks, sometimes to what appears to be an incredible degree, standing in front of a mirror for hours fixating sounds like the condition called body dysmorphic disorder. This condition is akin to obsessive-compulsive disorder and usually manifests itself in a young person fixating on one particular area of the body (hair, eyes, skin, facial asymmetry, and so on) and becoming preoccupied to a degree that far outlasts the usual teenage concerns. Bodily defects are exaggerated far out of proportion. Sometimes so-called defects are impossible for an outsider to even see. The obsession takes increasing amounts of time from normal activities and sometimes body areas are covered (with hats and sunglasses) as well. It often leads to social withdrawal and academic problems as school becomes a place to avoid. Family life sometimes begins centering around the suffering teen's condition. Often such a teenager suffers from anxiety, depression, or obsessive-compulsive disorder. The teenager with this condition needs a professional consultation to be sure there aren't more serious problems that need attention. In most cases there is a gradual diminution with time; in others treatment will be necessary in the form of therapy and possibly a course of psychotropic medication.

My sixteen-year-old son continues to misbehave despite what I try. He has been suspended from school almost each week, hangs out with the worst kids in the neighborhood, and has started to come home drunk and stoned. We tried school counseling and therapy to no avail. What do we do? Do we have to send him away?

It sounds like your son needs what we call a higher level of care than you can provide at this time. There are many teenagers whose behavior continues to deteriorate despite parents' efforts. Each locale in this country provides social services to its citizens. Your local social service organization, family court system, or foster care organization can help lead you to getting your son the help he needs. After a determination is made that your son needs special help and monitoring he might be put on temporary probation and/or be forced to attend certain therapy centers and abide by household rules. If he is able to benefit from these he will be allowed to stay home and continue to go to school, and can try to become a productive member of society. If he fails at probation it will be in his best interest to enter a residential setting before its too late and his antisocial tendencies become ingrained and unalterable. At a residential facility he will receive a comprehensive treatment approach including a focus on education, behavior, and psychological functioning. I have seen many teenagers benefit from such an experience despite the many trepidations that parents have when they have to "send away" their children.

I asked my son if he uses drugs and he said "No, just pot." Isn't marijuana a drug?

Yes, marijuana is a drug. Teenagers often say they do not use drugs and then go on to say they use marijuana regularly. Its use is common, it is glorified in the media, and as a result some feel that it isn't "really a drug." In fact, marijuana has serious effects on a teenager's capacity to exercise appropriate judgment, to remember things, to organize his world, to do well in school, to drive a car, to perform athletically, to perceive things around him, and to function in a family setting. In some cases it leads to addiction, despite the fact that we hear that it isn't a "real drug." While there continues to be debate about whether marijuana necessarily leads to other drug use we are sure that most users of other drugs started with marijuana. If you feel that your teenager is using marijuana in more than an infrequent experimental fashion get some help—at school or your local mental health/substance abuse association, or find one of the hundreds of Web sites (i.e., drugabuse.gov) that can be of great help in finding you the appropriate resources.

I'm worried about our son, who gets angry easily and has often threatened to run away. My wife and I did not take this seriously, but recently we saw a note on his floor in his room with details of where he would go. What should we do?

Immediate action seems necessary. The good news is that you are still in an early stage with a potential runaway teen. He hasn't gone yet, and indirectly he "let you know" by "accidentally" leaving a note in clear view. Most teenagers who run away do so because they feel misunderstood. That is not to say that you aren't trying. He sounds like he might be impulsive and impatient and unable to sit down quietly and discuss things. You might also be frustrated with his anger or other behaviors and might be acting a bit impatient with him. Whatever the mixture of causes, you want to prevent his running away; although many teenagers return home quickly, some don't and increase their risk of being hurt or getting involved in dangerous and risky behaviors. Prevention is the most important intervention.

You have to find a way to sit down and communicate with your son and let him know that you are listening. It might mean a family meeting where everyone gets a chance to be listened to or even going to a third party (a close family member or a professional) who can intercede and keep the "verbal traffic" moving so people listen to each other. Teenagers who feel listened to, not necessarily agreed with, usually don't have to run away.

Our daughter has been talking about getting her body pierced and even getting a tattoo. Should we let her?

At least your daughter has been talking about it and not presenting it to you after completion. Tattoos and piercings are quite common among teenagers (estimates of 10 percent are common) and are not necessarily a sign of being in a gang or of severe rebellious pathology, although in rare instances they might be (there will be many more signs of such problems). In most cases these activities are simply a rite of passage of adolesence. If the subject is brought up for discussion, the general dangers should be discussed such as the transmission of diseases such as hepatitis or even HIV during the procedures and the permanence of tattoos. Great care must be exercised and the person must do the tattoo or piercing using appropriately sterilized instruments. This discussion might be enough to dissuade your youngster. If not, don't worry. Most piercings can be removed without much if any residual scarring and most tattoos can also be lightened at least and are often in spots not visible when dressed.

I know divorce affects young children because they often don't understand all the changes, but don't teenagers handle it better?

Divorce affects children of all ages, even adult ones. While younger children experience divorce more forcefully—they cannot process all the painful information and often see the world through egocentric eyes, thus sometimes feeling that they caused it and only focusing on their own pain—teenagers do a bit better. Usually they can understand the more complex problems of divorce and the complexities of relationships, but don't underestimate the affect that divorce has. Teenagers whose parents get divorced or were divorced at an earlier time can suffer from feelings of loss, abandonment, depression, hopelessness, and grief. This can go on for a long time. Divorcing parents who ensure their post-divorce relationship runs as smoothly as possible do the best thing for their teenager. Your relationship with each other is the best predictor of your child's future adjustment.

We were recently told that our thirteen year old has attention deficit hyperactivity disorder. We thought that was usually diagnosed in younger children. Can teenagers get it too?

Attention deficit disorder with or without hyperactivity is a common disorder that is usually diagnosed during the primary school years. It consists primarily of inattention, impulsivity, and sometimes hyperactivity. There are often learning disorders present as well. It is often missed in the early years and only diagnosed later on. Treatment is still effective and consists of a combination of educational, psychological, and in some cases medication therapy. Recently there has even been a big upsurge in adults who are being diagnosed with this disorder for the first time, although nearly anyone who has it has been afflicted since childhood.

X

Additional Resources

General

American Academy of Child and Adolescent Psychiatry
3615 Wisconsin Avenue, NW
Washington, DC 20016-3007
800-333-2676
www.aacap.org

Federation of Families for Children's Mental Health
1021 Prince Street
Alexandria, VA 22314-2971
703-684-7710

Medscape
http://www.webmd.com

National Alliance for the Mentally Ill
Colonial Place Three
2107 Wilson Blvd.
Arlington, VA 22203-3754
800-950-NAMI

National Institute of Mental Health
5600 Fishers Lane
Rockville, MD 20857
301-443-4536

National Mental Health Association
1021 Prince Street
Alexandria, VA 22314-2971
703-684-7722
Toll free 800-969-6642

Focused

Anxiety Disorders Association of America
600 Executive Blvd.
Rockville, MD 20852
301-231-9350

National Alliance for Research on Schizophrenia and Depression
60 Cutter Mill Road
Great Neck, NY 11021
516-829-0091

National Council For Post-Traumatic Stress Disorder
215 North Main Street
White River Junction, VT 05009
802-296-5132

National Depressive and Manic Depressive Association
730 North Franklin Street
Chicago, IL 60610-3526
800-826-3632

Stepfamily Association of America
650 J Street
Lincoln, NE 68508
800-735-0329

Obsessive Compulsive Foundation
PO Box 70
Milford, CT 06460-0070
203-878-5669

Social Phobia/Social Anxiety Foundation
5025 North Central Avenue
Phoenix, AZ 85012

Attention Deficit Information Center
475 Hillside Avenue
Needham, MA 02194
781-455-9895

CHADD Children and Adults with Attention Deficit Disorder
8181 Professional Place
Landover, MD 20785
301-306-3070

Suicide Prevention
www.rmhc.com/mis/suicide_prevention/

Alcoholics Anonymous
PO Box 459 Grand Central Station
New York, NY 10163
212-870-3400

Learning Disabilities Association
4156 Library Road
Pittsburgh, PA 15234-1348

Overeaters Anonymous
6075 Zenith Court, NE
Rio Rancho, NM 77124
505-891-2664

Educational Resources Information Center (ERIC)
1-800-LET-ERIC

Office of Juvenile Justice and Delinquency Prevention
www.ojjdp.ncjrs.org

The National Center for Conflict Resolution
www.nccre.org

Atlas Program
3181 SW Sam Jackson Park Road
Portland, Oregon 97201-3098

Substance Abuse Info

American Council for Drug Education
    800-488-Drug
Families Anonymous
    800-736-9805

National Council on Alcoholism and Drug Dependence
   800-622-2255
National Clearing House for Alcohol and Drug Information
   800-729-6686
National Families in Action
   404-034-6364
Center for Substance Abuse Treatment and Referral Hotline
   800-622-HELP
Steroid Issues Web site drugabuse.gov

About the Author

DR. HENRY A. PAUL is the author of *Is My Child OK? When Behavior Is a Problem, When It's Not, and When to Seek Help* and *When Kids Are Mad, Not Bad*. He is a psychiatrist and educator who has helped thousands of young patients and their parents for more than twenty-five years. He is the Executive Director of the Karen Horney Clinic in New York, he is also the past president of the American Institute for Psychoanalysis, is a member of the American Academy of Child and Adolescent Psychiatry and the American Academy of Psychoanalysis, and is in private practice. He has appeared on *Good Morning America, The Early Show, The View, Dateline, NBC Nightly News,* and is a frequent guest on *The O'Reilly Factor* and many other national network television programs.